ANDRÉ MALRAUX

Modern Critical Views

Continued at back of book

Modern Critical Views

ANDRÉ MALRAUX

Edited and with an introduction by

Harold Bloom
Sterling Professor of the Humanities
Yale University

CHELSEA HOUSE PUBLISHERS ◇ 1988
New York ◇ New Haven ◇ Philadelphia

© 1988 by Chelsea House Publishers, a division
of Chelsea House Educational Communications, Inc.,
345 Whitney Avenue, New Haven, CT 06511
95 Madison Avenue, New York, NY 10016
5014 West Chester Pike, Edgemont, PA 19028

Introduction © 1988 by Harold Bloom

Printed and bound in the United States of America

10 9 8 7 6 5 4 3 2 1

∞ The paper used in this publication meets the minimum
requirements of the American National Standard for
Permanence of Paper for Printed Library Materials,
Z39.48-1984.

Library of Congress Cataloging-in-Publication Data
André Malraux.
    (Modern critical views)
    Bibliography: p.
    Includes index.
    1. Malraux, André, 1901–1976—Criticism and
interpretation. I. Bloom, Harold. II. Series.
PQ2625.A716Z5624   1988   843'.912   87-11625
ISBN 1–55546–291–X (alk. paper)

Contents

Remembering Malraux: On Violence
and the Image of Man   151
    Victor Brombert

The Orient as Western Man's "Shadow" in Malraux's
La Tentation de l'Occident   165
    Nina S. Tucci

The Model Relativized: Malraux's *L'Espoir*   173
    Susan Rubin Suleiman

La Voie royale and the Double Time of Art   181
    Rhonda K. Garelick

Editor's Note

This book brings together a representative selection of the best criticism available in English upon the writings of André Malraux. The critical essays are reprinted here in the chronological order of their original publication. Where the critics have chosen to leave their quotations from the French untranslated, their practice has been followed. I am grateful to Rhonda K. Garelick and Frank Menchaca for their assistance in editing this volume.

My introduction centers upon the novel *Man's Fate*, tracing in its heroes a sense of revolutionary belatedness, and partly interpreting that sense as a trope for Malraux's awareness of his condition as a novelist.

W. M. Frohock begins the chronological sequence with an overview of Malraux's first novel, *The Conquerors*, which is seen as a study in psychic anxiety and the metaphysical Absurd. In an interpretation of *Man's Fate*, Geoffrey Hartman emphasizes the dialectic of inward solitude and imposition of the will that dominates the book's heroes.

R. W. B. Lewis surveys Malraux's entire career as a novelist, emphasizing the vagaries of critical reception and expressing an aesthetic preference for *The Walnut Trees of the Altenburg*.

In another consideration of *Man's Fate*, David Wilkinson finds in the book the Myth of "the Bolshevik hero," more Malrauvian than Marxist. Roger Shattuck, in an appreciation of *Anti-Memoirs*, assigns Malraux's autobiographical reflections to the genre of travel writing, and evokes the shade of Henry Adams. A very different account of *Anti-Memoirs* is given by Michael Riffaterre, who exposes the structure of Malraux's obsessions, and concludes that: "He does not write about a reality remembered" but rather a reality that symbolizes his own mind.

Days of Wrath is judged by Thomas Jefferson Kline to be a celebration of the artist as Prometheus, rather than an exaltation of the Communist hero. Lucien Goldmann reaches a very different conclusion in a Structuralist study of *Man's Fate*, where his sociological insight is that the hero's individual struggle is transcended by the laws of the revolutionary community.

In a reading of *The Walnut Trees of the Altenburg*, C. J. Greshoff sees the novel's ultimate ethos as being the solidarity of men against death. The later Malraux, philosopher of art, is placed in historical perspective by the great historian of art, E. H. Gombrich, who reveals Malraux's limitations, yet ventures to compare him to John Ruskin.

Victor Brombert, in a retrospective view of the totality of Malraux's career, praises him both for the courage of action and for his tragic courage as novelist and aesthetician. The early epistolary work *La Tentation de l'Occident* is read by Nina S. Tucci as a prelude to Malraux's projection of the "shadow" of Western man upon the Orient in his first three novels.

Man's Hope, Malraux's novel of the Spanish Civil War, is seen by Susan Rubin Suleiman as a tendentious if moving work, since it emphasizes the need for discipline in the struggle against Fascism, while neglecting the crucial conflict between the Communists and their more idealistic allies. In this book's final essay, published here for the first time, Rhonda K. Garelick analyzes the early novel *The Royal Way* as an autobiographical meditation upon Malraux's own generation, trapped in an alienation or detachment from its own history.

Introduction

L*a Condition humaine* (1933, known in English as *Man's Fate*) is judged universally to have been André Malraux's major novel. Rereading it in 1987, sixty years after the Shanghai insurrection of 1927 which it commemorates, is a rather ambiguous experience. One need not have feared that it would seem a mere period piece; it is an achieved tragedy, with the aesthetic dignity that the genre demands. What renders it a little disappointing is its excessive abstractness. Malraux may have known a touch too clearly exactly what he was doing. Rereading Faulkner always surprises; there is frequently a grace beyond the reach of art. Malraux's fictive economy is admirable, but the results are somewhat schematic. Clarity can be a novelistic virtue; transparency grieves us with the impression of a certain thin quality.

The idealistic revolutionaries are persuasive enough in *Man's Fate*; they are even exemplary. But, like all of Malraux's protagonists, they are diminished by their sense of *coming after their inspirers*; they are not forerunners, but belated imitators of the Revolution. Malraux's protagonists designedly quest for strength by confronting death, thus achieving different degrees either of communion or of solitude. Their models in fiction are the obsessed beings of Dostoevsky or of Conrad. *Man's Fate* cannot sustain comparison with *Nostromo*, let alone with the anguished narratives of Dostoevsky. There are no originals in Malraux, no strong revolutionaries who are the equivalents of strong poets, rather than of philosophers. Geoffrey Hartman, defending Malraux's stature as tragedian, sees the heroes of *Man's Fate* as understanding and humanizing the Nietzschean Eternal Recurrence:

> The tragic sentiment is evoked most purely not by multiplying lives . . . but by repeating the chances of death, of unique, fatal acts. A hero like Tchen, or his fellow conspirators Kyo and Katov, dies more than once.

1

But is that the Nietzschean issue, the Nietzschean test for strength? Do Malraux's heroes take on what Richard Rorty, following Nietzsche, has called "the contingency of selfhood"? Do they fully appreciate their own contingency? Here is Rorty's summary of this crucial aspect of Nietzsche's perspectivism:

> His perspectivism amounted to the claim that the universe had no lading-list to be known, of determinate length. He hoped that, once we realized that Plato's "true world" was just a fable, we would seek consolation, at the moment of death, not in having transcended the animal condition but in being that peculiar sort of dying animal who, by describing himself in his own terms, had created himself.

Nietzsche understood that political revolutionaries are more like philosophers than like poets, since revolutionaries also insist that the human condition bears only one true analysis. Malraux's heroes attempt to escape from contingency rather than, like the strong poets, accepting and then appropriating contingency. Though the heroes of *Man's Fate* and of Malraux's other novels meditate endlessly upon death, if only in order to achieve a sense of being, they never succeed in describing themselves entirely in their own terms. This is a clue to Malraux's ultimate inadequacy as a novelist, his failure to join himself to the great masters of French fiction: Stendhal, Balzac, Flaubert, Proust, or the international novelists he most admired: Dostoevsky, Conrad, Faulkner. Would we say of the protagonists of Stendhal and Balzac that the death which overcomes them "is no more than the symbol of an ultimate self-estrangement"? Hartman's remark is valid for Malraux's heroes, but not for Stendhal's or Balzac's.

Malraux, a superb and wary critic, defended himself against Gaëtan Picon's shrewd observation that: "Malraux, unlike Balzac or Proust, in no way seeks to give each character a personal voice, to free each character from its creator." His response was: "The autonomy of characters, the particular vocabulary given to each of them are powerful techniques of fictional action; they are not necessities. . . . I do not believe that the novelist must create *characters*; he must create a particular and coherent world." *Man's Fate* certainly does create such a world; is it a liability or not that Kyo, Katov, Gisors, and the others fall short as characters, since they do not stride out of the novel, breaking loose from Malraux, and they all of them do sound rather alike. I finish rereading *Nostromo*, and I brood on the flamboyant Capataz, or I put down *As I Lay Dying*, and Darl Bundren's very individual voice haunts me. But Kyo and Katov give me nothing to meditate upon, and

Gisors and Ferral speak with the same inflection and vocabulary. Fate or contingency resists appropriation by Malraux's heroes, none of whom defies, or breaks free of, his creator.

Despite Malraux's defense, the sameness of his protagonists constitutes a definite aesthetic limitation. It would be one thing to create varied individuals with unique voices, and then to show that they cannot communicate with one other. It is quite another thing to represent so many aspects of the author as so many characters, all speaking with his voice, and then demonstrate the deathliness of their inability to speak truly to another. Malraux confused death with contingency, which is a philosopher's error, rather than a strong novelist's.

This may be why the women throughout Malraux's novels are so dismal a failure in representation. Unamuno ironically jested that: "All women are one woman," which is just the way things are in Malraux's fictions. A novelist so intent upon Man rather than men is unlikely to give us an infinite variety of women.

What redeems *Man's Fate* from a reader's frustration with the sameness of its characters is the novel's indubitable capture of a tragic sense of life. Tragedy is not individual in Malraux, but societal and cultural, particularly the latter. Malraux's Marxism was always superficial, and his aestheticism fortunately profound. The tragedy of the heroes in *Man's Fate* is necessarily belated tragedy, which is fitting for idealists whose place in revolutionary history is so late. That is why Gisors is shown teaching his students that: "Marxism is not a doctrine, it is a *will* . . . it is the will to know themselves . . . to conquer without betraying yourselves." Just as the imagination cannot be distinguished from the will as an artistic tradition grows older and longer, so ideology blends into the will as revolutionary tradition enters a very late phase. Tragedy is an affair of the will, and not of doctrine. Kyo and Katov die in the will, and so achieve tragic dignity. Gisors, the best mind in the novel, sums up for Malraux, just a few pages from the end:

> She was silent for a moment:
> "They are dead, now," she said finally.
> "I still think so, May. It's something else. . . . Kyo's death is not only grief, not only change—it is . . . a metamorphosis. I have never loved the world over-much: it was Kyo who attached me to men, it was through him that they existed for me. . . . I don't want to go to Moscow. I would teach wretchedly there. Marxism has ceased to live in me. In Kyo's eyes it was a will, wasn't it? But in mine, it is a fatality, and I found myself in

harmony with it because my fear of death was in harmony with
fatality. There is hardly any fear left in me, May; since Kyo died,
I am indifferent to death. I am freed (freed! . . .) both from death
and from life. What would I do over there?"

"Change anew, perhaps."

"I have no other son to lose."

The distinction between a will and a fatality is the difference between
son and father, activist and theoretician, latecomer and forerunner. For Malraux, it is an aesthetic distinction, rather than a psychological or spiritual
difference. As novelist, Malraux takes no side in this dichotomy, an impar-
tiality at once his narrative strength and his representational weakness. He
gives us forces and events, where we hope for more, for access to conscious-
nesses other than our own, or even his. As a theorist of art, Malraux brilliantly
grasped contingency, but as a novelist he suffered it. He saw that the creator
had to create his own language out of the language of precursors, but he
could not enact what he saw. *Man's Fate* is a memorable tragedy without
memorable persons. Perhaps it survives as a testament of Malraux's own
tragedy, as a creator.

W. M. FROHOCK

The Metallic Realm: The Conquerors

"A hopeless conflict . . . prepares us for the metallic realm of the Absurd."
—*La Tentation de l'Occident*

Malraux's own esteem for his first two novels is strictly limited. He has called *The Conquerors* "the book of an adolescent"—which, since he was twenty-five when he wrote it, can only mean that he finds the book itself immature—and he omits *The Royal Way* entirely from the Pléiade edition of his novels. He is right.

At least he is right to the extent that these two novels constitute a dry run. He had a basic theme: the Absurd—and some subsidiary ones as well. He had a basic magma of material: what he learned about life and about himself from his first experiences in the Orient. And he had a basic fable: a man goes out to the East, meets another man, somewhat older, with whom he has a special bond and watches his friend go through the calvary of discovering his limitations as human being. He had discovered his basic, tragic mood. What he did not have was a corresponding experience of techniques which would allow him, on the first try, to put everything else he had into one book; he still had to practice his hand and clarify his vision. After he had done so, but only then, he could start *Man's Fate*.

He conceived *The Conquerors* as political by its setting and action, tragic by its tone, and metaphysical by its implications. Since revolutionary events move fast, he had to find a form and a style that would keep up with their fundamental rhythm and preserve the feeling essential in all his novels up

From *André Malraux and the Tragic Imagination*. © 1952 by the Board of Trustees of the Leland Stanford Junior University. Stanford University Press, 1952.

5

to *Man's Hope*, that history will not wait for an individual to settle his destiny at leisure.

Actually the shape he gave *The Conquerors* is the exact opposite of the one he finally settled upon for *Man's Fate*. The latter novel opens with its focus entirely upon one character and broadens until it encompasses the whole revolutionary picture. But in 1928 he starts from the widest possible focus and narrows it through the three parts of the narrative until at the end one individual occupies the whole scene. The first part, labeled "The Approaches," takes in the whole play of revolution in Southeast Asia; the second, called "The Powers," studies the fighting at Canton which his hero, Garine, is directing; and the third, "The Man," studies Garine himself. As the narrator's ship moves up out of the Indian Ocean toward Hong Kong and Canton, characters are introduced, issues at stake made clear, and the apprehension of the passengers, coupled with the narrator's impatience to reach the scene of action, builds up the nervous tension and unifies the feeling of the novel as a whole. Next the story moves in upon the battle for Canton and follows the detail of revolution. Finally it turns to Garine, who is the nerve center of the fight, and fixes upon him. Thus the perspective moves, evenly, from wide pan to close-up.

The narrative itself is entrusted throughout to the same first-person narrator. He is unnamed and his personality is kept intentionally unobtrusive; though he is a participant, his acts are always the carrying out of orders and are not significant. He has known Garine a long time, and the latter has put him to doing some vague sort of liaison work for the Communists, but his one real function is to be the Jamesian "central intelligence."

His record is virtually a diary. Action is noted in the present tense and as though at the narrator's first moment of leisure, as soon as possible after it has taken place, *and without his knowing what will happen next*. The device adds greatly to the effect of immediacy and to the reader's feeling of being present at the action. The account starts *in medias res* and with a rush. (This is not a novel where events grow out of contacts between characters; the events would happen anyway even if these characters did not exist.) Radio bulletins alternate with fragmentary explanations and bits of conversation. Each notation bears a date (from June 15 to August 18, 1925) and often an hour. As the story hurries along the reader is always kept aware of time, not the time which wears men away and in this sense works upon and changes characters, but the time which sets a limit in which a man must do what he has to do. The characters rarely relax, sleep fitfully, hardly eat, and are always under dramatic tension.

The style of the diary is impressionistic, in places telegraphic, and rarely in need of the grammatically complete sentence.

Silence. Dès que nous attendons quelque chose, nous retrouvons la chaleur, comme une plaie. En bas, une faible rumeur; murmures, socques, inquiétude, la cliquette d'un marchand ambulant, les cris d'un soldat qui le chasse. Devant la fenêtre, la lumière. Calme plein d'anxiété. Le son rythmé, de plus en plus net, de la marche des hommes qui arrivent, au pas; le claquement brutal de la halte. Silence. Rumeur. . . . Un seul pas, dans l'escalier. Le secrétaire.

(Silence. As soon as we expect something to happen we feel the heat again, like a sore. Below, a quiet stirring; murmurings, shoes, nervousness, the clatter of a street vendor, the cries of a soldier driving him off. Opposite the window, the light. Stillness full of uneasiness. The rhythmic sound, clearer and clearer, of men marching up, in step; the heavy stamp of the halt. Silence. Stirring. . . . A lone step, on the stairs. The secretary.)

Such writing can do with a minimum of syntax because impressions noted in series require little to link them. There is no need to subordinate some to the others, because all have the same value, i.e., the value of events. The rhythm of this particular series goes: silence, noise, silence again, new noise, significance of the noise (the last handled by the event of the secretary's entrance which explains the new noise). The development of the series is dramatic: silence comes over the room; during the wait they become aware of the heat; then a noise brings a tension; tension falls when the source is recognized; they are calm again but still tense when the soldier has driven off the pushcart man. A new noise comes, but is too quickly recognized for tension to mount; there is silence again, then another noise which registers after a moment (note the comma between *pas* and *dans*) as a step, and then in walks the secretary. The punctuation serves, most frequently, to separate stimulus from interpretation: one step (comma for a pause while they ask themselves *where*) in the stairway (period while they ask themselves *who*) and then the answer. Naturally the whole book does not maintain this pace or this impressionistic brevity, but there are many other passages as loaded and as rapid as this one, and the net effect is to add to the feeling of haste and to the nervous tension.

Whenever possible, running narration is avoided in favor of dramatic scenes, even when doing so calls for real ingenuity. To introduce Garine, for example, the narrator is made to dig a captured British Secret Service dossier out of a trunk, and read it aloud, supplying the hero's motives as he reads and arguing with the document when the information is faulty. This in spite of the fact that he has known Garine for years and might well simply tell us the essential facts on his own authority—except for the nagging question: what happens to the dramatic excitement of the book while he does so? The concern for dramatization is carried so far that when, because of its confidential nature, the narrator cannot plausibly hear a conversation, Garine reports it to him later in dialogue and even imitates the voices.

Malraux sees his scenes much better than he hears them; in places the dialogue may be too smooth to be true, and too elliptical for the characters to have understood each other, but his eye is as true as Hemingway's, and his study of gesture so complete that at times he can get on without dialogue. The scene where finally the captured terrorist Hong is brought before him is handled without a spoken word. Hong enters between two soldiers, with marks on his face from the fight; he stops, arms behind his back, feet spread; Garine looks at him, waiting, fatigued by his fever, his head moving slowly sideways; he pulls in a deep breath, shrugs. Hong catches the shrug, lunges toward Garine, is brought down by a rifle butt on the head. And that is all: each movement is significant and motivated, and—remembering Garine's instinctive sympathy for Hong and his saying that he has few enemies he understands so well—the gestures translate without loss the emotions of the scene.

Malraux sees the scene with the precision of a good movie lens, and to what extent his eye is cinematographic becomes clear in the pages directly following the confrontation with Hong, when Garine and the narrator go to see the mutilated bodies of their murdered friends. They are in a shed where a Chinese sits at the door, kicking away a dog that persistently tries to get in. The dog leaps and dodges, and keeps coming back. Garine and the narrator approach. The Chinese leans his head against the wall, eye half-closed, pushes the door open for them. The large, dirt-floored room has dust piled in the corners. In spite of the blue shades the light is too strong and blinds them. The narrator drops his eyes, raises them again, and sees the corpses *standing up*, not laid out but leaned against the wall. Garine tells the guard to get covers. The guard has to be told three times before he can understand; Garine lifts a fist, then tells him that he will get ten *taels* for bringing covers within half an hour. The narrator's muscles relax when he hears spoken words, but tighten again as he sees that the mouth of a dead friend has been mutilated, widened with a razor. He squeezes his arms against his sides and leans against the wall. A fly lights on his forehead and he does not drive it away. . . .

Recent criticism says much about this kind of immediacy of sensation. The visual detail and the narrator's visible reaction to the detail are passed on to the reader for interpretation: no need to tell the reader what the fly's remaining on the narrator's forehead means. And because the reader interprets he participates. He is as close to the action as he can be, and seems to live it rather than contemplate it. In other words, aesthetic distance has been cut to a minimum.

The effect is one of compelling authenticity. Malraux seems quite aware of what he is doing, and even introduces a gratuitous but particularly striking and immediate image on occasion to reenforce the reader's feeling of being present. Thus when Borodin reveals to Klein and the narrator how he has worked on Hong's emotions, so as to be sure that Hong will murder the Gandhi-like Tcheng-dai without delay, and adds that from that moment Hong's terrorists will have the Communist group on their list of prospects: "Borodin, chewing his moustache and buckling the uniform belt that bothers him, rises and leaves. We follow. Stuck against the light bulb a large butterfly projects upon the wall a great black stain." The shadow of the butterfly is completely irrelevant to the action and has no symbolic significance, but after Borodin's speech about Hong, full of implications about impending murder which naturally project the mind into a near and ominous future, the image pulls one back into the reality of the present with great force.

The sharpness of Malraux's visual imagination is of course a vast advantage. When he is ready to write *Man's Hope* ten years later, he will return to the device of telling his story in brief, sharply cut episodes like these and make the most use possible of the visual effects. But the Spanish War novel is a complicated one, and much of its meaning is conveyed through juxtaposition of scenes that vary greatly in tone, color, and emotional mood, whereas the story of *The Conquerors* is simple and rectilinear, a matter of aligning the scenes one after the other in the order of the chronology of narration—from the passage of the ship up the South Asia coast to the moment when Garine realizes that his strength is exhausted and he must leave Canton while he still can, in public victory but in private defeat.

Technically, so far as telling a story is concerned, *The Conquerors* was a success. The sharp-focused point of view, the skillfully maintained pace, the extremely immediate imagery, are achievements which Malraux has never bettered.

But Malraux's technique is one that makes the presentation of character inordinately difficult. Personal relations such as the traditional novel exploits can hardly exist here. The only event that could be alleged to develop out of a personal relationship—Garine's refusal to let Hong be tortured—can be attributed more accurately to his understanding a human case very like his own. Otherwise the important relationship for each character is his political role, and his connection with the other characters is professional.

The characters are primarily types, defined by their attitudes toward life and politics. Borodin is the man who has submerged his individuality in the Revolution. Hong is the Terrorist. Nicolaïeff is the Torturer. Tcheng-dai is the Moral Force. Rebecci is the Anarchist who has talked away his energy. The fact that they are also men emerges very slowly, even in the case of Garine.

Like Tartuffe in the play, he is familiar long before we see him, but familiar as a type. At Saigon, Rensky, the art collector, drops the tempting remark to the narrator that he doubts that Garine is really a Marxist Bolshevik. At the next port of call another minor character adds that Garine has joined the Revolution for the same reason men join the Foreign Legion: he cannot abide life in ordinary society. He also remarks that where Borodin is a man of action, Garine is a man *capable* of action, and pays tribute to Garine's ability as organizer. Still a third minor character later adds that Garine seems to him a sick genius and not entirely dependable. Thus in the first seventy pages of a 215-page book we learn about the central figure only what kind of man he is.

Here the narrator breaks out the Intelligence report on Garine and gives us a biography, with footnotes on motives, yet even now the emphasis on Garine as an individual human being is not complete. We learn why Garine's type is not Borodin's—why he is a Conqueror rather than what Malraux will later label a "Curé" of revolution, a maker rather than a custodian. Only when we reach Canton, enter Garine's office, see him, feel the presence and power of the man's personality, does the type recede behind the image of the driving, intense, desperately earnest, desperately sick individual. The fact of his being a type remains in the background through the tense days of the fighting, maneuver, murder, and torture, but it is still there and emerges again in the final pages, when Garine has decided to leave Canton rather than die on the scene of his triumph. We are reminded by a series of dialogue passages that it is just as well he leave, since the Revolution has no permanent berth for the Conqueror: such types are too undisciplined.

The key to Garine's character is his Angst, which has its source in his violent awareness of the vanity of life. His "dedication to a great action" has been an escape, to let him live in awareness of the Absurd without giving in to it. As a student in Switzerland he had financed a number of abortions. Tried as an accessory, he had felt his trial to be a grotesque, unreal farce. The (to him disproportionate) penalty for his offense had finished the job of convincing him of the absurdity of his plight. "I don't think of society as evil—and thus capable of improvement—but as absurd. Not the absence of justice itself bothers me but something deeper, the impossibility of accepting any social form whatsoever." He had not served his jail sentence, but the

First World War had brought him again face to face with the Absurd and he had deserted: the knives issued for a trench wipe-up had reminded him too powerfully of kitchen knives. Later he had joined the Bolsheviks while they were still in exile, preferring them to the Anarchists because they were technicians rather than preachers, and feeling that the Bolsheviks were likelier to offer the experience of a great action and the experience of power. This hope had overweighed his knowledge that he could not tolerate party discipline, had no interest in social amelioration, and, in general, disliked people. He had arrived in the Orient in time to plunge into the young revolution "with absolute absence of scruple," to build a propaganda service, combine it with the police, and have it ready to deliver to the International after the death of Sun Yat-sen. He and Borodin *are* the Canton revolution. But dysentery and swamp fever have wasted him to the point where he has had to choose between returning to Europe and seeing the victory at Canton. He has chosen to stay. The success of the Canton enterprise attests his sustained vitality. But with his decline in strength, the awareness of the Absurd has returned and he is now persuaded that not merely society but life also is absurd. His driving energy collapses when Hong's terrorists murder Klein and his companions; the sight of the tortured, mutilated faces plunges him back into the emptiness of his accomplishment. At most he is able to affirm that one thing still counts—not to be conquered. Occasionally he rouses from his despair, but the final collapse is inevitable. As his health weakens, he grows increasingly obsessed by the Absurd. He becomes increasingly a private individual struggling with a private problem rather than the leader of great action. Then when he refuses to make a political speech at Klein's funeral—disobeying Borodin's order—the individual asserts himself completely: "I didn't throw Europe into a corner like a pile of rags and take the risk of ending up like some Rebecci just to teach people obedience. Or to learn to obey, myself, either."

This is his ultimate *non serviam*.

We are a long way from Communist orthodoxy here. Technically Garine is no anarchist, but his sensibility is anarchistic: his ultimate authority is the satisfaction of his intimate, private needs. This is why he has been able to understand young Hong's rejection of the party discipline in favor of direct personal action. Either of these men could have said what Garine does say: that action had made him indifferent to everything else, including its outcome, and that if it was easy for him to join the Revolution, that was because the result was distant and always uncertain.

Consequently, Garine's plight is sad; the Revolution offers him the best available possibility of meeting his private needs through participation in a "great action," but at the cost of his own destruction: there is no permanent place for the transcendent ego of the Conqueror type in the revolution he makes. There is no exit from the dilemma.

What Garine needs, said Leon Trotsky in his resounding article, is a good dose of Marxism. To Trotsky's mind, the character with real stuff in him is not this "revolutionary who scorns Revolutionary doctrine," but young Hong, whose refusal to compromise is the beginning of virtue. He makes no bones of calling Malraux amateurish and doctrinally timid, and alleges that his sympathies have been corroded by excessive individualism and aesthetic caprice.

(What Trotsky really means is that in letting the bourgeoisie of Canton share the Canton revolution, people like the historical Borodin and the fictional Garine were playing Stalin's hand and not Trotsky's. Malraux has gone wrong by not having read his Trotsky.)

Malraux's reply amounts to an ex post facto statement of intention: he meant *The Conquerors* to be a novel and not a declaration of faith. The judgments represented in the book are not his, but those of distinct, autonomous individuals, in particular circumstances, at a particular time. The purpose of the book, he declares, is less to picture a revolution than to make clear the nature of man's eternal fate. Trotsky has mistaken the human and fallible characters of a novel for immutable archetypes of political allegory.

This interchange beteween Malraux and Trotsky does much to reveal the essential nature of Malraux's book. To Trotsky, Garine is merely a defective revolutionary; his trouble is quickly reduced to excessive individualism; and man's fate, as Malraux calls it, is nothing but Garine's inability to adjust himself to the brave new world—whereas Malraux's "aesthetic caprice," as Trotsky calls what we would call the intention of the artist, is to show a man in a situation he has created, the only situation in life which he finds tolerable, and one which is absolutely certain to work the ruin of its creator. Trotsky is looking for a revolutionary, and Malraux is giving him a tragic hero who happens to be involved in a revolution.

Now the reason for the incessant haste of the style becomes clear—the story must hasten toward its outcome with something of the rush appropriate to tragedy. *And the point of view must be focused relentlessly upon Garine because he is meant to have the general significance of a tragic hero.*

But does he? Trotsky, for all his special predispositions, was an intelligent reader, and he took what Malraux meant for tragedy to be the report of a revolution. (Trotsky even puts quotes around the word *roman*.) And the other critics who read the book as Trotsky did were numerous. Were they so terribly wrong in neglecting the tragic aspect of the book?

Not entirely. For putting men in the situation of revolution reveals many other aspects of the fundamental human situation besides Garine's, and the book is evidence that these other aspects were extremely interesting to Malraux. These subsidiary interests are what spoil in some degree his technical success. If the speed of the narrative made difficult the job of transforming Garine from type into human being, it made doubly hard the task of bringing alive these other characters who did not benefit by the direct and continuous attention of the narrator.

Hong, for example, is animated (we are told) by an all-inclusive hatred, bred from the misery he has known. And a killer has his secret: he must see things differently from other men just as a torturer like the policeman Nicolaïeff must have had special experiences which now make him enjoy his cruel profession. Klein, the old hand at revolution who has had all the experiences of torture and imprisonment, and knows at first hand the difference between killing from a distance with a gun and killing intimately with a knife, and who in his deathly fatigue gasps out how hard it is merely to be "ein Mensch . . . a man," also possesses a secret. So does Tcheng-dai, who has sacrificed all his possessions to build his moral prestige, and, in his seeming detachment from everything, is providing for his own immortality ("taking care of his biography"); he can render the Revolution ineffective with a nod, and if he cannot achieve his ends and stay alive, he will achieve them by committing suicide.

There is also Rensky, the collector for museums, whom we see only once but long enough to learn that he has gone to the Temple of Angkor Vat to carve on a wall a smutty inscription in Sanskrit, just for the pleasure of baffling some future, presumably serious, archaeologist. And Gerard, the former high-school principal, who leaves the narrator full of surmises about a curious sexuality that has absolutely nothing to do with anything that will happen or can happen in the rest of the story. There is also Rebecci.

This little Italian anarchist has wasted his life in talk; he now runs a shop in Saigon where he sells "pacotille"—cheap junk like the mechanical birds that are his speciality—and kills time telling impossible yarns to a little circle of Chinese girls. A consuming curiosity makes him an authority on erotic literature, but, like his politics, his eroticism remains theoretical—in this case because of the presence of his alert Chinese wife. His futility seems absolute, and yet this is the man whose teaching has produced Hong.

There is not one of these people who is not interesting to Malraux in his own right. We know this because we know that Malraux will investigate similar types, sometimes at considerable length, in *Man's Fate*. But in *The Conquerors* the unvarying point of view makes it impossible for the reader to see life through their eyes. And the pace leaves no time for us to see them, even as they look to the narrator, for long.

Originally Malraux had written a ten-page scene in which Garine discusses Borodin at length with the narrator. Borodin here sounds much less the typical functionary than he does in the finished book. The propagandist, we learn, is in the Revolution because he enjoys the activity; he wants the Revolution to go on and on. Success is not the object. He lives for his role. The doctrine not only has to be spread, but it must be spread *by him*. This Borodin is far and away more interesting than the one in the finished novel, and there is no doubt, after these ten pages, that Malraux was deeply interested in Borodin as one kind of human being. There is also no doubt that the passage had to be suppressed. These were ten pages in which, because of the requirements of point of view, nothing could happen—and a ten-page stretch with no action is awkwardly long, given the rhythm of the narrative. Coming so late in the action, long after the exposition was finished, this scene would have broken the stride of the story. Technically speaking, Malraux had no choice. The passage was published separately a year after the novel.

GEOFFREY H. HARTMAN

"The Silence of the Infinite Spaces"

Malraux entitles his . . . greatest novel *La Condition humaine*. Political in subject, it is, like *The Conquerors*, more than political in range, and deepens the definition of Man explored in the previous books. Of the novel's seven chapters, the first two tell of the quick success of the Shangai insurrection, while the remainder portray an ironical, protracted series of events, reducing the characters one by one to solitude. Because, in the first part of the story, they can still impose their world on the world, they also succeed in imposing their will. Yet, from the outset, a contrary pattern prevails, ripened by apparently external circumstances. Soon every character suffers an experience of self-estrangement through which he becomes aware of the radical gap between the world and his view of it. A moment of "the silence of the infinite spaces" mocks his deepest dreams, and, though it may not alter his will to act, suggests a contradiction, inescapable in its nature, between Man and History.

In this book Malraux's architectonic vigour surpasses any shown before; it almost convinces us that the form of the novel is the natural medium for his view of life. The premise that Man inevitably imposes his world on the world, that thought and act are fictional in essence, grants the slightest event the same expressive potential as the greatest. It is true, at least, that Malraux's power of *development* has advanced. We can take, as an example, his treatment of what was probably the germinal incident of the novel. Towards the end of *The Psychology of Art* he remarks:

From *André Malraux*. © 1960 by Geoffrey H. Hartman. Hilary House, 1960.

Every man's self is a tissue of fantastic dreams. I have written
elsewhere of the man who fails to recognize his own voice on the
gramophone . . . and because our throat alone transmits to us
our inner voice I named the book *La Condition humaine*. In art the
other voices do but ensure the transmission of this inner voice.
The artist's message owes its force to the fact that it arises from
the heart of silence, from a devastating loneliness that conjures
up the universe so as to impose on it a human accent.

The incident to which the author refers occupies an unobtrusive section
at the beginning of the novel. Kyo is listening to records prepared by the
conspirators, which purport to teach a foreign language but actually transmit
secret messages. Kyo, who does not recognize his own voice in recorded
form, thinks the disks have been changed or that the phonograph distorts,
but the matter is quickly dropped. Malraux allows the event to interpret
itself by haunting the consciousness of Kyo, who associates more and more
persons with it. When, for example, he tells his father (Gisors) about the
estranged voice, the latter explains: "We hear the voices of others with our
ears, our own voice with our throat." And he adds, astonishingly: "Opium
is also a world we do not hear with our ears." Thus one germinal detail
gathers momentum and begins to symbolize the human condition in its
entirety. Gisors himself takes opium, and it seems that every man, wittingly
or unwittingly, finds a way to overcome an irreducible solitude. The world
of Man's perceptions is, like that of the artist, a second birth, a world conjured
up to impose on it a specifically human accent.

As with the detail so with the persons. There are many characters now,
none really minor, and all affected in various ways by a radical experience
of estrangement. Kyo fails to recognize *his* voice; Tchen did not recognize
his arm. Some, like Gisors, are always aware of an inner desolation; others,
like Kyo, the man of action, who distrusts his father's tendency to convert
every experience to knowledge, only by usurpation or chance. The death
which overcomes Malraux's heroes is no more than the symbol of an ultimate
self-estrangement. And even those who survive do not always escape it.

Malraux is, at last, in full possession of his idea. He has found a law
encompassing all "fatality," and can give each of his characters an individual
and widely varying fate because they are still instances of that law. Man, as
The Royal Way had implied, is defined by the world he imposes on the world,
not potentially but actually. Man's fate, the present novel adds, follows from
his nature. What is *fate* except an inextricable involvement with the world,
one which comes about because of the nature of Man, who wants to make
the world inseparable from his life?

That this attempt, however vital, must fail, is the *condition humaine* out of which Man's greatness and tragedy spring. Malraux stands close to the existentialistic thesis that we "invent" our fate in order to be irremediably bound to the world. But even though every such "invention" reveals a specific power in Man to impose his world on the world, it is also an escape from his intrinisc solitude, and leaves an anguish that tells he is greater than the sum of his acts.

The multiplication of individual destinies is also part of a more relaxed and "epical" narrative manner. Tchen still runs to his fate as if action were a drug against solitude which wears off and had to be increased. But others move at different speeds, and reach their fulfilment at different points in the plot, which is no longer in a state of continuous high tension. The specifically *literary* problem which Malraux solves in the present novel is how to convey Man's pursuit of fate without the artificial, fantastic tempo of *The Conquerors* or the conglomeration of synthetically staged adventures we find in *The Royal Way*. His problem is of the same order as that of an artist who strives to obtain a three-dimensional effect with two-dimensional means, to show that the medium does not have to be of the same nature as the thing it represents. All problems of this order are essentially aesthetic and imply that artistic freedom consists in the power to represent an experience without being subject to its law.

If we compare two incidents, of how man runs towards his fate, one from *La Condition humaine* and the other from *The Conquerors*, Malraux's new artistic freedom will appear in greater relief. In the latter, Klein, a friend of Garine's and fellow-worker in the strike, is taken hostage by the terrorists and killed. Garine and the narrator are told that a number of bodies have been found and go to identify them. As a morbid joke the terrorists have propped the bodies upright, and for once the narrator's speed of perception fails: "As soon as I raise my eyes I see the four bodies, *standing*." The author here suggests two things: an event too quick for human eyes, and that Klein's body *is* death, as if death had been within him as a hidden fatality. The slashes on Klein's face, perceived later, express a further trick of fate: Klein was always terrified at the idea of knife-killings. Then Garine wants to close his comrade's eyes, and, with a blindly foreseeing gesture, puts two fingers "stretched apart like scissors" on the white eyeballs—realizes the murderers have cut the eyelids off.

The scene described above is one of the finest in *The Conquerors*. It haunts the mind by its compression and its obsessive emphasis on the faculty of sight. It seeks to show that fate is quicker than Man, and yet within Man, who anticipates and even conspires with its action. A very different scene, expressing the same idea, occurs just before Kyo listens to his voice and does not recognize it. Very casual, it is enlivened by a single naïve gesture. Tchen has just informed his comrades of the completed murder, and feels a great need to leave them and confide in Gisors, because no one else, except perhaps Katov, is really close to him:

> The Russian [Katov] was eating little sugar candies, one by one without taking his eyes off Tchen who suddenly understood the meaning of gluttony. Now that he had killed he had the right to crave anything he wished. The right. Even if it were childish. He held out his square hand. Katov thought he wanted to leave and shook it. Tchen got up. It was just as well: he had nothing more to do here; Kyo was informed, it was up to him to act. As for himself, he knew what he wanted to do now. He reached the door, returned however.
>
> "Pass me the candy."
>
> Katov gave him the bag. He wanted to divide the contents: no paper. He filled his cupped hand, chewed with his whole mouth, and went out.
>
> "Shouldn't 've gone 'lone," said Katov.
>
> A refugee in Switzerland from 1905 to 1912, date of his clandestine return to Russia, he spoke French almost without accent, but he swallowed certain of his vowels, as though to compensate for the necessity of articulating carefully when he spoke Chinese. Almost directly under the lamp, very little light fell on his face. Kyo preferred this: the expression of ironic ingenuousness which the small eyes and especially the upturned nose (a sly sparrow, said Hemmelrich) gave to Katov's face, struck him all the more as it jarred with his own features and often troubled him.
>
> "Let's get it over with," said Kyo. "You have the records, Lou?"

The passage effects a transition from one personal focus to another, from Tchen to Kyo. In so doing it swiftly illuminates the relationship between both and the third main character, Katov. Though the latter is a pivot he appears momentarily in greatest relief: his personality is an *unknown* which Tchen and Kyo (and Hemmelrich) cannot solve. Katov is often kept opaque, and he does not hold the centre until the last great scene of his sacrifice and death. Still, we are often shown into his thoughts, and if he remains mysterious here it is because Malraux always chooses some opaque pivot around which actions or thoughts turn. In Tchen's first scene it is the victim shrouded by the white gauze; in Katov's last scene the strangely empty space of the prison compound; and often such an obscure experience as that which Tchen wishes to clarify with Gisor's help, or that which Kyo puzzles over after hearing his voice in recorded form.

Malraux's characters are defined by their different reaction to this "unknown." All are drawn towards it like Perken to the idea of torture, or Claude to his map, or the conquerors to "China." But now Malraux varies more skilfully the structure of each fascination, its momentum, form and quality. Both Tchen and Kyo subtly transform the other man, make him less strange, more at one with their wishes. The manner in which each imposes his world on the world is, however, quite different.

Tchen is strongly conscious of his solitude, his increased familiarity with death, and wants to deny it. He thinks he understands Katov's "gluttony," but when the latter misinterprets his outstretched hand, we are reminded of the distance between any gesture and its interpretation, as well as of the distance between Katov and Tchen which the latter would have liked to deny. Yet Tchen accepts Katov's misunderstanding too quickly, and his returning for the candy, and gulping all of it, has something equally hasty about it, this time wilful rather than spontaneous. It may reflect the speed with which he moves towards his "fate." As for Kyo, he tends to pass over differences in character, proceeding by the quickest route to the next item: "Let's get it over with." He too, therefore, displays a certain haste. Katov, finally, appears kind and relaxed, but there is the suggestion of gluttony and that curious "swallowing of vowels." The whole scene has a great deal of humorous strength not found in any of Malraux's previous work except his fantasies.

The estrangements of which we have talked always occur in the midst of the secret haste the above passage hints at. When the records are played, Kyo hears a voice he does not recognize as his own. Despite the fraternal effort of revolution, all the characters, by the end of the novel, come to face death or destiny alone, strangers to themselves and to the world. The moment of death is, in fact, associated with this leitmotif of the strange voice. Just before Kyo joins Katov in the prisoner compound and takes poison, he passes through an experience in which it plays a deeply disguised role.

König, Chiang Kai-Shek's police chief, in charge of rooting out the Communist revolutionaries, has heard that Kyo is a believer in the "dignity of Man." He therefore has Kyo brought from prison and plans to make him betray his belief. During their interview the telephone rings and a voice asks whether Kyo is *still* alive. Soon it rings a second time with, apparently, the same query. König, in the meantime, has begun an aimless interrogation. Does Kyo want to live? Is Kyo a Communist through . . . dignity? Kyo, who does not see a purpose to these questions, tensely expects the telephone:

when it rings a third time König lets it ring, hand on receiver, asking where the Communists have hidden their arms—another pointless question, since he already knows the answer or does not need Kyo for it. Then, suddenly, Kyo understands that the telephone is merely a piece of stage-business.

What business Malraux does not say, but König is obviously not inter-rested in specific information. He wants merely the gesture of betrayal, and later offers Kyo his freedom in exchange for it. The business of the telephone, a devilish variant on the game of one two three . . . gone, is rigged up to achieve this end. For the repeated ring suggests more than a limit to Kyo's life which König (the name perhaps symbolic) has the power to suspend. It evokes the *indifference* of the world—that repetitive machine, that strange anonymous voice—to Man's existence and will. The real temptation faced by Kyo is not König's power or his humane offer but the subtler suggestion of this voice. It demands nothing except the sacrifice of an idea, the idea of Man. The inhuman whistle of the locomotive which later pierces the prisoner compound, the scene of Kyo's and Katov's death, is the image of König's telephone raised to the height of impotent terror.

The tragedy Malraux depicts, and which the world of *Man's Fate* em-bodies most clearly, does not stem from any special flaw in the protagonists. It comes, at first sight, from the brutal confrontation of Man with external fate. Yet each of the novels shows a reversal in which external forms of fate appear as invited or even invented by Man. A later work such as *Man's Hope*, in which the author feels even freer towards his idea, suggests this reversal also in occasional images, as when Loyalist aeroplanes appear to *seek* the enemy's antiaircraft fire. Malraux's view should, however, be distinguished from religious and psychological concepts of fate. The former may hold that a person creates what he deserves, the latter that he creates for himself what he most deeply wants or is compelled to want because of early experiences. For Malraux there is a fatality prior to every individual fate, and this lies in the specific nature of Man, who cannot accept a world independent of his act, and so aspires to identify himself with forces greater than his being, even at the risk of losing part of his humanity. This risk is expressed in the general theme of self-estrangement, as well as by the symbols of alienated or inhuman face and voice. König with his telephone and the atrocious whistle of the locomotive has donned the mask of fate: he is assimilated to what has crushed him and propagates its horror compulsively. But the tragic, rather than demonic, figures show their greatest strength as they stand alone, be-trayed by the forces they have called up, deeply conscious of their power not to be seduced. Katov and Kyo wear their own faces and speak with their own voice.

R. W. B. LEWIS

Malraux and His Critics

"Malraux is interested in painting," Maurice Blanchot remarked in 1950, "but we know that he is also interested in man." What is beguiling about the remark is not only its deceptive simplicity—in an essay not otherwise notable for simplicity—but the ordering of its key terms. Blanchot to be sure, was engaged at the moment in appraising Malraux's interest in painting as reflected by *The Psychology of Art*; even so, his formulation was, and I think, remains essentially correct, especially when he continued: "To save one through the other—[Malraux] was unable to resist this great temptation."

Not many readers were as quick to grasp the point: the intimate relation between Malraux's supposedly new concern with the total world of art forms and his abiding concern with the condition and the destiny of man. Writing in 1957, Armand Hoog remembered "the outburst of surprise . . . and bafflement that accompanied the publication, in 1948, of the *Musée imaginaire*," the first part of *The Psychology of Art*. "More than one critic," Hoog said, "marveled, however admiringly, that such an excellent novelist should turn into an art historian." No novelist of his generation had been more closely associated, in the vague consciousness of the reading public, with the raw violence of contemporary events. Malraux had dramatized the 1926 uprising in Canton (*The Conquerors*, 1928), his own penetration of the Siamese jungle with something of the tribal warfare going on there (*The Royal Way*, 1930), another and larger phase of the Chinese revolution (*Man's Fate*, 1933), aspects of brutality and enslavement in Nazi Germany (*Days of Wrath*, 1935),

From *The Trials of the Word*. © 1965 by R. W. B. Lewis. Yale University Press, 1965.

the Spanish Civil War (*Man's Hope*, 1937), and most recently a poison-gas
attack on the German-Russian front in World War I, preceded by a glance
at the Young Turk revolutionary movement before the war and framed by
memoirs of World War II (*The Walnut Trees of Altenburg*, 1943). No writer,
not even Hemingway, could seem less likely to the unknowing to devote
himself to researches into Sumerian or Gothic art.

But the surprise occasioned by Malraux's art studies was due of course,
as Hoog says, to an inattentive reading of the novels just mentioned, and to
popular ignorance of Malraux's several interrelated careers. It is now clear
that there is an astonishing unity to everything Malraux has written; one is
inclined to add "everything he has done," since his first significant book, a
sort of epistolary novel bearing the Spengler-echoing title *The Temptation of
the West* in 1926. A main element of that unity has been a persistent preoc-
cupation with art: with works of art and the cultures they comprise and
express; and with the role of art in a generally "absurd" universe. It was
Malraux who, in *The Temptation of the West*, introduced the word "absurd"
into the modern philosophical vocabulary: in a contention that to the eye of
modern man the universe appeared fatally bereft of meaning because of the
loss of compelling and explanatory religious belief and, with it, the collapse
of any direction-giving concept of man; because of the successive "deaths"
of the idea of God and the idea of man. Most of Malraux's novels have been
symbolic assaults upon history, in an endeavor to wrest from history a
persuasive definition of human nature and a dependable guide and measure
of human conduct; while in his life, Malraux has been committed to intensive
action and to what Picon calls "the myth of the great individual" as sources,
perhaps of insight but certainly of compensation. But he has also and ever
more strenuously been committed to the great art-work as performing, more
satisfactorily yet, these same functions. If Malraux evidently still believes
in the efficacy of the master, he believes even more in the saving power of
the masterpiece.

The play of these terms—man, the absurd, action, history, and art—
has been constant in Malraux's writing from the beginning. But before
criticism could arrive at them, it had to get beyond a prior misapprehen-
sion—namely, that Malraux was primarily a chronicler of contemporary
revolutions, a skillful journalist of the political and economic upheavals
peculiar to his age.

I

Leon Trotsky posed the issue in 1931 when he said about *The Conquerors:*
"The book is called a novel. What in fact we have before us is a fictionalized

chronicle of the Chinese revolution during its first period, the Canton period." Trotsky, as we know, had an uncommonly quick perception of literature; he was among the first, a couple of years later, to detect the achievement of Ignazio Silone's *Fontamara*—in which, he said, revolutionary passion was raised to the level of art. He felt that *The Conquerors* was itself a work of considerable art and made some acute and generous observations about its beauty of narrative. But he felt that the author's revolutionary passion was flawed; that Malraux's effort to give a faithful portrait of insurrectionist China had been (in Trotsky's word) corrupted, both by an "excess of individualism" and by "aesthetic caprice." Even in retrospect, the charge (which Trotsky supported with considerable and pressing detail) is not without substance and pertains to a wider problem: for there has always been a sort of murky imbalance between Malraux's political affinities (the presumptive ones in his novels and the actual ones—communist and then Gaullist—in his life) and his stated or implied beliefs about literature. Nonetheless, Malraux had reason to say, in answer, that his book was not intended and should not be judged as a fictionalized chronicle, and that, in effect, it was just the individualism and the aesthetics that made it a novel. As to the former, the book's stress was placed "on the relationship between individual and collective action, not on collective action alone." As to the latter, Malraux made the crucial remark that the novel was dominated not by considerations of doctrinal loyalty and historical inclusiveness, but by the vision, the way of looking at things—in Malraux's French, by *"l'optique"*—proper to the novel as an art form. The entire critical "problem" of Malraux—the "Malraux case," as some French commentators have called it—lies, implicit but bristling, in this early exchange.

Still, when *The Conquerors* was followed by a more full-scale narrative of the Chinese revolution, the betrayal and defeat of the communist effort to seize Shanghai in *Man's Fate*, and that by an account (manifestly firsthand in part) of the Spanish Loyalist rebellion in *Man's Hope*, it became generally agreed that Malraux, even more than Silone or Koestler, was *the* novelistic historian of the great social agitations of the century. However original he might be as a craftsman, his subject, it was agreed, was the specific contemporary battle between socialism and capitalism—"the central struggle of modern times," according to Haakon Chevalier in his introduction to his own English translation of *Man's Fate*, "the struggle of a dying order with the forces within it that are molding a new world." That opinion, too, now strikes us as limited rather than misguided: and limited exactly in its failure to see Malraux's passionate hostility to limitations. For Malraux's heroes, as Joseph Frank has observed, "were never simply engaged in a battle against

a particular social or economic injustice; they were always somehow struggling against the limitations of life itself and the humiliation of destiny."
The socialist revolts loomed, in Malraux's view, as instances, urgently important in themselves, of a much grander revolt; and he took them as occasions
for depicting in fiction the revolt of man against his spiritually and intellec-
tually hemmed-in condition. This was why Malraux's writing had so immense an impact during the thirties upon the rebellious spirits of so many
different countries with their so different modes and objects and strategies
of revolt, and why he was able to enlist a far-flung loyalty that has persisted
with a sometimes unsubdued fierceness.

Malraux's main characters really are protagonists: that is, etymologi-
cally, primary combatants. What they do about the human condition is to
take arms against its historical embodiments; and they will go to the ends
of the earth to seek them out. The point has been noticed more than once:
Garine, son of a Swiss father and a Russian mother, comes in *The Conquerors*
to southern China; Perken, in *The Royal Way*, literally as well as psycholog-
ically *heimatlos* (his native state, Schleswig-Holstein, has been annexed by
Denmark), probes uncharted areas of Siam on a crusade against death; in
Man's Fate and *Man's Hope*, persons from many nations foregather in Shanghai
and Madrid, as they did in actual fact, at the moment of supreme historical
crisis; the Alsatian Vincent Berger, in *The Walnut Trees of Altenburg*, pursues
a mirage of Ottoman nationalism through central Asia. Berger's mission is
a failure: the holy war he believes in is not to be kindled; but the others find
and take part in the (losing) battle of their deepest desire. In short—and the
commonplace is worth repeating, since it applies more unequivocally to
Malraux than to any other modern novelist—Malraux's heroes make their
test of life in those places and times where human experience is most intensified, where indeed it has become most decisively embattled. It is on a
succession of darkling plains, where ignorant armies clash by night, that
Malraux's characters attempt to find an explanation of man's essential nature,
a justification of his condition, a glimpse of his destiny, a reason for his
being.

But as they do so, we move with Malraux into perplexities which, if
not wholly philosophical in nature, are at least sources of logical anxiety.
Time and again, Malraux has implied that it is in *action* that the strong-
willed individual may hope to find not only assuagement but revelation.
Victor Brombert reminds us that many of Malraux's key personages are
intellectuals—former university professors and the like—but intellectuals
who for the most part have lost faith in the values of ideas as such and who
have come to distrust the pure exercise of mind. They have therefore aban-

doned the contemplative or the teaching life and have turned to some arena of explicit action—usually by attaching themselves to a revolutionary cause where the cause is undergoing trial by warfare—in search of some truth more vital than the truth of ideas. It is a belligerent version of the perennial pragmatic strategy. Chiaramonte remarks that Malraux "pushed to its extreme consequences the modern pragmatic impulse which tends to see in the world of action the only reality, and, what is more, to reject any proposition which cannot be directly translated into a force, an act, or series of acts." The word "modern" in that admirable sentence might well be replaced by the phrase "ancient and traditional," for it has always been the hallmark of the pragmatist that he sees "in the world of action the only reality." Customarily, moreover, the pragmatic temper not only rejects propositions that cannot be translated into actions; it also dispenses with any branch of thought and despises any activity of mind that is not involved with—cannot be tested by—human experience. So it is that *history*—that is, precisely, "the world of action"—history in both its first and second intentions, as a series of actual events and as the record of events: history, in the usual pragmatic scheme, takes the place of metaphysics and of any independent theory of knowledge. The tumult of history becomes the one accessible context of truth and value; and inspecting it, the pragmatist has often been able to disclose some developing and meaningful shape, some gratifying or alarming design of things past and passing and to come. His chart of that design is the pragmatist's account of reality. The very troubling question about Malraux and for Malraux is whether he has ever managed to suggest in his fiction any such disclosure.

But Malraux is or has been a novelist, a person dedicated (as he told Trotsky) to *l'optique* of fiction rather than that of history or philosophy. The literary issue here is at least as complex as the philosophical one, and goes far beyond the confines of this essay. It has to do with that level of a work of literature—that is, of any work that aspires to such a level—on which the literal incidents and characters, the actual clashes and conversations, can be seen enacting an allegory of some large and generalized historical process: a process in which an entire social order may be caught up, or even a whole world; and a process which may or may not be "true" in the perspective of a scientific historian as it fixes on the historical period where the process is allegedly unfolding. Conrad's *Nostromo*—to stay simply with the modern novel (and apart, that is, from the tradition of epic poetry)—is a splendid example; and so of course is Dostoevsky's *The Possessed*.

In *Nostromo*, the various convulsions that rend and then reshape the little South American republic of Costaguana, the assortment of plots and pur-

poses, the interaction of a host of ambitions and devotions: all this secretes
an appalling myth of modern economic, political, moral, and even religious
history. It is the history, most generally, of the devious and yet absolute
conquest by "material interests" of the spirit and energy of modern man;
more particularly, of the process by which material interests, trusted and
supported as a source of order and justice in a repressive and unstable
backward society, bring in their own brand of intolerable injustice and
repression and thus assure further upheavals in the future. One looks in vain
for anything like so powerful if so grim a pattern in *The Conquerors* or *Man's
Fate* or *Man's Hope*, or in the three taken together. Nor can one make out in
those novels the tremendous and still more emphatic kind of historical pattern
(the inevitable spawning of nihilism by liberalism in mid-nineteenth-century
Russia) set forth in *The Possessed*. Nor, at an opposite extreme of fictional
stress, do we find the sort of faraway but sizable implications about social
and moral history that exist somewhere in the depths of James's *The Golden
Bowl*.

Malraux's dilemma, if dilemma it be, is caused in part by the very
subject—contemporary historical violence—which he has been brave enough
to deal with. When, as in *Man's Fate*, he remains faithful to the historical
outcome of the struggle, he concludes with a disaster which is not, *within
the novel*, invested with any particular significance. But when, as in *Man's
Hope*, he shapes historical fact to his fictional purposes (by concluding with
the Loyalist victory at Guadalajara), he suggests an outcome and a meaning
other than those history was already bleakly providing. Chiaramonte, who
makes this latter point, relates it to what he describes as Malraux's evasion
of "the implications of tragedy"; but I am not so sure. The case of *Man's
Hope* is problematic; but it may well be that in most of his novels, Malraux,
far from evading the implications of tragedy, was resolutely facing up to
something more terrible yet—to the absence of tragedy as discernible and
determining form at work in modern historical experience. Needless to say,
one great way to find and to make evident an illuminating design within the
confusions of history is to subject the course of the events in question to the
organizing power of the tragic imagination. Herman Melville did exactly
that when he confronted the turbulence of the American Civil War in his
loosely epic volume of war poems, *Battle-Pieces*. Most of those poems were
written while the war was still in progress; but looking back both at the war
and the poems after the pacification, Melville (in a prose supplement) could
draw upon Aristotle's definition of tragedy in the *Poetics* to define the war
as a "great historic tragedy" which he prayed had not "been enacted without

instructing our whole beloved country through terror and pity." But Malraux has not felt or envisaged the civil wars he has participated in as genuine tragic actions: not, at least, on any scale beyond that of a few driven and defeated individuals.

The importance, indeed the artistic and spiritual "value," of those individual destinies should not be minimized. It is true, as several critics have noticed, that there are no truly evil figures in Malraux's novels: no persons who either are evil through some private wayward impulse or who represent the force of some evil principle in the universe. But it is not true, as Claude-Edmonde Magny would have us believe, that Malraux has never created a character who "changes and really grows." Malraux does not concentrate his narrative on the change and growth of an individual psyche with the patience, say, of a Flaubert or a Proust. Change, in Malraux's fiction, is a regular phenomenon, but it occurs spasmodically, with earthquake speed and shock, and almost always during moments of greatest intensity. Ch'en in *Man's Fate* has grown into an altogether different phase of being before the novel is ten pages old; Vincent Berger's very soul turns over in the midst of the apocalypse on the plains of Russia. And, in fact, all those persons whom Frohock has called "Neophytes" (the narrator of *The Conquerors*, Claude Vannec in *The Royal Way*, Kassner in *Days of Wrath*, and so on) change and grow to a greater or lesser degree, and in fits and lurches; and the mark of their development is the acquisition of insight. It is an insight, customarily, into the solitary, mortal, spiritually blinded and fundamentally helpless condition of individual man; and with it, a conviction about the supreme value of human companionship, "virile fraternity." This is one of the great themes of contemporary fiction, and no writer has handled it more efficiently (and influentially) than Malraux. But these insights do not arise, so to speak, as the lesson of history: for example, as its tragic import. They are much rather the individual human response to history's failure to deliver any lesson at all.

That failure is acknowledged with devastating rhetoric in the extraordinary debate that occupies the center of Malraux's last novel, *The Walnut Trees of Altenburg*. Here Malraux's entire personal and fictional endeavor, the whole "action" of his life and his novels over two decades, is recapitulated in terms of intellectual discourse: when the question of the definable nature of man is posed as a question about the continuity and coherence of the *history* of man. The debate seems at least, via the somber climactic speech of the anthropologist Möllberg, to set the seal on incoherence as the only fact, as it were the truthless truth, discoverable in history. One might still turn to human fraternity as a form of consolation, on the edge of this abyss of meaning. But had no other truth been seized from the plunge into action, the long encounter with history?

II

In one perspective, the answer has to be in the negative. Insofar as it aimed at anything more than sheer nervy excitement, the pragmatic impulse had been defeated along with the revolutionary causes in which it had variously exerted itself. Contemporary history had proven to be as shapeless and discordant as the vast history of human cultures so bleakly examined by Möllberg; from neither could those passionately sought-after explanations be extracted. But if Malraux's pragmatic strategy had failed, what we might call his romantic strategy had been faring a good deal better; and in another perspective, the perspective of art, a very different and decidedly affirmative answer had long since begun to issue. Malraux had learned—the hard way, as the saying goes—and had shown his characters learning that, in E. M. Forster's phrase, human history "is really a series of *dis*orders"; but he had also learned with Forster that "[Art] is the one orderly product which our muddling race has produced." Perhaps he had always known this. It is implicit in a part of his reply to Trotsky; and it is even more implicit in his developing style. For, as Geoffrey Hartman remarks, from *Man's Fate* onward "the style itself intimates the author's freedom from the law to which his world remains subject, so that if the idea of Man remains inseparable from the idea of tragedy"—or, as I would prefer to say, of incoherence and absurdity, seen perhaps as tragic fatalities—"the idea of the artist pairs with the idea of freedom."

About this contention, however, there has been a significant disagreement: significant because it bears upon the nature and degree of Malraux's own artistic achievement, and on the relation between it and the absurdities he has confronted in his subject matter. Mme. Magny, for example, before registering her deep disapproval of what she takes to be Malraux's message, warmly and brilliantly praises Malraux's style, and exactly on the grounds that (far from being "free" of the world it treats) it is a splendidly contrived equivalent of its own setting—that the syntactical disjointedness, the jerky cadences, the rapid transitions, and the startling juxtapositions in Malraux's novels serve as a precise enactment of the discordant realities they describe. Malraux's best novels, this critic says without any detectable trace of irony, are "beautiful, disconnected and truly *decomposed*." Mme. Magny, in short, endorses Malraux's effort to commit what American criticism sometimes calls the fallacy of imitative form: the fallacy of trying to render a decomposed world by a decomposed book. Gaëtan Picon appears to agree with Mme. Magny; he tells us that "Of all the novels, *Man's Hope* is the one that vibrates most with discordant voices (and perhaps for that reason it is the greatest)." But Picon is satisfied that one can locate the source of harmony in Malraux's novels—in a virile fraternity, as we might say, of ideas and attitudes. Although Malraux "never stops dramatizing inimical truths," and though his is unmistakably "a universe of debate," nonetheless "all those enemies are brothers," because all of them "unite in the one who animates their dialogues," in the creative consciousness and the narrative voice of André Malraux.

In this view (which approximates Hartman's), what provides wholeness and harmony in Malraux's writings is not so much the arrangement of the incidents or the patterns of characters and relations between characters, and even less the control and shaping power of some dominant idea. It is rather a style, a presence, what Henry James would call a tone: some quality of artistic expression, however we name it, that works against and away from the images of chaos and defeat that the novels otherwise contain. Such, certainly, has been Malraux's increasingly dedicated purpose. "The way to express the unusual, the terrible, the inhuman," he has said, talking about Goya, "is not to represent carefully an actual or imaginary spectacle but to invent a script capable of representing these things without being forced to submit to their elements." Nor was this any casual matter. For Malraux, everything—his own literary achievement, his view of the human condition and of the possibility of human freedom—hang on the capacity of inventing that "script." This is, finally, the grand "truth" that emerges from the debate at Altenburg.

The Walnut Trees of Altenburg is probably the best place to test any claim one would wish to make about Malraux as a novelist. For my part, I can only hope that Malraux's reputation will not stand or fall on *Man's Hope*, which, despite some uncommonly fine individual episodes, strikes me as a showy and ultimately a rather tiresome performance, and one in which the style is held captive by the subject; though the reader (who will have his own opinion anyway) is invited to consider the high estimates cogently argued elsewhere. *Man's Fate* has, of course, been Malraux's most widely admired novel, and it is no doubt his major contribution to the history of literature in his generation; beyond that, and beginning with its original title (*La Condition humaine*), it is so impressive and enduring a challenge to its own content that it is likely to endure long after that revolutionary content has ceased to agitate the mind of readers. But the work of Malraux's which best fulfills the requirements of art—in Malraux's terms or anyone else's—seems to me to be *The Walnut Trees*.

The accomplishment of *The Walnut Trees* is the more astonishing, since it consists of only the first third of a novel called *La Lutte avec l'ange*, the remainder (which Malraux may yet rewrite) being destroyed by the German Gestapo during the war. (Another mystery, as Frank says, is that the book "should still not have appeared in this country seventeen"—now twenty— "years after it came out in French.") I have elsewhere suggested certain reasons, in part extraliterary, for the special significance of *The Walnut Trees:* mainly, the handsome way it crystallizes and gives final shape to themes and human figures that between them define the age of fiction represented by Silone, Camus, and others. The themes include those of isolation and alienation, and of companionship as expressed most decisively in an act of unmistakable charity; and the chief figure is the one I have described as a sort of saintly picaro—a human being who is at once all too human, corrupted and corruptible, but who also possesses the modern humanistic form of sainthood which is, precisely, charity in action. In *The Walnut Trees*, this vitally contradictory character appears as a "shaman"—a type which, as a Russian soldier explains to the hero's son, is represented not less by men of action (like Trotsky) than by artists (like Hölderlin and Poe), not less by persons who effect national or world history than by pure visionaries; not less in idiots than in geniuses.

Action and art, history and vision, involvement and transcendence: we are back where we started, even to the citation of Leon Trotsky. Or, rather, *The Walnut Trees* throws light backward on Malraux's career, illuminating that early exchange with Trotsky and clarifying the precarious and continuing combination in Malraux of the adventurer and the artist, the minister of state and the art historian. It does so because it is constructed in such a way as to throw light forward and backward on itself. We should not forget that Vincent Berger and the poison-gas attack, as well as the discussion of shamanism, are *elements in a novel:* that is, in a work of art, and in one which has at its center Malraux's most forthright statement about the nature and function of art as the means of escaping the human condition, as man's greatest resource for achieving freedom from history. It is presumably no longer possible for anyone to suppose, as some of the novel's first readers did, that when Möllberg asserts the utter discontinuity between human cultures he speaks for Malraux: or, anyhow, that he is the whole voice of Malraux; for, like the other characters, Möllberg is a part of Malraux and one way of looking at the history Malraux had lived through. But a much larger part of Malraux is bespoken in the midst of the Altenburg debate in the quiet voice of Vincent Berger, saying what Malraux had tried to say to Trotsky before he had himself quite grasped the principle:

> To me, our art seems to be a rectification of the world, a means of escaping from man's estate. The chief confusion, I think, is due to our belief—and in the theories propounded of Greek tragedy, it's strikingly clear—that representing fatality is the same as submitting to it. But it's not, it's almost to dominate it. The mere fact of being able to represent it, conceive it, release it from real fate, from the merciless divine scale, reduces it to the human scale. Fundamentally, our art is a humanization of the world.

What Berger says (and what, later, Malraux would say in reference to Goya) is precisely what the novel illustrates and enacts. The real answer to the despair of Möllberg lies in the novel he inhabits: in the movement and texture, the composition and tone of *The Walnut Trees* itself. The novel is the final confirmation of its own stated conviction.

III

In the light of that conviction, Malraux's subsequent and voluminous art studies are so little surprising as to be altogether inevitable. *The Psychology of Art* and *The Voices of Silence* are vast discursive demonstrations of the theory about the relation between art and man's estate of which *The Walnut Trees* was the great fictional presentation. This is what, for us, lends a strangely moving accent to Maurice Blanchot's discussion of Malraux's "museum" as standing for "the end of history." The American reader will notice in Blanchot's expert account certain parallels between Malraux's views and those espoused in Anglo-American critical theory, parallels that help clarify the idea of art as escaping from history. There is, for example, something like T. S. Eliot's notion about the literary tradition, and the way every new masterpiece subtly reorders the body of past literature. More striking yet is the parallel with Northrop Frye's *Anatomy of Criticism* and its concept (spelled out more emphatically than it had been by Eliot) of the self-contained nature of literature, the sense in which the *literary*—or, more broadly in Malraux, the artistic—element of the artwork exists outside of time, and belongs to the timeless transhistorical order of art itself. But it is not easy to find any sort of parallel to the sheer passion (reflected in Blanchot) with which Malraux has proclaimed and elaborated these principles. It is the passion born from the encounters with history—those of Malraux's life and those of his fiction—and its form is the passionate conviction that, while history has to be reckoned with, has to be entered and participated in and investigated, it also has to be transcended; for when all is said and done, the truth is not in it. The knowledge provided by the "museum," says Blanchot, "is historical, it is the knowledge of histories, and of a series of histories that we accept"; but "at the same time, it is not historical, it does not concern itself with the objective truth of history . . . and this is the knowledge we accept and even prefer." We prefer it, according to Malraux, because the knowledge discoverable in the timeless, transhistorical world of art forms (the museum without walls) is a definition of man as free, heroic, creative, and purposeful. Art restores the definition that had been questioned and shattered by history: restores it and gives it an unassailable permanence. "To save one through the other— [Malraux] was unable to resist this great temptation."

DAVID WILKINSON

The Bolshevik Hero

Malraux's two novels [*Man's Fate* and *Days of Wrath*] completed in 1933
and 1935 (at the height of his own period of cooperation with the Communists) represent a distinct phase in his development. Not a party member,
he rejects both the organizational methods of the party and a key aspect of
Marxist dogma. But the central figures of *Man's Fate* and *Days of Wrath* are
Communists because in this period Malraux has accepted without any re-
luctance the value of fighting the same fight as that of the Communists. *Man's
Fate* arrives at this conclusion by debating what Malraux sees as the alternative ways to lead one's life at a moment of revolutionary crisis. *Days of
Wrath* dispenses with the debate entirely. Both works present mythic, exemplary heroes—figures not to be rejected, like those of the preceding works,
but worthy of imitation. Malraux has reached his first resting point here,
his first partly stable notion of what is man's political good. This abstract
idea of the good life is rendered concrete in the successful lives of Kyo Gisors
and Kassner, in the successful figure of the Bolshevik hero.

 Man's Fate (1933) appears to employ a plot structure familiar to Malraux:
action, apparent success, failure. But at the opening of *Man's Fate*, as if to
differentiate it from the works that come before, stands not a journey but a
murder. At the end, there is not death or departure but a succession, a new
and yet renewed debate, a continuation into the future. If the future has
ever until now had any meaning or real existence for Malraux, his readers
have not been made aware of it. With all its similarities, real and apparent,

From *Malraux: An Essay in Political Criticism.* © 1967 by the President and Fellows
of Harvard College. Harvard University Press, 1967.

to its predecessors, *Man's Fate* is a different book. Still an enormous explo-
ration and lesson in the tragic shape of human destiny, it constitutes a new
lesson, breaking new ground.

The plot is more complex than earlier ones (though this point is not
significant for the present investigation), and the action will demand and
accept the summary of "success and later failure." The greater complexity
simply consists of the larger involvement of those characters other than the
central figure in the movement of the novel; more attention must be directed
to them; and this orientation becomes the ostensible reason for a more basic
search into these other figures than the highly concentrated focus of *The
Conquerors* permitted. The time is March 1927, the place Shanghai. The
Kuomintang, which now holds Hankow as well as Canton, is moving north-
ward over the hopeless opposition of various forces; those that matter briefly
in the novel are the "White" forces associated with the Shanghai government.
The immediate issue is over the seizure of Shanghai—will it fall to the
organized Communist groups within or to the "Blue" Nationalist army of
Chiang Kai-shek? For Chiang is on the verge of splitting with the Communists, until now his allies in the Kuomintang, and the question of who
takes Shanghai points beyond itself to the question of which will be victorious
in China in the struggle which both know must come. More to the reader's
interest are the problematic relation between the hierarchical Communist
party (centered now in Hankow) and the Shanghai revolutionaries (who are
still psychological individualists, if individualist in no other way) and the
general relation between order and the person in a situation of revolt. And,
inevitably, the destiny of men, taken one after the other, as a clue to the
destiny of man.

A Communist insurrection, led by Kyo Gisors and the Russian Katov,
captures Shanghai in about a day and a half. The Communists divert a
government arms shipment to themselves and by distributing the weapons
turn a general strike into a revolution. The Shanghai Communists have won,
Chiang is forestalled. But already in the first day of the uprising preparations
are being made by the President of the French Chamber of Commerce,
Ferral, to deal with Chiang Kai-shek and to turn him against the Communists.
As the city falls, the deal is closed; and one portion of the action ends with
the presentation to the Communists of a Blue order to surrender their arms
and leave themselves helpless. Kyo and his friend Ch'en, a terrorist, make
a journey to Hankow, trying and failing to receive the support of the International in a refusal to give up their weapons and an immediate break
with Chiang. Ch'en returns, to be killed in an unsuccessful attempt on
Chiang's life. Kyo also returns, to organize combat groups and await the

inevitable repression. When it comes, he is arrested and later commits suicide; Katov is taken and executed, along with all the other revolutionaries except for a few who escape to continue the fight or to muse upon it. The plot itself, like that of *The Royal Way*, ends in a defeat. But an analysis of the characters individually leads to a different "conclusion."

The apparently stable plot is dominated by the new method of constructing the actual argument. Instead of examining the life of one moral prototype, finding the elements of strength and weakness in that type, the reader is exposed to a large set of important characters. Each of them displays a certain perception of the Absurd and a certain reaction to it: all are figures searching for some enduring value in the face of isolation, defeat, and death. Though they do not argue the case for the lives they lead with as many words as do the figures of *Man's Hope*, *Man's Fate* is nevertheless a debate among many possible responses to the Absurd—a debate in which the characters argue with their lives.

The point at issue is the response of the hero to his predicament. Each character becomes aware of a particular mask of the Absurd, a manifestation of destiny which stands in his path. How does he react to it? Does he attempt to blind himself to its existence? Does he submit to it and become an instrument? Does he revolt against it, attempt to conquer it, and turn it to use? And is his conquest merely a pretense, the verbal screen for a hidden surrender or a real failure? To this interrogation the figures of this political novel must be subjected, to discover which of them, if any, is indeed its hero.

Each key figure has his own special ordeal. König, Chiang Kai-shek's police chief, cannot forget that once, when he was captured and tortured by the Reds in Russia, he wept before them; now he is forever obsessed by that memory, driven literally to lose himself, unable to forget his disgust with himself and his humiliation, unable ever to recapture what he was. The Baron de Clappique has fallen out of his social place into a sordid subterranean life on the fringes of the night world of Shanghai; he cannot think of his degradation without renewed anguish. Old Gisors, Kyo's father, is an intellectual, anguished for a more Malrauvian reason: the constant perception of his own solitude, the fear of death. Ferral, President of the Franco-Asiatic consortium and the French Chamber of Commerce, in terror of being dependent upon the will of another, is beset by the craving for power and the fear that it will escape him. The phonograph seller Hemmelrich, who has lived an atrocious life of poverty and wretchedness for thirty-seven years, writhes at the thought of a future like his past, in which he cannot afford to die because he has a family but cannot alleviate the misery of his wife or the constant pain of his sick child. The young Westernized Chinese, Ch'en, has received from a Lutheran pastor a deep religious anxiety, an agony of sin and shame, a consciousness of isolation from the world, a need to fulfill an apostleship—but no love, no religious vocation, no faith. This variety of human torment is in sharp contrast to the morbid unity of Perken's obsession: some of these maladies look superficially more curable than the consciousness of death. But in fact it is mainly those who are doomed to die who make the best of life, those who want something from life who live on contemptibly and in despair.

The responses to the human lot in *Man's Fate* fall into three broad groups: some men, like the Conquerors, seek their defense in power and violence; others seek to escape by transforming their consciousness, overcoming their perceptions of the world; still others are revolutionaries who find the causes of their condition in the social order and attempt to amend it.

König, Ch'en, and Ferral belong to the first group. König's memory of humiliation by torture can be wiped away, for a moment only, by torture and murder, by the killing of a whole class of men whom he holds responsible. He was tortured by the Reds: now "*my* dignity is to kill them"; he believes that he can live the life of a man again only when he feeds his solitude with blood. And even to kill is not enough—first he must degrade and humiliate the victim just as he has been degraded. He is exacting retribution, but not retribution alone. König denies that he is a free man, free to choose his own way of living. Because the Reds drove nails into his shoulders, and because he wept before them, he lives by punishing them; because he insists on blood, he must not admit to himself that he could have lived otherwise. Only if he can persuade his victim to degrade himself—as had König— during the ordeal can he prove—as he must prove again and again—that men with a dignity of their own do not exist. If no one can withstand his torture, then dignity consists merely in being torturer rather than victim, and König possesses all that life can afford a man; if no one can withstand his torture, then the humiliated cannot choose their lives, and König could not have chosen to become anything but what he is. His justification of and satisfaction from his life require a certain submission from all his prisoners. König captures the revolutionary Kyo Gisors, converses with him humanely, hears him talk of his decision for the revolution as the product of "a will to dignity." König determines to pull him down, as he must. He interrogates Kyo; he cajoles him, threatens him, tempts him to change sides and save his life; "only I will know it"—know again, that is, that men in torment are *all* without dignity. Kyo refuses and is sent to be killed. König has not had his full measure of satisfaction: his solution to the problem of his own pain has been violated, for he has only captured the body of his victim. Worse still than this outrage is the fact that a man should have endured the same atrocious condition that distorted and destroyed König: for now König can know that it was not his condition but his choice of a cure for it that deformed him as a man and made his loss of dignity permanent. He might have recovered himself, but his defense was both unworthy and unsuccessful.

By the time König comes onstage, the independent elements of his personality have long since vanished and he has been swallowed up by his role: counterrevolutionary in politics, policeman in society, killer in existential reality. Ch'en Ta-erh is swallowed up before our eyes by the role of anarchist assassin, terrorist, Conqueror and murderer. He appears first as a revolutionary conspirator who stabs a sleeping man as a matter of duty; he dies in political and actual solitude as a man who has parted with revolution in order to make terrorism into the meaning of his life. To possess himself he must become a lonely executioner. Killing—political killing of certain men, as for König—is what will free him from his absurd burden.

The Absurd presents itself to Ch'en as religious Angst without the comforts of religion. Like the pastor, his teacher, Ch'en is driven to forget himself in action, to justify his life by making a sacrifice of it. But Ch'en's religious version of the unhappy consciousness lacks the charity that might direct him to sacrifice for others, and it lacks the inner life and sense of the presence of the divine that might permit a religious renunciation: since he has no faith, religion cannot be his defense. He is seduced away from Pastor Smithson by an intellectual recruiter for the revolution, who plays on his illusion of heroism to bring him into political activity.

In the course of this activity Ch'en becomes a decisive influence, setting off both the revolt and the repression. To him this is only by the way, for he is entirely involved with the meaning of his acts for himself, for his own life. He begins by murdering a man so as to steal a paper which will get the insurrection the arms it must have to start. But for him the political meaning of the act vanishes as it is performed and is replaced by an entirely personal, religious one. He feels that the murder has thrown him into a world from which there will be no escape. By his bloody act he is in his own mind set apart from "men who do not kill," cut off from the realm of the living, absorbed into a world of murder, of imprisoning solitude and increasing anguish. He struggles to return, but he cannot. Neither in conversation nor in action can he convey what he has felt, his sudden familiarity with death. As his combat group attacks a police station, they link arms in a chain on its roof (the top man holding to a roof ornament so that the bottom man can hurl grenades through a window): "In spite of the intimacy of death, in spite of that fraternal weight which was pulling him apart, he was not one of them." The murder means, to him, the revelation and the seal on his utter solitude.

But this world of solitude that he has discovered is created by a specific act and can only enfold him completely when he repeats that act. Ch'en becomes obsessed with the idea of terrorism. His sleep is poisoned with new anguish, with terrible monsters conjured from his memories of murder, that only a new plan and a new murder will relieve. He begins to draw away from the other revolutionaries, to defy discipline as well as doctrine, to insist upon the assassination of Chiang Kai-shek. He breaks with them and makes an attempt on Chiang's life.

Politically this is the provocation that sparks the repression. For Ch'en the decision to kill has (again) a personal meaning only. He tries to give it a political meaning as well by fabricating an ideology of terrorism: the individual without hope, says this ideology, must find an immediate meaning to his life, not through an organization, but through an idea—the idea of martyrdom; the terrorist mystique will require every man in solitude to assume a responsibility, to appoint himself the judge of an oppressor's life, to decide alone, to execute alone, and to die alone. But this mystique is without political end, is intended to achieve nothing beyond the deaths of the "accused" and his "judge." The only meaning available to the individual is, therefore, the immediate meaning: he kills; he dies. Ch'en makes no serious attempt to convey this mystique to others or to judge whether or not Chiang or some other should be killed. An ideology which cannot survive its author has a merely personal meaning. The decision to make an attempt in which he must die silences Ch'en's nagging anguish and replaces it with a "radiant exaltation," a complete possession of himself. Thus it appears that his true object is in his own death, met amid a ritual of sacrifice. He achieves his objective.

Ch'en's reaction to his "human condition" has in common with those of the other Conquerors, which otherwise it hardly resembles, that it takes the form of a sickness, and of a submersion in sickness, rather than a cure. His self-destruction does not even pretend to free him. His world, so alien to that of men, is finally dominated, not by men, but by death and by fatality. Yet on one occasion it seems to Kyo that Ch'en embodies man himself, a moth that creates the very light in which he will destroy himself. No argument in *Man's Fate* denies it: only the lives, and even more the deaths, of Katov and of Kyo himself.

The entrepreneur Ferral, the third of the Conqueror-types in *Man's Fate*, is what Garine might have become by living to associate himself with

England. Ferral is an ex-intellectual and former deputy, using his enterprises in the Orient as the stairway back to power in France. The revolution menaces the Chinese portions of his empire, and he reacts vigorously even while it is in progress, routing out the money which will enable Chiang to pay his army and break at once with the Communists. He is successful in buying off Chiang, but at the moment of success his financial troubles grow; though he has beaten the nearest enemy, he is in turn vanquished in his own field, and his consortium is finally dissolved.

Ferral is thoroughly devoted to power seeking. Intelligence for him is "the possession of the means of coercing things or men," and he thinks of other men not as persons, but as part of a network of mechanisms to be operated. " 'A man is the sum of his action, of what he has *done*, of what he can do. Nothing else. I am not what such and such an encounter with a man or woman may have done to shape my life; I am my roads.' " Yet he vaguely suspects how thoroughly dependent he is on forces which he does not control, and it is made inescapably plain to him when, after his victory, a roomful of candy-chewing "sedentary nonentities"—the representatives of the French banks—in a long, incomprehensible ritual deny him the funds needed to save the consortium and the power for which he has fought.

Old Gisors identifies Ferral's real urge, one that is both endless and hopeless.

> "Men are perhaps indifferent to real power . . . the king's power . . . the power to govern. . . . What fascinates them . . . is not real power, it's the illusion of being able to do exactly as they please. . . . Man has no urge to govern: he has an urge to compel . . . to be more than a man, in a world of men. To escape man's fate, I was saying. Not powerful: all-powerful. The visionary disease, of which the will to power is only the intellectual jus-tification, is the will to god-head: every man dreams of being god."

Gisors also remarks that "there is always a need for intoxication: this country has opium . . . the West has woman. . . . Perhaps love is above all the means which the Occidental uses to free himself from man's fate." For Ferral, if we read "eroticism" for "love," this is true: his ideal "power" is really the complete sexual possession of a woman, and he carries out operations in that sphere in just the same manner as in those of counterrevolutionary and financial maneuvering, with the same absorption—in fact, with the same ending. This will to possess dominates his relation with his mistress, Valerie: by giving her sexual pleasure and by humiliating her, he believes, he triumphs over her. But this triumph is not lasting, for she responds by making him ridiculous in public; in turn, furious with humiliation, he imagines fantastic punishments, finally fills her rooms with animals and satisfies himself by humiliating a prostitute in his turn. "His will to power never achieved its object"; he could never possess another completely nor completely penetrate the consciousness of a woman; "in reality he never went to bed with anyone but himself." His activity is frenzied and meaningless, and a wash-drawing he has placed on his wall is his emblem: "on a discolored world over which travelers were wandering, two exactly similar skeletons were embracing each other in a trance." And to give the lie to all the activity which is only a disguise, there is his strange, superficially inappropriate craving for sleep:

> Sleep was peace. He had lived, fought, created; beneath all those appearances, deep down, he found this to be the only reality, the joy of abandoning himself, of leaving upon the shore, like the body of a drowned companion, that creature, himself, whose life it was necessary each day to invent anew. "To sleep is the only thing I have always really wanted, for so many years."

Games of power which defeat him, craving for an omnipotence which he can never reach, the need to inflict humiliations which end in his own humiliation, the need to possess and to possess what forever escapes him, a flight at last from himself into sleep where he finds only nightmares and, once more, himself: all are forms of the attempt to be released from "man's fate," and all, equally, fail.

Ferral and König each yield to an obsession growing out of past humiliation, Ch'en to one with which his mentor infects him. Each permits his obsession, with power or violence, to create an inner anxiety that is relieved only in the anticipation or the act of damaging, indirectly or directly, some other person. But the compulsion to rule, to torture, or to kill grows insatiable and boundless. They must fail to satisfy it sooner or later. But only Ch'en discovers the true end toward which the impossible desire points: permanent peace; self-destruction. In the earlier stages of this passage from obsession to death, Ferral and König (who leave their victims alive) no doubt transmit their disorders as Ch'en's pastor transmitted his own, for they present to others the same experience of humiliation that molded them. They are the carriers of the Absurd, as they are its victims. This latter quality at least they share with those who would defend themselves through changing their ways of looking at the world. If those who choose to be intoxicated with action destroy others as well as themselves, those who choose other forms of intoxication (that touch themselves only) are perhaps to be preferred.

That they turn against themselves at least suggests that those who turned against society did so by choice rather than by necessity: that, despite the seeming logic of their lives, they could have done otherwise.

As Malraux continues to explore the question, "How can a man live?"—which is to say, how can one contend with one's human lot—he encounters answers that are as futile as they are fascinating. One answer that fascinates is the Baron de Clappique's: mythomania. Clappique is a fugitive, expatriate, penniless, fallen member of a deteriorated upper class. His normal existence is sordid: he is first found playing the fool in a jazzhall, the Black Cat, between a pair of dance girls. He appears simply whimsical, but he is like the other denizens of that fringe world, "in the depths of an identical despair." He drinks, throws away all his money in one night, concocts variegated and fabulous tales about himself, with one object: the denial of his life, of his decline. Wealth does not exist, poverty does not exist; " 'Nothing exists: all is dream.' " Kyo and his father have an occasion to discuss him: " 'No man exists by denying life.' . . . 'One lives inadequately by it. . . . He feels a need to live inadequately.' 'And he is forced to.' 'He chooses a way of life that *makes* it necessary.' " Old Gisors claims that Clappique's affliction has no more depth than the man himself; but if Clappique's is not deep, it is still the same malady that belongs to all men. He cannot think of the manner of life from which he has fallen without one form of anguish, and his simple confrontation with the serenity of the Japanese painter, Kama, brings him another: "the atrocious sensation of suffering in the presence of a creature who denied suffering."

Like the others Clappique senses the presence of an Absurd; he tries to defend himself against it by outperforming it in absurdity, by means of his fantastic vagaries. He suffers and denies it as best he can—though absurdity personified never thoroughly outfaces the Absurd even in his normal life—by making everything into an alcoholic or outrageous dream, even his own being: " 'Baron de Clappique does not exist.' "

Clappique becomes involved with the revolutionaries by chance, because he runs out of money and can be of some service to them in obtaining the arms shipment; the police, for whom he has usually provided information, discover this, and his connection with Kyo leads one of his contacts, on the day before the repression, to warn Clappique to leave Shanghai. Instead, Clappique warns Kyo; the latter, who has long since made up his mind to stay and fight to the end, asks Clappique to go back to try to obtain more information; Clappique arranges to meet him at the Black Cat. Before the appointment, with time to spare, Clappique is attracted to a gambling house; the information he has, vital to Kyo, is forgotten as Clappique suddenly seems to find himself in the world of true and unconcealed reality, a man confronted by destiny in the form of a roulette wheel, with the clarity of a revelation. From a man with no depth, he becomes one who seems to comprehend everything in Malraux's philosophy, in one experience.

> He had the feeling of seizing his life, of holding it suspended to the whim of that absurd ball . . . the living reality . . . of everything by which men believe their destinies to be governed. . . . Through its agency he was embracing his own destiny—the only means he had ever found of possessing himself!

Yet a sense of wrongness, of a false twist in his revelation, seeps through to us: he is gratifying "at once the two Clappiques that composed him, the one who wanted to live and the one who wanted to be destroyed"; he tries to win "no longer in order to take flight, but to remain, to risk more, so that the stake of his conquered liberty would render the gesture even more absurd!" He finds in gambling "a suicide without death." Knowing that his play will lead to his own inability to leave Shanghai and to Kyo's capture,

> he threw Kyo back into a world of dreams . . . he was sustaining that ball . . . with his own life . . . and with the life of another.
> . . . He knew he was sacrificing Kyo; it was Kyo who was chained to that ball, to that table, and it was he, Clappique, who was that ball, which was master of everyone and of himself—of himself who was nevertheless looking at it, living as he had never lived, outside of himself, held spellbound and breathless by an overpowering shame.

His liberation begins to seem false to him the moment he leaves the gambling house; "anguish was returning"; he tries to defend himself by going from prostitute to prostitute, concocting a tale of his own coming suicide, becoming drunk on his fabrications of "a world where truth no longer existed . . . neither true nor false, but real." Again his old metaphysics argues that since this new universe did not exist, "nothing existed. The world had ceased to weigh upon him. Liberated, he lived now only in the romantic universe which he had just created."

Much later he returns to his room, trying to banish torment and solitude with whiskey. He spies a mirror and, in a weirdly terrifying scene, "as if he had found a way of expressing directly in all its intensity the torment which words were not adequate to translate, he began to make faces transforming himself . . . into all the grotesques that a human face can express," then suddenly recoils from the "frightful mirror" whose "debauchery of the grotesque . . . was assuming the atrocious and terrifying humor of madness."

He feels no remorse, only a fear of death; having lost his money, he destroys his identity by passing himself off as a sailor on a vessel about to depart, preferring, as a stowaway, a voyage that will probably lead to prison to his real physical annihiliation; and aboard ship he returns to his continuing round of mythomania and alcohol. He stands firm on his conviction that "men do not exist" because "a costume is enough to enable one to escape from oneself"—even though that escape is only the construction and reconstruction of a series of prisons. Clappique might have been able to alter his life, to emerge from his self-imposed regime of degradation, if he had cared to notice the chance and to will the change. Instead, and despite a series of insights into the sources of his anguish, he had chosen—and knows he would choose again—one more, and the grandest, of a series of abject illusions of liberation, "the most dazzling success of his life," since he is no longer telling a lie but existing as one. He is a figure out of surrealist quietism, and his nonviolent confrontation with destiny, his absurd reaction to absurdity, is a form of subjection and submission that scarcely pretends to be anything else.

Another character who follows an escapist road away from his own overwhelming Angst is Kyo's father, Old Gisors. An intellectual, he has organized revolutionary cadres but avoids action himself. Quite unlike his son (or Garine), he is a contemplative, interested in what is deepest or most singular in men rather than in what can be used to make them act, in individual men rather than in the moving forces of the world of flux. His meeting with other major characters—Clappique, Ch'en, Kyo, Ferral—all turn into analyses which the reader may accept as true but which lead to no conclusions. And these disjoined analyses are but one step away from a total lack of contact; it is only his son who binds him to the world of men and makes them matter at all, and after Kyo's death human individuals no longer exist for him at all.

At the outset Old Gisors is a Marxist for reasons precisely opposed to those of Kyo, for a fear of death brings to him a consciousness of fatality; rather than revolt against this fatality, he wishes to bring himself into harmony with it; while Kyo lives and men still count for something to him, Gisors is therefore attracted to Marxism, not by the will it contains, but by its element of fatality. As for the men he scrutinizes, however much he knows or deduces about them, he does not know them. He begins with the abstract cognition of the distance lying between himself and others. As the revolution begins, he comes to apply this realization, to feel the gap, to understand that he does not know his own son, that there is no point of contact between them even though they are on the same side of a political contest. As a former professor, he can be sure only of what he has taught or given to a man, and it is not he who has taught Kyo to follow the life of action. He loves his son ("One never knows a human being, but one occasionally ceases to feel that one does not know him"), he teaches his students to give themselves wholly to the *willing* side of Marxism, solely to give Kyo allies; but his love cannot overcome the separation he perceives between them, his own consequent solitude, anguish, and obsession with death.

A photograph of Kyo lies under the tray which holds Gisors's real escape: opium. Since he cannot escape his total solitude, since he can neither reach nor be reached by another consciousness, he chooses to plumb the depths of his own "furious subterranean imagination" clothed in the benign indifference of the drug. The oppressive world loses its bitterness to his perceptions: "His eyes shut, carried by great motionless wings, Gisors contemplated his solitude: a desolation that joined the divine, while at the same time the wave of serenity that gently covered the depths of death widened to infinity." When Kyo is captured, Gisors makes hopeless attempts to secure his release; after Kyo's death he is plunged into grief but refuses at first to smother it with opium. He watches near his son's body and allows the meaninglessness of the world to burn out and destroy all the bonds which had linked it to him; "he felt the basic suffering trembling within him, not that which comes from creatures or from things, but that which gushes forth from man himself and from which life attempts to tear us away."

But at the last he flees to Japan and to opium again; he abandons his Marxism and becomes indifferent finally to life and death. " 'Men should be able to learn that there is no reality, that there are worlds of contemplation—with or without opium—where all is vain . . . !' 'Where one contemplates what?' 'Perhaps nothing other than this vanity. . . . That's a great deal.' . . . 'All suffer, and each one suffers because he thinks. At bottom, the mind conceives man only in the eternal, and the consciousness of life can be nothing but anguish. One must not think of life with the mind, but with opium.' " He becomes able to view Kyo's death without torture. " 'It takes fifty years to make a man, fifty years of sacrifice, of will. . . . And when this man is complete, when there is nothing left in him of childhood . . . when he is really a man—he is good for nothing but to die.' " He contemplates men whom he no longer resembles and achieves an understanding from his distance of

> all those unknown creatures who were marching toward death in
> the dazzling sunlight, each one nursing his deadly parasite in a
> secret recess of his being. "Every man is a madman . . . but what
> is human destiny if not a life of effort to unite this madman and

the universe. . . . Every man dreams of being god." . . . Humanity was dense and heavy, heavy with flesh, with blood, with suffering, eternally clinging to itself like all that dies, but even blood, even flesh, even suffering, even death was being absorbed up there in the light like music in the silent night . . . human grief seemed to him to rise and to lose itself in the very song of earth; upon the quivering release hidden within him like his heart, the grief which he had mastered—slowly closed its inhuman arms.

He sees men, but he has lost them; his escape has cut him off from all that is human in them: "for the first time the idea that the time which was bringing him closer to death was flowing through him did not isolate him from the world, but joined him to it in a serene accord. . . . Liberated from everything, even from being a man, he caressed the stem of his pipe." Like his son's dead body, he is "already something other than a man."

Clappique and Old Gisors seek to escape by transforming their awareness of the world. Clappique's weapons are alcohol and lies, Gisors's are drugs. Clappique concocts fabulous tales about himself to deny life, to support his principle that "nothing exists: all is dream." He drinks to create a dream, he gambles to achieve the sense of victory and liberation. By mythomania and alcohol he constructs a series of spurious illusions of freedom—a series of degradations and submissions and self-imposed humiliations, lies which at last he can neither believe nor escape. Gisors, like Clappique, resolves the struggle between man and the world, between self and otherness, by merging man with world, self with otherness. Like Clappique, he escapes by a voluntary destruction of himself, akin to suicide: he is finished with the struggle and pain of being a man. Men must strive and suffer always, if not the one then the other; those who leave off doing either become foreign to mankind. And whether the escape is effected by self-brutalization or self-transcendence makes no difference, for a completely successful escape, like a death, closes the books on a human existence.

Power, violence, lies, and dreams do not escape the judgment of destiny. The third group of characters, the true revolutionaries, even in the face of their own humiliations and deaths grasp human and permanent values. Malraux, with a new "social" consciousness, discovers a human type for whom human isolation is neither necessary nor eternal: in the present it can be broken in a common struggle, even in a common defeat; in the future, toward which that struggle is directed, it may be withered by the transformation of civilization.

In his life Kyo Gisors fights for a value that will outlive him—the "human dignity" that is the just common property of all man. He conceives of dignity primarily as a negation, the absence of the humiliation of man by man, the end of the absurd cycle of being humiliated and of humiliating, of being tortured and torturing, that describes the life of König or of Ferral, or of Garine. The implication of a struggle for "human dignity" instead of for "my dignity" (which for König lies in "humiliating them") is a utopian anarchism, an opposition, not to government, but to the urge of the powerful to compel. Garine knows of only one way not to be beaten—to conquer. Kyo subscribes to a third path. He does not elaborate on the changes that would have to be made in the social order or in the psyches of individuals of the conquering and escapist types before the utopia of dignity could come to be. But he cannot take the problem of the future as seriously as he might because physical victory in the present is not achieved in the novel. Therefore the utopia of human dignity remains at the level of a Sorelian myth, emphasizing and driving a will to act in the present rather than describing in detail the future brought by victorious action.

Yet the hopeful future is not left so vague as this. Malraux himself reveals a subdued utopianism, introducing hope, not only through Kyo, but also through Old Gisors and Hemmelrich. In one of his detached analyses Gisors declares that a civilization becomes transformed when its most oppressed element suddenly becomes a *value* and that for modern civilization this will occur when the worker ceases to attempt to escape his work and finds in it his reason for being—when the factory becomes what the cathedral was, and men see in it, not gods, but human power struggling against the earth. And Hemmelrich, driven into Russia after the suppression of the Shanghai uprising, fulfills Old Gisors's prophetic words by discovering his own dignity in the work that had previously crushed him—because for the first time "I work and know why I work." The inference is that the transformed future will involve not merely sociopolitical transformations of an anarchist sort (the abolition of the institutionalized opportunity to dominate) and psychological changes (the healing of the Conquerors), but new cultural myths as well.

Myths appear in many forms in Malraux's work. Myths about the heroic life of an individual inspire initiates to imitate him; such myths, thus far, have only appeared as damaging, since they have attached themselves only to Conquerors (as in the Grabot-Perken-Claude chain). Myths about a new future and a good life therein have been manipulated by psychotechnicians to procure them power (Garine). Such myths, of a future in which the content of the good life is absolute personal power, accepted by the Conquerors, have stirred them to action and struggle but have always yielded defeat, though at moments the presence of the other men whom he is using in the fight has broken through to the Conqueror and has revealed to him some real value, which he normally passes by. Myths about men and the world dominate whole cultures: the Western myth leads to anguish and despair for those who believe it (according to Ling) and for those who do not (according to A.D.). But Malraux, perhaps because of his early anthropological training, cannot espouse the impossible—a civilization without myths. Instead he has begun the search for new, potentially creative myths (in J. E.), at all three levels: hero myths, political-utopia myths, and cultural myths. The first possible hero myth (Conqueror-type) has been tried and found wanting; Malraux is now examining the second type. He has only just begun a reflection on a political utopia of dignity: one feature of that utopia will be a cultural myth that destroys the alienation of the worker from his work by explaining it, not as something he must do to keep alive and get cash, but as a role in a common struggle. Since this is a peaceable utopia, the worker is to be animated not by a class-struggle myth (as with Sorel and Stalinism) nor by one of national struggle, but by a myth of the struggle of man against the earth—a humanist myth. Gisors's lecture on the transformation of a civilization is the first sign of what is to become Malraux's humanist position, in which the Western cultural myth described by Ling ("men" as separate from and in conflict with "the world," and the "individual" as separate from and in conflict with all other "individuals") is to be supplanted by a myth of "man" as a naturally harmonious unity separate from, and as a whole in conflict with, "the world."

But, because the political order of the moment offers no immediate chance to bring about the better world, the mythic heroes of *Man's Fate* do not conduct a revolution to victory and build a new order: they follow it to defeat and find a new value. The political utopia they seek is not within sight: but, in making them struggle for a good future, it yields them part of its values in the present. This situation is partly exemplified by Hemmelrich and by the Russian Organization Man, Katov, and fully by the death of the Franco-Japanese intellectual, Kyo Gisors.

The shopkeeper and phonograph seller Hemmelrich is an ambiguous character: almost the counterpart of König, through half-ironic and uncontrollable, half-unexplained means he has managed to hold back and win over the dehumanizing forces around him. For thirty-seven years he has lived unable to rise above wretchedness, "a blind and persecuted dog." If he could, he would "offset by violence—any kind of violence . . . this atrocious life that has poisoned him since he was born, that would poison his children in the same way." But he cannot join the revolution and die, because of his wife—whom he married because she was as wretched as he—and their child, sick with mastoiditis and in constant pain. He cannot strike back; out of fear for them he cannot even give shelter to his friends.

> If he had had money, if he could have left it to them, he would
> have been free to go and get killed. As if the universe had not
> treated him all his life with kicks in the belly, it now despoiled
> him of the only dignity he could ever possess—his death.

But when the repression begins, his shop is "cleaned out" by grenades in his absence, his wife and child are killed; an ironic fate has freed him. "He could not banish from his mind the atrocious, weighty, profound joy of liberation . . . now he was no longer impotent. Now, *he too could kill*." He runs to the nearest Communist strongpoint to help in its defense. There is an explosion; he recovers consciousness to see a Blue scout coming toward him through the barbed wire, an opportunity to kill. "He was no longer a man, he was everything that Hemmelrich had suffered from until now. . . . 'They have made us starve all our lives, but this one is going to get it, he's going to get it. . . . You'll pay for it!' " He kills the man and escapes in his uniform.

Hemmelrich might now be ready to join König as a man capable of nothing but killing; yet, inexplicably, this one murder appears to bring his second, and real, liberation. His hands, covered with the blood of his family, had been horrors which could only be forgotten if he held a knife or a machine gun in them; but now two drops of blood from the man he has killed fall in turn on the victim's hands, "and as if this hand that was being spattered with blood had avenged him, Hemmelrich dared at last to look at his own, and discovered that the blood-stain had rubbed off hours before." Unlike König, Hemmelrich is able to stop at this juncture without making himself once more a subject of the Absurd. He leaves China, and the reader is told that he has finally found what becomes in this novel Malraux's foremost value—his dignity—in work.

> "He is a mounter in the electric plant. He said to me: 'Before,
> I began to live when I left the factory; now, I begin to live when
> I enter it. It's the first time in my life that I work and know why
> I work, not merely waiting patiently to die.' "

Hemmelrich has been freed; more importantly, he has been able to free himself.

Malraux's Organization Men (Comintern professional revolutionaries) have tended to be moral mediocrities who are skillful at explaining why revolutionaries must compromise to survive and why foreign revolutions must be subordinated to the welfare of the Soviet Union. But Katov (and Kassner of *Days of Wrath*) transcend mediocrity through suffering. By the time of the Spanish Civil War all the old questions and more arise: but in these two novels the Organization Men are permitted to surpass themselves.

Katov, unlike the other Shanghai insurrectionists, has already been freed of his burden of anguish. This burden, like that of Hemmelrich, was the suffering of others whom he could not relieve; as Hemmelrich is freed in the course of the novel, Katov had long since been liberated by death to fight. He knows what he is fighting for: every battle now recalls to him a memory from the Russian Civil War—the capture of his battalion in winter, the digging of their own graves, their taking off coats and trousers in the cold before the White firing squad, the uncontrollable sneezes "so intensely human, in that dawn of execution, that the machine-gunners waited—waited for life to become less indiscreet." The other Organization Men act in the name of a fatality, the inevitable Revolution; Katov acts in the name and memory of men. With his fellows, Katov is captured in the repression. Almost nothing is known about him when he finally appears in a schoolyard, used to hold the wounded prisoners waiting to be shot, and is put with Kyo in a space reserved for those who are to be tortured to death by being thrown alive into the boiler of a locomotive—their deaths signaled back to those in the schoolyard by the shriek of the locomotive whistle. It is the way of his living those last hours which says all there is to be said about him. "Katov was lying . . . beside him, separated from him by the vast expanse of suffering" which separates all, but also "joined to him by that absolute friendship, without reticence, which death alone gives . . . among all those brothers in the mendicant order of the Revolution: each of these men had wildly seized as it stalked past him the only greatness that could be his." When Kyo dies beside him, Katov is thrown back into solitude, but without suffering. He too has cyanide with which to end his life; but next to him are two of his fellows without it, and in the grip of fear.

> In spite of all these men who had fought as he had, Katov was alone, alone between the body of his dead friend and his two terror-striken companions, alone between this wall and the whistle far off in the night. But a man could be stronger than this solitude and even, perhaps, than that atrocious whistle: fear struggled in him against the most terrible temptation in his life.

He gives them the cyanide and condemns himself. Katov is a doctrinaire among the revolutionaries, but nothing in his doctrine obliged him to make

that sacrifice, and it puts him on a plane above both those who decline to
act and those whose action relates to themselves alone.

His Japanese education gave Kyo Gisors the conviction that "ideas were
not to be thought, but lived." He has taken up his manner of living through
a conscious and voluntary act rather than under a compulsion (like Ch'en).
"Kyo had chosen action, in a grave and premediated way, as others choose
a military career, or the sea: he left his father, lived in Canton, in Tientsin,
the life of day-laborers and coolies, in order to organize the syndicates." He
is a different type from the nihilist-adventurers and terrorists. He is not
restless; since he is not secretly in love with death, he does not use the idea
of a heroic life to justify continuing to live; the heroic sense merely gives
him a form of discipline in action. The Absurd is not his constant companion:
"His life had a meaning, and he knew what it was: to give to each of those
men whom famine, at this very moment, was killing off like a slow plague,
a sense of his own dignity." Thus he rejects the most debilitating element
of Western cultural consciousness and affirms its most humanistic potential
values. The oppression that was grist for the propaganda mill of Garine—
who only half understood the value he was communicating to the Chinese
masses—becomes for Kyo the real enemy, and Old Gisors's utopian hope
in a sense becomes a destination. " 'There is no possible dignity, no real life
for a man who works twelve hours a day without knowing why he works.'
That work would have to take on a meaning, become a faith." Katov co-
ordinates the insurrection along with Kyo; but Kyo has more of a sense of
its possible meaning: the revolt is intended "to conquer here the dignity of
his people."

The author shows more of Kyo, who is the deeper character, and therefore the reader becomes aware that this new type of hero is not someone
who has had a fortuitous escape from his humanity. He too can be tormented:
a phonograph becomes the symbol of his transient obsession. Having made
a recording of his own voice, he finds that he cannot recognize it when it is
played back to him. The occurrence nags at the depth of his consciousness,
and he questions his father about it. " 'It's undoubtedly a question of means:
we hear the voices of others with our ears.' 'And our own?' 'With our throats:
for you can hear your own voice with your ears stopped.' " And then:
" 'Opium is also a world we do not hear with our ears.' " And later the event
comes back to him in a moment of self-doubt:

> His torment returned, and he remembered the records: "We hear
> the voices of others with our ears, our own voices with our
> throats." Yes. One hears his own life, too, with his throat, and
> those of others? . . . First of all there was solitude, the inescapable

aloneness behind the living multitude. . . . "But I, to my throat, what am I? A kind of absolute, the affirmation of an idiot: an intensity greater than all the rest. To others, I am what I have done."

But there is a reason for this torment, and it passes when Kyo is able to overcome its real cause.

Kyo—the first of Malraux's heroes able to feel toward a woman more than an eroticism which is really a relation of himself to himself—is deeply in love with his wife, May. She is, like him, a revolutionary (and it is not by chance that the ability to love is combined with a commitment to revolution). "For more than a year May had freed him from all solitude, if not from all bitterness." His brief convulsion of despair and futility is brought on when she tells him on the morning of the insurrection that in the face of suffering and death she has just gone to bed with another man. He is consumed, not be real jealousy or hatred (since he understands her only too well), but by a feeling of being suddenly separated from her, of being unable to find her: she has returned him to solitude.

In his tormented meditation Kyo stumbles on a suggestive psychology of love: it is to May only that he exists as something more than a biographical summary of his actions; in the same way that Old Gisors is able to know in others what he has changed in them and made of them, Kyo and May are able to know each other because they love each other, and this ability has been their mutual defense against solitude.

> "My kind are those who love me and do not look at me, who love me in spite of everything, degradation, baseness, treason— *me* and not what I have done or shall do—who would love me as long as I love myself—even to suicide. . . . With her alone I have this love in common. . . ." It was not happiness, certainly. It was something primitive which was at one with the darkness and caused a warmth to rise in him, resolving itself into a motionless embrace . . . the only thing in him that was as strong as death.

Not until the collapse of the revolt, when Kyo goes out to be captured, does he regain this relation with May: he refuses to allow her to accompany him, under the guise of protecting her; there is a moment of total separation, until she motions to him to go; finding that his torment only recurs, he returns for her, having learned "that the willingness to lead the being one loves to death itself is perhaps the complete expression of love, that which cannot be surpassed." Because this love is sufficient for him, before he dies—alone—

he regrets only that May, who is weaker than he, must be left alone with her grief. That Kyo is able to build, and to rebuild, such a relation is enough to show his difference from those who can only suffer or "triumph" alone.

As with Katov, more is revealed about Kyo when the apparent victory of the insurrection is transformed into defeat, and he determines to die for it, than before. He is captured and faced first with humiliation—the same sort of humiliation which has brutalized his interrogator König—and then with death. The humiliation comes when he is thrown into a temporary prison: darkness, the odor of a slaughterhouse, wooden cages, and within them "men, like worms," and the warder with his whip. Because all the prisoners are utterly powerless before him, the warder takes on the shape of a bestial incarnation of fatality. Kyo witnesses the flogging of an old harmless lunatic, is helpless to prevent it, and horribly and ignominiously must struggle against a desire to watch the torture. But he is able to stop the beating, then to ensure his own whipping and then to have his slashed hand shaken by the torturer. "Life had never imposed upon him anything more hideous"; yet, simply by departing from the prison, he is able to leave behind that "loathsome part of himself" which has been created there. After this, it is not merely a pompous gesture when he tells König:

> "I think that Communism will make dignity possible for those with whom I am fighting. What is against it, at any rate, forces them to have none. . . ." "What do you call dignity? It doesn't mean anything." . . . "The opposite of humiliation. . . . When one comes from where I come, that means something."

Like Katov, like Hemmelrich after the death of his wife and child, Kyo Gisors is a free man. He is aware of the presence of the Absurd, but he is not obsessed by it, he is not a compulsive killer or liar or addict or master. When he does feel anguish, it is for a specific reason, not because he is an unhappy consciousness, and if the reason passes, so does anguish. At the last he knows that dying in the common fight for dignity can be an act as exalted as any act in life and that there would have been no value in his life had he not been ready to die for it.

> He had fought for what was in his time charged with the deepest meaning and the greatest hope; he was dying among those with whom he would have wanted to live; he was dying, like each of these men, because he had given a meaning to his life . . . . It is easy to die when one does not die alone. A death saturated with this brotherly quavering, an assembly of the vanquished in which

multitudes will recognize their martyrs, a bloody legend of which the golden legends are made!

Kyo has made a success of his life. He cannot avoid, as no man can avoid, the final fatality, but even that he seizes, rather than accepting as it is thrust on him. His life, which could have been made meaningless if he had let fatality or events, oppression or despair or discipline, make it so, has a meaning because he has made a meaning for it. He exists in solitude because he is an individual, but he overcomes that solitude in the company of those who had shared first victory and then defeat and who, prisoners, are now to share death. One bond links them in spite of all the movements of events that tend to separate or degrade them: "fraternity," the immediate communion among human persons converted into a fellowship by direct confrontation with a common fate. Kyo's life is an image to others because he has not merely had a hope, as Gisors had, but has fought for its realization, and because its realization would involve a value above self-concern and self-love and even self-fulfillment. He has struggled to procure for others a dignity which is native to him; his death is as worthy of him as is his life; he is, in short, a political hero of the highest type shown in Malraux's works.

That type may be called the Bolshevik hero. His solitude is a contingent condition, with which he breaks by action. If his action is successful, it may lead to a new social order in which isolation and malaise will be contingent and conquerable for all men. Because his action is directed to that end, his will has given a meaning to his life; because his life has a meaning, he is not perpetually restless. Because he fights in common for a common hope, he can even in physical defeat breach solitude and attain fraternity, the present good that is his reward for seeking the future good. From the display of human types and ways of life a high myth, a political commitment, has emerged.

The mythic Bolshevik hero collects and reconciles fragments from Malraux's past. He captures the fraternity that Claude felt by chance and the meaning in life and death that Perken grasped for one single moment. He creates men's souls as Garine did, but he possesses the hope that Garine manipulated. He holds the values that the Conquerors overlooked. One may wonder about some of his more obscure features. Can he remain a Communist when the party is run by the Organization Men? What will really happen to a society where the Bolsheviks are victorious? On such a day, what will become of the fraternity of the elite revolutionary intellectuals? The workers will find meaningful work: what will the dignity of the few consist in, once the persecutors whose repressions aroused their fraternal sentiments are

gone? But in Malraux's next novel such questions are not relevant because
victory is still not in sight. His second hero-type thus attains a temporary
stability, and his political thought finds a first resting place.

Days of Wrath (1935) returns to the single-main-character pattern, this
time with a positive figure at the center. The work deals with nine days
spent by a German Communist, Kassner, in a Nazi prison cell. Days of Wrath
is a natural successor to Man's Fate; it contains none of the ideological conflict
of the earlier work, but it contains the resolution of that conflict. Kassner,
like Katov, is a man committed without the constancy of anguished doubt
that has rightly accompanied the commitments of others. Because he is not
so deep a man as Kyo, his book is a lesser one; but he adds more substance
to the figure of the Bolshevik hero.

The intellectual structure of Days of Wrath is unlike that of the previous
single-hero books. Instead of an anguished vision, a revolt, and a defeat,
there is a revolt, a sacrifice, an escape, and a new revolt. Kassner is an
organizer of the German Communist underground. He is arrested when he
deliberately springs a police trap to save his comrades. He is imprisoned,
questioned, tortured, and isolated. If the insane fantasies born of his solitude
do not kill him, the Nazis will. But an unknown comrade saves him from
madness by establishing communication with him through the cell walls;
another saves his life by assuming his identity and his place in prison. Outside
Germany Kassner is reunited with his wife at a mass meeting of his comrades,
and he prepares to return to Germany.

At one level this book is a work of propaganda: the brotherhood of
mutual sacrifice in which the Communists are united preserves them from
the impacts of life and death, permits them to overcome the fear of death,
to overcome torture and solitude. The party (whether or not it ever existed
on earth) makes its men into brothers and heroes. At this level Days of Wrath
is a skillful lyric peroration to the dramatics of Man's Fate. The only question
of special interest is why Kassner is an Organization Man, why the movement
proceeds from Kyo, who rejects the dead weight of the apparatus of the
International, to Kassner, a man wholly within the organization, with no
sense of conflict between its objectives and his own, no qualms about his
position.

Malraux's heroes, like Malraux himself, seek a good in political action
which they cannot secure by their own power. Repeatedly they must choose
as allies political forces stronger than themselves. The force chosen is that
which comes closest to providing the desired goal; the intimacy of the alliance
depends upon the similarity of the goals of individual and movement. Garine
wanted to overthrow an older order of power and take it for himself. He

allied himself with the Kuomintang Communists because they were both passionate and competent: but after a joint success he and they would have become rivals. By 1927 and the Shanghai affair the Comintern had lost its passion, but the revolutionaries on the spot had not. And Kyo wants something different—"human dignity": he believes that the Communists may supply it while their enemies will certainly not. In 1934–35 the Comintern had a short-lived "humanist" outburst which suggested that its explicit positive goal might not be far from Malraux's (it was at this time that he was honored in Moscow); that trend was followed by the policy of the popular front, which recaptured for the Communists in the eyes of many the "will" and activism they had lost at the time of *Man's Fate*. On the basis of the behavior and misbehavior of the Communist apparatus alone, therefore, it was valid to portray Kassner as a Communist, because at this time there existed no other political force which could or would do what Malraux wanted done. It was on the same ground that in 1948 Malraux defended his alignment with De Gaulle. In 1935 it was the Communists who, in carrying on the struggle for a valid future, permitted even such ordinary men as Kassner to live heroic lives and to enjoy the fraternity of heroes. To convey that fact is one intention of *Days of Wrath*.

But at a level less bound to current events there is a more universal intent, which can outlast the conditions of a current alliance. (Like the elements of the first two novels that are preserved and developed, this aspect is present in fragmentary form.) At this universal level the matter of chance that Kassner is at a certain moment a Communist is unimportant. In the preface Malraux speaks of "the world of tragedy, the ancient world," composed of man, what oppresses him (the elements, isolation, destiny, death) and what defends him. Kassner is simply fundamental man: his successive trials are meant to be typical of the ordeal of men before the everyday risk of death, and his defenses—comradeship, fraternity, love—are meant to be recourses universally and eternally valid. Kassner is a worker by social origin, an intellectual only by self-education—Malraux's first such hero. Even the most oppressed of men in the most oppressive of states can have what is needful to combat his suffering; even he can choose the right life and death.

When doubts return about the virtues of the apparat, the almost serene acceptance of a conclusion to political debate will not persist. *Man's Hope* explodes the passing resolution of all political problems expressed in *Days of Wrath*. But Kassner was able to transcend his isolation outside as well as inside the frame of politics. He feels a sense of communion, not only with his fellow sufferers, but also with the woman he loves, with a crowd, with a pilot in a storm. Politics is not essential to personal "salvation" in every case: for the Absurd has many faces, as Garine knew very well. The revolutionaries in *Man's Fate* have almost forgotten this truth, for each of them is the victim of one chief form of absurdity, its political form. Kassner sees many forms again: in the face of oppression and torture, of the inhuman power of nature, of the madness of the crowds, of the certainty of death, he is able to work an inner change by reflection, to conceive in each case a different communion and a different defense. Where there are brothers, therefore, it will be possible for men to transcend their isolation by political action so long as they are subjected to a common and indiscriminate oppression; but it does not necessarily follow that where oppression is not felt in common or where isolation is not political, isolation and oppression cannot be transcended. Communion comes through politics in *Man's Fate*. Some other areas of life afford it in *Days of Wrath*, though only peripherally.

The moments of self-transcendence afforded to the insurrectionists of *Man's Fate* turn into a lifetime of such moments in the permanent underground of *Days of Wrath*. So long as a vigorous, united, and consciously repressive state machine confronts, persecutes, but cannot destroy an organized resistance, these rebels and brothers can be compelled to lead short, happy lives as individuals and a long, lyrical existence as a group. Because victory is not in sight, they need not trouble themselves with difficult political questions. Because circumstances permit them to identify a certain ruling class as oppressors, and a certain oppressed class as brothers, they have only to act, only to keep the faith, and they are healed. Their health depends on the existence of a cruel, deliberately oppressive, but inefficient regime (for so the Nazis are presented). If the revolutionaries were to win, they must needs take thought, as becomes clear in Malraux's next novel. But what if the Kassners (and the Kyos and the Katovs) had no such oppressive order, no such clear-cut enemies and comrades? Such was the situation of Garine: he traveled to find a revolution, but it was not his; he attained no lasting communion. And what if there is no "clearly" just cause, no self-evident and self-conscious community of the oppressed, no painstaking and deliberate persecution?

When the historical circumstances require it, Malraux turns to answer these questions. New means of transcending the human situation will continue to reveal themselves, far more fully than they do to Kassner. So long as a delicate balance of social forces permits it, the Bolshevik remains a hero. Either victory or tolerance would derange that balance. When they do, the Bolshevik becomes an incomplete hero, and another replaces him—a more rounded and varied human type.

ROGER SHATTUCK

Malraux, the Conqueror

"What books are worth writing, except Memoirs?"
—The Conquerors, 1928

In 1965 President De Gaulle sent his Minister for Cultural Affairs to visit the Chinese leaders in their heartland. André Malraux had staked his spiritual claim on the Orient more than thirty years earlier with four books, and no one had challenged it. The move was an obvious one for De Gaulle, and a mission not without excitement for Malraux. Probably in order to find rest and resume his writing, interrupted since 1957, he traveled by water. The name of the liner, *Cambodia*, recalled his earlier trips to the Far East. That corruptly administered French colony was the scene of his arrest and trial in 1924, actions which provoked strong protests from many Paris writers. Moreover, the opening sequences of his first two novels take place at sea.

Malraux carried on board with him in 1965 a small library, including his most recent novel, *Wrestling with the Angel (La Lutte avec l'ange)*. The first part had been published in 1943 as *The Walnut Trees of Altenburg*: the second part, of which an unfinished manuscript had been destroyed or lost by the Gestapo, was announced as still "in progress" in 1965. He had almost a month to work on it in the privileged calm of shipboard life. But instead of returning to the novel, he found himself writing an extended, self-revealing, magnificently eloquent log of the trip, a reweaving of his life back into his work. He chose a countertitle, implying a new genre: *Anti-Memoirs*. It is as if, beneath the keel of that slow boat to China and inside this substantial volume, Malraux's past began slowly surfacing, like an unknown creature

From *The Innocent Eye: On Modern Literature and the Arts.* © 1968, 1984 by Roger Shattuck. Washington Square Press, 1984.

from the deep. When it did, as in the China sequence recounting his conversation with Mao Tse-tung over the fate of the hemispheres, the pace of
things slowed and deepened in order to encompass that past. Malraux completed his circumnavigation by air over the Pole and returned to Paris a
changed man, not so much because of the trip as because of the unexpected
book the trip had spawned.

This much information, at least, can be deduced readily from internal
evidence. This much, and possibly more—barely discernible, bringing a
note of private lyricism that is unexpected in Malraux. Granted the mood
is half shrouded in rhetoric. I quote from the second page of the French
version in my own translation:

> Why do I remember these things?
>
> Because, having lived in that uncertain country of thought and
> fiction that artists inhabit, as well as in the world of combat and
> history, having discovered in Asia when I was twenty a continent
> whose turmoil still illuminated the meaning of the Occident, I
> have encountered at intervals those humble or exalted moments
> in which the fundamental enigma of life appears to each of us as
> it appears to most women on looking into an infant's face, as it
> appears to most men on looking into the face of a corpse. In all
> forms of whatever draws us on through life, in every struggle I
> have seen against humiliation, and even in you, sweetness so pure
> that one marvels how you can walk upon the earth, life seems to
> spring forth as from the gods of vanishing religions, like the
> libretto for an unknown music.

Unaccountably, the only words that seem to have been dropped from
400 pages of the American edition are the two personal pronouns, *toi* and
tu. But the American edition does contain something not in the French
edition: a prominent dedication "For Mrs. John Fitzgerald Kennedy." Malraux's friends have known for some time of the deep attachment he formed
for *la Présidente*, whom he escorted in 1961 to the Jeu de Paume museum
and to Malmaison and saw several times after that in the United States. She
must have appeared to him a complex creature: a living statue, the star of
stars, a person more scarred by history than he will ever be, the very embodiment of sweetness.

Toward the end of his career Malraux's position in French intellectual
life was a curiously ambiguous one. Young activitists and revolutionaries
admired his exploits in China and Spain and the books that grew out of
them. They could not bear his apparently unwavering association with De

Gaulle, with a party, and with a governmental office. As Minister of Cultural Affairs, Malraux initiated reforms that had little originality. The Maisons de la Culture in the provinces were, even in name, a page out of the Communists' ideological battles of the thirties. Commissioning Chagall to paint the ceiling of the Opéra seemed quite a coup until someone pointed out that Lenin had employed him for the same purpose in Moscow thirty years before.

The promotional campaign that surrounded the Paris publication of *Anti-Memoirs*, including radio and television appearances and a long-playing record, was widely interpreted as a kind of official propaganda effort designed to cover up unrest and use Malraux's prestige to bolster the government. When he intervened in the administration of the Cinémathèque and tried to relieve its director, Langlois, of his responsibilities, Malraux had to back at least halfway down. He summarily fired Jean-Louis Barrault for turning over the Odéon theater to students in May 1968. Malraux himself played no public role during the May Days until they were practically over. Then, on June 21, he appeared on Europe I in an interview that came as a kind of summation: "First of all, there has been a real crisis over the idea of hierarchy. It is not easy to see because theoretically what people put forward against hierarchy is the idea of disorder." He went on to speak of the drama inherent in the fact that Christian culture continues even though Christian faith has disappeared as a sustaining force. "Today, in a way, civilization exists in a vacuum and is going nowhere." As a minister Malraux was not listened to very attentively. As a writer, however, he never lost his audience.

II

Anti-Memoirs opens with ten pages that rise like a bright rocket and then go out before we have glimpsed much of the surrounding terrain. The effect is tantalizing. A country priest gestures in the night and speaks of hearing confessions. We hear many voices, Malraux's above all. He has wise words about death and sincerity, about dying gods and rising cities. "I hate my childhood . . . I do not find myself very interesting . . . how [can one] reduce to a minimum the theatrical side of one's nature." In the last paragraph, Jung, of all people, is climbing down a ladder in New Mexico. The surface provides little continuity. Malraux seems to back systematically away from the very subjects the title promises. But be patient. The journey has not yet begun.

Almost everything, of course, comes back transfigured. These pages form an elliptical preview that distorts and truncates what will later be made whole. The priest does have something portentous to say about age and greatness. Malraux does not really hate his youth or disdain his past. Sincerity is a doubtful ideal, found least of all in memoirs. To kill the playactor in oneself may mean abandoning the game. Jung is as culture-bound as any poor Indian. There is no recapitulation, but by the end of the book we recognize the landscape of Malraux's many-mansioned life. In the course of this opening chapter he tells us that the Berger family, which he chronicles through three generations in *The Walnut Trees of Altenburg*, is in reality a transposition into the Alsatian forests of his own seafaring forebears from Dunkirk. The second chapter of *Anti-Memoirs* consists of a twenty-page condensation of the middle 150 pages of that novel. Such a radical telescoping destroys the story line in order to pick out what are apparently the auto-biographical elements. From the start we are suspended between fiction and non-fiction, between the already recorded and the unascertainable.

From this point on, the book might be called "Ports of Call." Each place evokes its memories. Egypt, the first stop, carries him back to his first discovery there thirty years earlier of the "two languages" in art: appearance and truth. Halfway between East and West, Egypt is the desert out of which everything came forth, the culture which discovered the human soul and built the first great tombs. Moreover, Egypt reminds Malraux of his ar-chaeological stunt with the pilot Corniglion. Subsidized by a Paris news-paper, they had tried to locate the ruins of the Queen of Sheba's ancient capital in the desert east of Aden. That flight produced a stirring account of a near-crash they had in escaping from a local storm, as well as a few blurred snapshots, duly published in the sponsoring paper.

The memories that cluster about India, the next layover, take us further back and bring us further forward in time. Malraux had stopped briefly in Ceylon in 1923 and had visited a series of holy cities in northern India in 1929, including Jaipur, "the most dreamlike place of all." But the mention of a 1958 fence-mending mission to see Nehru for De Gaulle transports the narrative back to Paris. The next thirty pages are devoted to Malraux's meeting with De Gaulle. Apparently each was led to believe the other had asked for the interview. By divulging this fact at the end, Malraux contrives to extract a minimum of comedy out of this epic *malentendu*. By his own account Malraux seems to harangue the politely listening general about the primacy of the nation, the revolutionary spirit, and intellectuals in politics. After this first take comes a series of retakes of De Gaulle. Malraux char-acterizes him as the exact opposite of Trotsky. (Thereby hangs another tale, not told here, of how Malraux refused to admit in 1934 that he had gone to Royan to meet the exiled Russian. Malraux was very close to the Party then.) The story of another political mission for De Gaulle in 1958 turns into a semi-burlesque thriller. Malraux discovers himself on a platform in Guiana talking only to the first few rows of a vast audience while its outer edges are engaged in a well-organized uprising.

The narrative moves back now to India, where the ship is still docked, and gives an account of Malraux's 1958 conversation with Nehru. "So now you're a minister." Malraux's response is one of the nimblest literary leaps in the book. He recounts an anecdote that implies he is as much a minister as the cat that lived in Mallarmé's apartment was Mallarmé's cat: it's all a matter of pretending, like Sartre's waiter. They talk of many things, at the end of which Nehru says, "Tomorrow we shall learn from the newspapers what we said to each other"—a wistful motto for our times, just as much a theme here as it is in *Bonnie and Clyde*.

The Indian interlude with its multiple appendages is not yet over. A line from Gandhi about freedom being found in prison leads into the trumpet-like line "My prison began in a field." The following section (we are approaching the center of the book) picks up Malraux's "absurd" arrest by the Gestapo in 1944 north of Toulouse and his decision to reveal his real identity at his first interrogation. The Germans staged a mock execution to unnerve him and from then on everything, including his imprisonment in Toulouse, seems to turn on *malentendus*: Malraux shares a room with a man hideously tortured because the word "tourist" in his file had been read as "terrorist"; Malraux himself barely misses being tortured, and is possibly saved from death, because the Paris authorities sent down his brother Roland's file instead of his.

The subtitle of this long Indian section of the book now changes from "Anti-Memoirs" to "The Temptation of the West," the title of an epistolary novel or essay he published in 1926. The 1958 visit takes him to the holy towns of Benares, where he is mistaken for (so Raja Rao tells him) Vishnu, to Ellora, and finally to Bombay, where he recalls his brief combat service as a tank commander in 1940. These pages are lifted almost verbatim from the end of *The Walnut Trees of Altenburg*. The chapter closes with a romantic yet moving passage about an old peasant woman's smile bringing back all human realities to his crew, who have barely missed death in a trap.

The desultory conversation with Nehru that concludes this section reads like a reworking of ideas from *The Temptation of the West*. The discussion of values and action and culture circles slowly around the concept of trans-migration of souls, which resists assimilation into the Western view of the world. But Malraux is forever coming back to it as if it were a far more tempting solution to the conundrums of death and immortality than the Christian game of gambling all eternity on a single life. Nehru himself remains a shadowy figure, guru of all India. He should be the very soul of that nation which is not yet a victim of the Western disease of individualism. But such a country of the mind cannot be concentrated in one character of high relief; we glean its reality from a tempo and the patina of its places. "Remote from us in dream and in time, India belongs to the Ancient Orient of our soul."

The steamship *Cambodia* moves on toward Singapore and is rammed in the narrows. Malraux lingers a few days in that agonized city of refugees. Out of a real past and out of his own fiction emerges the character Clappique. (The narrative has now modulated into the present tense of a journal with frequent excursions into the past.) In *Man's Fate*, Clappique is the clownish talker and shady dealer whose forgetfulness at the crucial juncture leads to Kyo's death. This aging yet still vigorous character reads, mimes, and summarizes to Malraux the scenario of a film based on the life of Mayrena. He was a legendary adventurer—prince of his own private realm among the Sedangs and toast of Montmartre at the turn of the century. It makes quite a film, complete with witch doctors and elephant hunts, entitled *The Devil's Kingdom (Le Règne du Malin)*. Malraux, by including it, has signed it—a striking anticipation of *Apocalypse Now*.

Leaving the disabled ship, Malraux takes an airplane to Hong Kong and rereads his own novel, *The Royal Way*, about the Moï tribes, whose territory he is now flying over. A few miles further on, Da-Nang lies below him, another legendary place out of the fictions of Mayrena, Clappique, and Malraux himself. But now: "around the port, the American battle fleet lies motionless." Cut: to the last section, called "Man's Fate."

In Hong Kong, posters in the big Communist department store inspire a dramatic retelling of the Long March and the heroic crossing of the Ta Tu River by Mao Tse-tung's troops. Malraux flies to Peking and begins a series of conversations that rise steadily in significance and tension. First, Marshal Chen-yi, one of the founders of the Chinese Communist Party in France, expelled in 1921, now Foreign Minister. In a long discussion of Vietnam, the marshall states that the United States' escalation is Vietnam's Long March. Malraux suggests that the United States has no world strategy at present, imperialist or otherwise, and is simply repeating France's old errors. With Chou En-lai ("He knows as well as I do that in the United States he is thought to be the original of one of the characters in *La Condition humaine*"), the exchange moves far beyond Vietnam to China's sense of destiny, her newly found freedom, and her will to transform herself. Malraux thinks to himself of Sun Yat-sen's sentence about the word "freedom" being new in Chinese and therefore lacking the weight it has in the West. "It is always men who win in the end," says Chou at the end of the talk.

The official audience, with presentation of credentials to President Liu Shao-chi, provides the occasion, as everyone understands in advance, for the meeting with Mao Tse-tung. Malraux begins by talking about the Museum of the Revolution he has just visited in Yenan. We are now at the true summit, not of world power, but of wisdom and experience. On the walls, not propaganda posters but Manchu scrolls. At least that is the account Malraux gives, reconstructed like all the other conversations from transcripts and recollections, corrected, I feel sure, to register how it should have happened.

> MALRAUX: Gorky said to me one day, in Stalin's presence:
> Peasants are the same everywhere.
> MAO TSE-TUNG: Neither Gorky, a great vagabond poet, nor
> Stalin . . . knew anything at all about peasants.

Mao Tse-tung means the Chinese peasantry, in whom he puts his faith more than in professional revolutionaries. This is the true father of the country; unlike Chen-yi and Chou, he has never left China. He is concerned about the nationalist-bourgeois opposition and about his following among the young. A few sentences suggest the thinking that may have led to his five-month "disappearance" and subsequent developments—the Cultural Revolution and the Red Guards. But every stage direction implies a great immobility on Mao Tse-tung's part, "a bronze Emperor" with cigarette. The conversation, slowed to half-time by the pauses for translation, seems monumental even when it is trivial. Russian revisionism, French socialism, the possible Indonesian alliance—everything finds a place in the tapestry of world politics held between them quietly and pondered for its true meaning.

Obviously Malraux admires this "Old Man of the Mountain," who keeps repeating that he is "alone with the masses." Is Mao Tse-tung confiding anything to this emissary from another lonely chieftain? Malraux looks at him. "What an extraordinary power of allusion! I know that he is about to intervene anew. Through the young? Through the army? No man will have shaken history so powerfully since Lenin." It takes Mao Tse-tung a long time to walk his guest out to the car. Afterward, what Malraux remembers is the single emphatic gesture Mao Tse-tung made during the entire afternoon's exchange when his French guest, in reference to the United States, said, "We're independent, but we're their allies." Mao Tse-tung's arms rose into the air in surprise, or dismay.

"I return to France 'over the Pole.' " The last pages cut back and forth between a meeting to decide an appropriate monument for a Resistance hero, concentration-camp scenes of degraded humanity confronting total inhumanity, and the Lascaux cave. It was discovered by two boys and a dog in 1940 out exploring the countryside. The place was used by the Maquis to store arms. Its prehistoric paintings must now be protected against fungus. Lascaux is the first museum, and possibly the last. The death-resisting works it guards may still perish in spite of us. . . . The book ends in mid-air. We are promised more.

III

Three or four hundred years from now, what myths or legends will have precipatated out of our century? We may know better than we usually venture to say. The young liberal king who abdicated an ancient throne for love and liberty. The great international performer (a hybrid of Caruso and Nijinsky) who became a victim of his own astonishing talent and found a sad and lonely end. The laconic cowboy-mechanic who gambled everything on a single engine, his capacity to stay alert for thirty-three hours, and an oversize wing full of ping-pong balls. The gesticulating dictator who led a civilized nation into savagery with the brazenness of his lies and the hypnotic qualities of his voice. The new Oriental, sage and activist, a composite of Gandhi, Nehru, and Mao Tse-tung, who revived a sundered continent. The youthful President shot just when he was learning how hard it would be to fulfill the hopes the whole world had begun to place in his smile and in his words. The early astronaut who cannot readjust to living on the Planet Earth and comes to a shameful end. . . . The exact repertoire is not important. Here, however, is the company among whom Malraux sets out to measure his own role. Do not be misled. The tone is not megalomaniac or even mythomaniac; it is curiously self-effacing. But he has chosen his league.

In earlier days, every photograph showed Malraux with a cigarette— the intellectual as tough guy and mystery man. He carried the role well, as the illustrated pages of *Malraux par lui-même (Malraux on Himself)* amply demonstrate. Walter Langlois's book *The Indochina Adventure* leaves little doubt about the traumatic effect on Malraux of the Phnom Penh trial in 1924 which sentenced him to three years in prison (later reduced to one, and never served) and branded him a criminal for finding and wanting to keep some barely known and unclassified temple sculpture in Cambodia. The gangster surface wore off slowly through a long cohabitation with works of art and through gradual disenchantment with the power struggles of the

Communist Party. Between 1936, when he organized an aviation brigade to help the Republicans in Spain, and writing *Wrestling with the Angel* in 1941, a second crisis altered his thinking. It involved the Republican defeat in Spain, the Stalin-Hitler pact, the German invasion, and Malraux's own combat experience as a tank commander. *Wrestling with the Angel* is a title he took seriously. It appears again in the opening pages of *Anti-Memoirs*, followed immediately by the bluntly affirmative question "and what else am I undertaking?" When Jacob fought all night with the angel, he prevailed, earned the name Israel, and bore his battle scar in the hollow of his hip. Malraux has squared off here with the dark angel of his own past, which is all that remains for him of the expiring gods. Everything implies that his struggles may belong to legend. But do they?

Even reinforced by T. E. Lawrence, Saint-Exupéry, and Rimbaud, Malraux will not be given a new name by the angel of history. He has neither of the essential qualities: obsession and aura. Intellectual brilliance is not enough. "And it is not the role which makes the historic personage, but the vocation." The words tumble out after the first meeting with De Gaulle. Malraux's struggle holds us because of the quality he finds or creates in his encounters. He prepares the ground for them in an ominous sentence on the first page of *Anti-Memoirs*. Punctuating his statement by raising his arms in the air, the chaplain of Glières (he is the chorus and will be seen and heard again) declares: "le fond de tout, *c'est qu'il n'y a pas de grandes personnes*." Malraux underlines. Kilmartin translates: "There is no such thing as grown-up people." Too much is lost. Behind the cliché expression *"grande personne"*— grown-up—stands the bedrock meaning of "great man"—hero. "In the end you can't tell the men from the boys." Or: "When you come right down to it, there are no little people and big people—just people." The ambiguity is essential and far-reaching. There has been a mighty striving in the night, expressed in both the structure and the style of this volume. But its greatness resides in a subtle and ironic avowal that greatness may escape even the great.

IV

I have touched on the structural features that bind together this seemingly jerry-built book. The succession of datelines, some of them double or triple, establish the log-book format; it is fleshed out with flashbacks and time mixes into a kind of four-dimensional journal. The "transitions" make a further revelation. Writing in Bombay in 1965, Malraux recalls at length a 1958 trip to the same city during which he retired to the governor's seaside

bungalow to reread a text he had written in 1940 about tank combat. But
the different levels of reference are not merely thrown together by casual
association; they interlock and frame one another in a second structural
pattern—that of a building carefully refashioned out of an earlier structure,
with further materials added to complete the new design. The first version
of the Berger family story appears in Malraux's first novel, *The Royal Way*,
expands into a full-dress version in *The Walnut Trees of Altenburg*, and reappears in *Anti-Memoirs* drastically reduced in size and given both as a fiction
(i.e., transposed in a variety of ways) and as a true version of Malraux's
youth.

When old stones were reused in an Egyptian temple, the "usurped"
inscriptions carried a reference to their previous function and position. The
old structure is not forgotten but subsumed in the new one. *Anti-Memoirs*
has folded into itself not only fifty pages from *The Walnut Trees* but also an
execution scene from *Days of Wrath*, a rich store of images and ideas from
his writings on art, and a hundred pages in the middle of the deck lifted
from the scenario he was working on in 1945 about the adventurer Mayrena.
Everything is tightened and revised in small details as it goes in, yet it remains
immediately recognizable. The effect, and probably the purpose, of this self-
quotation will come clear in a moment. As structure, it carries an experimental and often disconcerting echo-chamber effect in which characters and
scenes return in fragments, reinterpreted and colored anew.

The third structural device is the use of recurring motifs. There are in
fact two major motifs, both of which are used like refrains. Stated in full
only once, they are invoked at intervals like the choruses of a song. I have
already identified the first refrain: the chaplain of Glières. He baptized Jews
left and right to save them from the Gestapo, never left the Vercors as Mao
Tse-tung never left China, and lifted his arms in the starry night to intone
the theme *il n'y a pas de grandes personnes*. Four times in the second half of
the book, Malraux, in almost identical sentences, "thinks of the chaplain of
Glières"—of his spirituality, his endurance, his sense of humanity before
evil and before death. The opening page of *Anti-Memoirs* is really a film
sequence, stated with an extreme economy of images and words. It is then
alluded to explicitly but fleetingly when such peasant perseverance seems
either furthest from or closest to the trajectory of the narrative.

The other refrain has to do with an elemental city world that is, if
anything, even more Malraux's than the open country. He calls it "coming
back to earth" *retour sur la terre*. Vincent Berger experiences it when he
returns to Marseille after several years' absence in Turkey and discovers that
"first of all Europe meant shop windows." Malraux went through that rediscovery of the familiar after his nearly fatal flight over the Aden desert.

By the side of the road there was a gate without a fence as in a
Chaplin film, with an inscription in huge Second Empire characters: *Ruins of Hippo*. In the town, I passed an enormous red
hand which was the glovemakers' sign in those days. The earth
was peopled with hands, and perhaps they might have been able
to live by themselves, to act by themselves, without men.

Malraux readers will recognize the *farfelu* mood of his early "Surrealist"
works, but here the whimsy is not gratuitous. Reenchantment with the
ordinary world follows a significant or spiritual adventure. In the preceding
sequence Malraux has already associated the wrinkled surface of the earth
seen from an airplane with the lines in people's palms: the latter are said to
face away at the moment of death. This disembodied, familiar, and ominous
red hand serves as the second refrain. When it recurs later in the book, it
recalls us to the magic of the simple things that lie around us at every moment
and that we can come home to. *Anti-Memoirs* has the extended, circular, yet
essentially domestic shape of the *Odyssey* or a fairy tale.

The fourth unifying factor lies very close to the third, but extends it in
a different direction. The lyric passage I quoted at the start about "humble
or exalted moments" is picked up a few pages later when Malraux speaks of
the nonchronological order of significant memories. They form "an unknown
constellation . . . the most significant moments in my life do not live in me,
they haunt me and flee from me alternately." Forty years ago in his essay
on the psychology of film, he spoke of "privileged moments" that emerge
unexpectedly out of the chaos of experience. The various comings back to
earth provide a whole series, particularly when the tank crew escapes from
its trap. Other "moments" are fairly sustained and cover as much as several
days' time: Nietzsche literally singing the words of his last poem as he is
being taken in the train through the St. Gotthard tunnel back to Basel; the
meetings with De Gaulle and Nehru and Mao Tse-tung; the sequence of
Malraux's arrest by the Gestapo and his final liberation. Malraux's privileged
moments fall between what Stendhal calls *moments probants* (he is referring
to Molière and implies that true drama presents encounters that test and
certify the characters) and Joyce's epiphanies.

In *Anti-Memoirs* when the camera pans off into the landscape, when a
conversation ceases in order to register a gesture or a distant sound, when
time itself seems to dilate, then we have reached a point of intersection
between the opposites Malraux can never forget—what you do and what
you are, deeds and secrets. It is a profoundly unsatisfactory division of the
act of living. Yet Malraux records scrupulously the occasions when these
two elements come into phase and reinforce each other. Without such mo-

ments, this voyage of rediscovery would have little to offer beyond the litheness of its language.

V

Everything I have said about the way Malraux has constructed this work, particularly his use of long passages salvaged from previous writings and his focus on privileged moments, suggests comparison with Marcel Proust. Now Proust is one of the greatest figures of literature. The novel form, European society, the French language, and the human sensibility itself have all experienced the tyranny of his feline mind. Malraux has no claim to such stature even though he is a powerful writer in several genres. But the comparison will bear examination. They are both mosaicists. True, Proust's densely involuted, mimetic style and his complex character development have little part in Malraux's universe. But both authors spend a lifetime rewriting crucial scenes and themes until they finally take their place in a single all-encompassing work. All Proust's writing before 1909 is a rehearsal for *Remembrance of Things Past*. To a somewhat lesser degree—after all, he is starting late—Malraux's thirteen previous books begin to look like trial runs for the final contest with destiny in *Anti-Memoirs*. Some of his readers will abandon him here; they will be the losers.

The development toward reappraisal and summation in Malraux points up the problem that has bothered the French critics: to what genre does *Anti-Memoirs* belong? Classification can be crucial. Malraux himself broaches the question right at the start, cites St. Augustine and Rousseau and T. E. Lawrence, and ends the chapter by stating: "I have called this book *Anti-Memoirs* because it answers a question which memoirs do not pose and does not answer those which they do." He appears to mean that he is concerned not with events exclusively but with a particular relation between them: privileged moments. Furthermore, one significant passage at the start implies that the book is oriented not so much toward memory as toward its opposite, *premonition*. In their work writers anticipate the fate they will go on to act out in life. He points to Nietzsche and Hemingway.

George D. Painter's description of Proust's undertaking may turn out to be close to the mark for Malraux: "not, properly speaking, a fiction, but a creative autobiography. . . . Though he invented nothing, he altered everything." The effects of such a literary project on the writing itself may be even more complex in *Anti-Memoirs* than in Proust's novel. In Malraux's palimpsest of fiction and non-fiction, the *je* becomes a chameleon. The *I* is narrator, character in his own narrative, and author of earlier works and deeds—and at other times a fictional narrator and character related to the "original" *I* and in a parallel situation. (We are approaching the territory of *The Counterfeiters*. But Gide's puzzle of authors within authors points by implication, and ironically, either to a divine agent or to the void. Not so Malraux.)

This identity game works out most neatly and paradoxically in the prison sequence in 1944. Malraux tells it tersely and well. It looks to me like the autobiographical and phenomenological heart of the book. Captured by surprise in uniform, Malraux decides to give his true identity as man and writer as well as his *nom de guerre*, Colonel Berger. (He had chosen the name originally for the hero of *The Walnut Trees of Altenburg* because it could be either French or German in origin.) The Gestapo is puzzled by the prisoner's apparent forthrightness and never does accept his unlikely story. Later, the French prisoners in Toulouse free themselves while the German tanks are still leaving. Malraux alone is in uniform. Out of the dangerous confusion in the courtyard someone calls out, "Let Berger take over!" And he does — yet he doesn't. For Malraux never enters the action directly as himself but acts through his surrogate and alter ego, through the character of himself as Berger, his pseudonymous creation brought to life. Stendhal played this game all his life. Malraux too, it seems, but without the same style and relish. A flesh-and-blood person is called to command liberated prisoners in the guise of one of his own fictional characters whom he usually casts in the role of his father—this is why the book moves so mysteriously through the straits that separate history from dream, and which connect history and dream. Colonel Berger became Minister of Culture in a highly flammable government.

Malraux's novels and especially his works on art are shot through with ill-defined hortatory words that have incurred the wrath of careful art scholars, such as Gombrich. Something is accomplished, I believe, by falling back on a concrete term: "conquest." It provided the title of his first novel. His career and writings turn on that theme. His first "serious book. *The Temptation of the West*, presents a confrontation of East and West in a context of conflict and domination. The characters in that book vigorously criticize museums as the repositories of dead trophies from the culture wars. In his political speeches of the thirties, Malraux retains the image of conquest, now enacted less against distant cultures than against our own unconscious. The heterodox speech he gave in Moscow to the first Congress of Soviet Writers (1934) was called "Art as Conquest." André Breton found Malraux's solution to the artist's political dilemma so convincing that he quoted a lengthy passage in one of his own speeches collected in *The Political Position of Surrealism:*

"Art is not a surrender, it is a conquest. Conquest by what? By feelings and means of expressing them. Conquest of what? Of the unconscious almost always; often of logic itself." The passage ends with the motto "More consciousness," lifted from Marx (early *and* late) and obviously alluding to Freud, who was by then anathema to the Soviets. Garcia, in *Man's Hope*, picks up the same theme in his widely quoted line about "transforming into consciousness the broadest possible range of experience." Möllberg, the ethnologist in *The Walnut Trees of Altenburg*, has written and destroyed a lengthy manuscript entitled *Civilization as Destiny and Conquest*.

If culture, the creative act, and even life itself can best be seen as a conquest, we still have one further step to go in order to understand the particular dilemma Malraux must face. To conquer implies a responsibility to dominate, to occupy, to assimilate or be assimilated. The conqueror in some way undertakes to live in relation to what he has conquered. But not so Perken and Ferral in the earliest novels. Their haughty and remote attitude toward a sexual partner is transferred in later books to other forms of knowledge and activity.

> The special pleasure one experiences in discovering unknown arts ceases once the discovery is made and does not develop into love.
>
> *(The Temptation of the West)*

> To transform society doesn't interest me at all. It's not injustice that puts me off, but something more basic, the impossibility of joining, of giving my loyalty to any form of society at all.
>
> (Garine in *The Conquerors* explaining why he is a
> revolutionary but not a Communist)

> The adventurer is obviously an outlaw; the mistake is to believe he breaks only the written law, or convention. He stands opposed to society to the full extent that it represents a pattern of life. He is opposed less to its conventions than to its very nature. To win is his undoing. Lenin was not an adventurer, nor Napoleon.
>
> (Malraux's marginal comments in *Malraux par lui-même*)

The curve can be traced across Malraux's works, whether they be concerned with archaeological prospecting, revolutionary struggle for power, aesthetic discovery and domination by means of museum or illustrated book, or a man's desire for a woman. His vocabulary is saturated with words like "wrest," "crush," "annex," "conquer," "victory," "triumph," "dominate." More widely circulated terms like "metamorphosis" are dignified versions for a title page. Notice that pleasure occurs only in the initial stage of conquest—even though the corpus of writings on art represents Malraux's resolute attempt to live with his empire. But he finally cannot.

> Our feelings seem to have a special charm while they are forming, and the whole pleasure of love lies in its shifting moods. . . . In the end nothing is so satisfying as to overcome the resistance of a beautiful woman. And on that score I have the self-feeding ambition of a conqueror who can never have enough victories or limit his desires.
>
> (Molière's Don Juan on himself)

In spite of his lifelong attempt to settle accounts with culture and art, in spite of the lucidity that reaches a high degree of intensity in *Anti-Memoirs*, Malraux remains a cultural Don Juan more excited by seducing than by possessing his prey. Is that a harsh judgment? I think not. Better we know ourselves than hide from ourselves. Furthermore, even Molière did not probe this passion-without-attachment to the full. Moral comprehension comes through the cool voice of Montaigne in his last revisions of the *Essays*.

> I feel weighed down by an error of soul which I dislike because it will not leave me in peace. Though I try to correct it, I cannot get it out of my system.
>   It comes to this: I underestimate my own possessions and correspondingly attach too much value to things that are strange, far away, or belong to someone else.
>
> ("On Presumption")

Here, according to my reading, lies Montaigne's secular account of original sin, our natural weakness. The inversion of pride distorts as fully as pride itself. Malraux has lived in constant struggle against this incorrigible soul-error. Every museum filled, every revolution won, every woman led to the bed of slaughter is a Pyrrhic victory unless our natural perverseness of mind can master itself. Here, in the context of our eternally empty conquests, arises the absurdity that prefaces every effort Malraux makes to reach lucidity or profundity. And here in the context of eternal enchantment and disenchantment, one should reread the opening of *Anti-Memoirs*. "*Il n'y a pas de grandes personnes.*"

In *The Temptation of the West*, Malraux develops the idea that "Every civilization molds its own sensibility." The following year he wrote an article in which he refers to a "grid" through which we apprehend the world. For thirty years a loose group of thinkers whom it is convenient to refer to as "Structuralists" has kept repeating to us that language forms and sustains the shape of experience, the pattern of available ideas and feelings within which we live. We cannot see the pattern except by an effort of personal and cultural transcendence, like that of visualizing the Milky Way as our own galaxy. Malraux can be regarded as one of the early Structuralists—*but not of language*. The mental grid he has increasingly devoted himself to mapping consists of *images*—forms, colors, simplifications, and their transformations. His temperament and his talent remain predominantly verbal. But his subject, his deepest fascination, is painting and sculpture. Gaëtan Picon, who writes with the authority of long friendship, concludes his portrait of Malraux with a flat statement: "The great admission of *The Voices of Silence* is that the author would have wished to manipulate colors and forms, not write sentences." The same book, *Malraux par lui-même*, reproduces eight of his drawings that display a surprising sensitivity to line and movement. By vocation and profession he manipulates words, yet he is forever telling us that thinking takes place by images in many of the greatest minds. For the past twenty years he has produced books whose profuse illustrations form the armature. It is so because he feels instinctively that a painting or a sculpture attests directly to and arises from an act. A nonverbal work of art detours the mental set inherent in language. Malraux speaks for himself in *The Voices of Silences*:

> The non-artist's vision, wandering when its object is widespread
> (an "unframed" vision), and becoming tense, yet imprecise when
> its object is a striking scene, achieves exact focus only when
> directed towards some *act*. The painter's vision acquires precision
> in the same way; but, for him, that act is painting.

The novels and *Anti-Memoirs* carry no illustrations. But the pictures lie in the text itself in the form of landscape, focused acts of seeing which express the character's freest thinking. *Anti-Memoirs* is a travel book because Malraux thinks through places—through the landscapes that punctuated the dialogue.

In respect to this radical insight into human consciousness, and in respect to a number of other preoccupations (politics, time, the novel as a vehicle of action, the faltering maturation of a man), there is one wistful figure who bears comparison to Malraux. Allow for at least three generations or sixty years of difference. He is not even a Frenchman: Henry Adams.

MICHAEL RIFFATERRE

Malraux's Anti-Memoirs

Even forewarned by the odd title, the reader must find this thick volume constantly disconcerting, especially if he is a Malraux votary. For at every step he stumbles upon pages he has read before. The five parts of *Anti-Memoirs* are linked together by the tenuous thread of Malraux's return to the scenes of his earliest adventures. Five parts, and four of them bear the titles of previous fiction, are all crammed with passages plucked out of the older works. Chateaubriand was peculiarly fond of resetting old pieces into his life story, but even he never went quite so far. Most of the time Malraux's borrowings from himself are extensively rewoven. *The Walnut Trees of Altenburg,* an unfinished wartime novel, contributes a number of episodes and its title to the first part; its postscript forms the core of part three. *The Royal Way* is remolded differently: a straightforward account of an expedition among primitive tribes becomes a film scenario that uses all the cinematic tricks—flashbacks, fade-ins, close-ups, etc. Of *Man's Fate* only the title and China remain: the Shanghai witness of the twenties returns to find that the once persecuted Communists are now the masters; Chairman Mao, a mere shadow then, withdrawn from the scene, is now planted center stage like the bronze statue of an emperor entombed. In *The Temptation of the West* we had an exchange of philosophies between two anonymous young men, vaguely representative, one from France, the other from China. The performance is now repeated, this time between Nehru, embodying at least one India, and Malraux himself, personal envoy of a Western rule and *the* French

From *Columbia Forum* 11, no. 4 (Winter 1968). © 1968 by the Trustees of Columbia University in the City of New York.

interpreter of the esthetics of both worlds. There is only one section of the book, also called "Anti-Memoirs," that might be regarded as reminiscences in the conventional sense, but even this is a far cry from most biographical literature. No revelations of the youth Malraux professes to have hated; no reply to his first wife's description, in *her* memoirs, of his early adventures; not a word about how he wrote his novels.

He does give fascinating insights into the great men he meets, especially that paragon of all men of action whom Malraux—yesterday's international revolutionary—now serves. There are many notes by the true insider on the collapse of one Republic of France, and of her empire. But even such eye-witness reports are given no greater importance than the author's visit to the Cairo museum, for instance, or his pilgrimage to the sanctuaries of India. Here again, incidentally, Malraux relies upon previous writings: his meditation before the Sphinx of Egypt is lifted almost verbatim from one of his long essays on art criticism, *The Metamorphosis of the Gods*. So is one of the apologues that substitute for personal confessions of faith—the story of Vishnu and the ascetic Narada. All this suggests that these memoirs of the man of action par excellence of French letters pertain rather to the history of his soul (or of Everyman's soul) than to his high deeds.

When this first of four volumes (those following will be posthumous) was being launched, excerpts leaked to the French press highlighted the role of the privileged insider revealing how history works. Quite obviously this was a publicity angle. The reader will certainly enjoy Malraux's portraits of great men (a new facet of his art), his humorous eye upon officialdom, the epic he makes out of his political speeches. But interesting as all this may be, it is not central to the nature of this work of art. Nor, for that matter, are style features that the reader recognizes from the novels—Malraux's skill at evoking the special exoticism of war scenes, the quasi oneiric quality of certain similes. The nub of the book is something else, which is made clear by the peculiarities of form and content I have just mentioned. These peculiarities attest the truthfulness of Malraux's declaration of intent in his first pages. The memoirs are antimemoirs because, unlike literary confession writers ever since Rousseau, Malraux does not believe we know more about a man if he admits what he has been hiding—which is usually contemptible or ludicrous "un misérable petit tas de secrets (a mean, pitiable heap of secrets)"—or that we get to know him better if he tries to uncover the recesses of his unconscious. Psychoanalysis, he feels, would be more effective and would have more savor. But above all, a man is not made of his weak points: he is what he makes himself into. Malraux does not think a portrait is truer if it is more "realistic"—that is, if it focuses on the petty, or on the anecdotal, or on the subject's tics. He hates the scrutiny of seams and linings known as "psychological" criticism: Sainte-Beuve had inevitably to misunderstand *The Red and the Black*, assuming as he did that it had been written by Monsieur Beyle, whom he knew; the author was Stendhal. Malraux does not go for that: "je ne m'intéresse guère (I am hardly interested in myself)." On the other hand, what a man makes himself out to be may be a sham. Malraux tries to reduce to a minimum what he calls "la part de comédie" in a human life—the "act." He strives not to be duped by any man's impersonation, by the romantic fantasies with which he may surround himself.

What interests Malraux, then, is neither what a man has no control over and would like to erase from his own image, if this were in his power; nor the act people put on to rationalize their instincts. His interest, rather, is in what he likes to call the deepest metamorphosis a man can achieve: turning a destiny you suffer into a destiny you master ("d'un destin subi en destin dominé"). Which does not mean, of course, that you can control your own destiny; but you can become fully aware of it, you can ask questions about it. There is no need to find the answers—perhaps we can never find them. It is the kinds of questions we ask that defines us. Such questions will not yield information about any given individual, but rather about a certain relation he has with the universe. They will not tell us what complexities or contradictions a great man or a saint is made of, but they will tell us about the nature of his greatness or of his saintliness. Throughout Malraux's dangerous life, it is the omnipresence of death that raises the essential question for him (the question "que la mort pose à la signification du monde"). For this practitioner of revolution, the existence of social oppression, starvation, especially torture (since that involves a more intimate and more individual contact between the torturer and his victim), raises another question: What does the fact of the systematic humiliation of man by man tell us of the meaning of the cosmos? It matters little that the questions may be hackneyed, commonplace. Everything literature is about is by this time commonplace. What matters is the form the poet shapes it into.

Malraux asserts his humanity whenever he asks these questions. The technique of the memorialist is to find himself by comparing his past to his present. Malraux practices this technique by revisiting all the times and circumstances that made him ask these questions. He is all the more certain that they lead him toward an understanding on his condition as man, because he has found that these same questions are everywhere on other men's lips, however different those men may be. Hence his long dwelling upon the experience of Asia, where he witnessed the death throes of civilizations; hence the inclusion in his memoirs of other people's memories so long as they pose the same questions (e.g., the experience of the concentration camps as told by inmates).

Questions grow deeper the more often they are asked. Malraux always found fiction convenient for asking them over and over again. Thus his continual excerpting from the imaginary experiments with which he duplicated in his novels the experiences of his life.

Malraux was bound to pick memoirs as the most practical vehicle for the three forms his constant questioning takes (meditation, asking others, asking his characters). The more so since for him the basic principle of art is the assumption that, as opposed to truth, reality is an appearance. He defines appearance as whatever is ephemeral, being subject to time, and truth as whatever transcends time. Because he held this concept, Malraux's choice of memoirs as a form of expression was the ineluctable outcome of his evolution, since as a genre memoirs are the perfect machine for sorting out what endures—that is to say, everything that art is about.

I insist upon this sorting metaphor because I believe it makes clear the essential mechanism of Malraux's anti-memorialism and because it emphasizes the fact that the author is returning to the inspiration of his long-abandoned novels, but armed this time with the new style that his practice of art criticism has taught him.

The genre *memoirs* is defined by two conventions: a dichotomy presenting the author as subject and the author as object; and a mimesis of reality organized along a time axis, which allows for comparison. Thus it can readily show what is repeated, i.e. what is similar in a sequence of various events.

Of these two defining characteristics, the use of the first person by the author is here the less important. Some critics make much of it, but it would be crucial only if it promised the unleashing of a tide of total confession that Malraux specifically repudiates. The first person does not make the confession more direct, or the contact more personal; it could easily be replaced by the third person speaking of a protagonist who is Malraux himself—as in his novels. In *The Walnut Trees* we have both: the story is told in the first person by a character. It is a marker, however, identifying the genre to which the book belongs, even if the work is a reaction against the prevailing, or more common, treatment of that genre. The first person also denotes the assimilation by one consciousness of what the author's varied experiences have brought him, no matter what their origin: contacts with others, learning through the experience of others, and experimentation through fictional characters. Malraux takes over and draws conclusions. Let us also emphasize the fact that the first person is not used here to record an evolution—the *je* of yesterday contrasted with the *je* of today. What strikes the reader immediately is that Malraux records what has not changed, that he uses a genre normally inseparable from the idea of change to underscore permanance.

This brings me to the fundamental structure of *Anti-Memoirs*—namely, what Malraux calls dialogue: "all my surviving memories dialogue together; as a matter of fact, my life's dialogues are all that is left of it." Some may see the dialogue as suggestive of man's inner contradictions: no such dichotomy in Malraux. For others, the dialogue sets illusions of the past opposite disillusions of the present. I fail to discern any disillusion in Malraux's confrontation of dates.

The dialogue is in fact often limited to an opposition of two dates at the beginning of a chapter: the date for today—1965; for yesterday, another date *and* the "story." No new version—which is to say that yesterday's version is still valid.

In many cases, however, there are two or more versions: a narrative retold, or the description of objects separated in time and space but connected by memory and therefore, it must be, somehow resembling one another. Whenever there is such a juxtapositon, the dialogue is very much an empirical application of comparative method to the analysis of structures: two comparable sets are superimposed on each other, so that it can be determined whether they evidence similar relations between their components, no matter how different the components may be semantically. If such similarities do show up, the two sets are said to be variants of the same structure. This is the very method Malraux uses in his art criticism: by juxtaposing paintings or sculptures, he is able to eliminate what does not keep recurring, and to underline by superimposition what does recur—a certain geometry typical of a given artist, for instance. In the same way certain distortions can be spotted in the treatment of themes or in the representation of reality that indicate that such structures underlie and modify forms which would otherwise be dictated only by the shape of things. Transposed into autobiography, this comparatism superimposes today's impression upon the memory it awakens, today's ways of perceiving the same object upon yesterday's ways, and so forth. If the superimposition yields invariants, these must be what is impervious to change and to time, what is truth in the midst of the ephemeral appearances of life. These invariants form a geometry of confrontation with death and with human degradation.

Consider, for example, the long episode of the plane that is caught in a storm and almost crashes: Malraux has carried this over almost unchanged from *Days of Wrath* to *Anti-Memoirs*. In the early novel, Kessner's flight adds suspense to the tale of an escaping prisoner—fate playing cat and mouse with

its prey. In *Anti-Memoirs* the incident is related as it was lived by Malraux
on his way back from the lost kingdom of Sheba: all that is left is Icarus
facing the archetypal void. The story of the flight is the same in both texts;
but what happens after the landing is now given straight, without the ad-
justments of setting required by the fictional plot. What is left is the inner
turmoil of a man back from somewhere else, for whom everything is astonishingly new, seen as through the eyes of a child, seen without meaning or
connection: hands living their own lives unrelated to bodies, dog unrelated
to master, everything just being there. This is of course the existentialist
experience, the truth we get at by removing the accidental. And Malraux
goes on reminiscing, comparing other comings back, from foreign lands or
from death, and each time there is the same basic component linking them,
the same structural sequence: return, rediscovery.

The process of isolating the essence of experience yields a stylistic bonus:
torn from its prior context, the surviving image takes on the absoluteness,
the immediacy, of explosions of affective memory. The more insignificant
the signal that triggers the explosion, the more subconscious the associations
that tie it to impressions of the past, and the more present the sensation.
Malraux's comparative method works something like this type of memory;
thus his reminiscences have the illuminating suddenness, the irrecusable
presence of accidental associations. Words seem to generate their own world.
The same suddenness is used to connect episodes, so that no hint of literary
artifact remains and the memoirs take on the shape of instinctive memory.
Malraux's memories of prison and of the Resistance are triggered by a remark
made by Nehru about British jails—other times, other places, epic dangers,
a whole chapter interrupts the tales of India. One word in the author's formal
address at a funeral: "the *prehistory* of Resistance"—and his mind wanders
back to a fantastic descent into the famed Lascaux caves, to check on a hidden
arsenal, or rather a descent into the triple night of time, fear, and Mother
Earth, which now in turn brings back and enriches his interrupted meditation
on the dead hero. Memoirs may follow chronology or the logic of events;
then they are narrative. The *Anti-Memoirs* are built upon analogy (the superimposition system is itself identical with metaphor); they are therefore
poetry.

When we speak of analogy we must not think only of superficial like-
nesses. These would not work, they would not produce their poetic effect
without the underlying structure: they work only if they are the concrete
medium which actualizes the structure's potentialities.

Thus, beholding the familiarity of the Indian poor with eternity, Malraux is reminded of the many humble men he saw facing death during the

Second World War. This is logical enough, but poetically it is a dud. Then follows the episode of the tank caught in a trap while he and his men wait endless minutes for the German shell that barely misses its target. So far, however, the superimposition of 1958 India upon 1940 France is only at a narrative level. But now suddenly the superimposition becomes our own poetic experience. After various lame efforts to draw parallels between burning Dunkirk and the cult of Siva the Destroyer, between the Elephanta pagoda and the cathedral of Chartres, Malraux hits upon a likeness (he calls it dialogue, of course) between two faces. The first is the face of one of his men in the tank, lighted by the moon through the periscope—a bizarre play of light that turns flesh livid as a corpse. Anguished, Malraux sees a portent of death. The second face is that of Siva's triple head, eyes shut in the pennumbra of the underground pagoda. The two, obviously, are not connected by an actual similarity: Siva's face is serene and beautiful (more than 100 pages have intervened between the description of Siva and this event for this impression to sink in and take root in our memory). The soldier's face is vaguely grimacing, almost toothless. But the two faces have one thing in common: both are lighted in darkness. That would be wholly insufficient to outweight the sharp disparities, and with no other link the comparison would be ludicrous. Not so where there is an underlying structure: this structure expresses the identity between two formally antithetical statements, on a model much like the joking "heads I win, tails you lose." It is actualized by the following variant: "the civilizations for which Death has meaning, the men for whom Life has no meaning"—a doubledecker signifying "the whole of mankind." Such a powerful latent equation will of course tend to overload any sign capable of carrying its meaning. The sign is the common "faceness" of the two faces. The contact is made, with the same powerful impact as if this were affective memory—a symbol is created.

A more complex example may clarify the operation of structural interferences. On the one hand, a systematic superimposition of memories is carefully worked out by the author as variations on a given structure. On the other hand, an aberrant element in one of these variants betrays the reactivation of another structure that may have been completely dormant in his mental storeroom, so to speak. As Malraux revisits the Pyramids and the Sphinx in Egypt, as his thought dwells upon graves as architecture and as sacred poetry, memory carries him back to the room in Nuremberg where Hitler used to meditate upon his speeches during the yearly Nazi party rituals. Hitler's cell comes to mind naturally enough, since the room was modeled after the sepulchral chamber inside the pyramid of Cheops. The Fuehrer's chamber also seems to him a kind of death symbol, since he visited

the room in the wake of Allied conquest, in April 1945. It struck him then
as the symbolic heart of Germany ablaze. The Nazi palace is strewn with
rubble and the torn limbs of the great bronze eagle. Skeletons inspired by
Dürer survey the scene from a balcony, blown there, it is true, by a mighty
blast, from the Museum of Natural History. All the same, this sort of
symbolism is a bit facile. The real source of the power Hitler's chamber
exercises over our minds is derived from the funeral chamber his room is
superimposed upon. The actual differences between the imitation and the
original are immense: on a rational level, Pharaoh's place of repose is all
purity, stone nudity, austere geometry; wheras Hitler's cell is mangled chaos.
But on the level of the imaginary, the two descriptions work as variants of
the same structure: the wild opposition of visual details and atmosphere gives
place, as we read, to the realization that Hitler's lair and Cheops's cenotaph
are both reached by way of a narrow initiatory descent into the depths, that
both are so locked up inside their architecture that the closure takes on a
maleficent symbolism, that both are haunted by baleful shadows. The actual
representations of death and destruction in the ruined city would be simply
good reporting, no more than the reflection of emotion-laden reality. Their
poetic force stems from the fact that Hitler's cell has become, in context,
the semantic equivalent (something like the *équivalent significatif* in Malraux's
terminology of art criticism) of its Egyptian prototype: the monument par
excellence of Death. The only difference is that in the Cairo context the
monument was described in what might be called Egyptian language, and
now it has been translated into a language of Apocalypse (with a touch of
Third Reich dialect).

It matters not that there may be a real architectural filiation between
the two actual buildings. The pertinent point, on the plane of literary representation, is that Malraux has seized upon that similarity and translated it
into the mutual substitutability of the two images. We have further evidence
in an addition that makes sure the reader will decode the message properly:
as Malraux reminisces about Nuremberg, he remembers that it was in the
spring of the year—amidst the debris he saw a fat German woman bicycling,
her handlebars loaded with lilacs. This again is a superimposition. In the
Tutankhamon tomb Malraux also notices the dried cornflowers which told
the archeologist that the young Pharaoh had died in the spring. The spring
flowers in the two cases are not mere coincidence; the similarity of motif
corresponds to a structural relation, the contrast between death and renascent
life, without which the representation of death would not be complete. It
serves the added purpose of reinforcing the parallelism between the two
descriptions and so imposes upon the reader a double reading of the Nu-

remberg passage: simultaneously, as an instance of picturesque prose and as a symbol.

Now *within* the Nuremberg variant another description seems at first to fall in the domain of facile contrasts, on a par with the skeletons on the balcony. As Malraux cautiously climbs down to the dictator's study, a red luminiscence gradually dissipates the darkness, while the harmonies of a subterranean choir resound. He finds himself in the presence of Negro American soldiers humming a spiritual—mankind finding its soul again in the midst of cataclysm. Maybe this is too good to be true—but whether the episode is invented or actual, it is a departure from the parallelism I have just been describing. As always happens, the distortion in the mimesis of the objects involved in the basic superimposition signalizes the pull of another structural scheme. For the *way* the incident is described denotes the presence of a structure in Malraux's experience anterior to his accidental Nuremberg encounter with the American Negroes. There is a significant sequence: evocation of a subterranean fire, its comparison with a Herculean pyre that had long been awaiting Hitler, this closely linked with the evil outside, and careful avoidance of any bifurcation toward Wagnerian possibilities. The sequence cannot be explained by the actual scene or even by the mechanisms of conventional antithesis taking off from such a scene. It is in fact exactly parallel to the description of Hell in one of Malraux's earliest texts, *Les Royaume farfelus* (1920–27), an unjustly forgotten allegory. There we find an omen of things to come—the depths, the fires burning in the depths and rising *de profundis*, the solemn chanting of the damned. Representatives of official religion deny that the damned sing; a visionary prince asserts they do. We must suppose that in *Anti-Memoirs* we have a variant, perhaps unconscious, of the 1927 image. In *Les Royaume farfelus* the song of the damned is undoubtedly a kind of metaphysical Internationale; it proclaims the rising of the world's oppressed. The recurrence of this structure in the Nuremberg reminiscences changes their meaning: the contrast now signifies the great historical constant of man's humiliation and of man's hope in its despite. This is Malraux's other basic obsession. This has *filtered* (another of his art criticism terms) the mimesis of the Nuremberg decor. A structure will generate symbols and filter reality whenever the reality described lends itself ever so little to a reorganization along the lines of the structure. Then, every time, the words used to describe that reality will change into a special vocabulary whose meaning will be regulated by the structure, not by the things depicted. In Malraux's own phrase (from *Voices of Silence*), the structure "is a nervous system looking for its flesh."

This is the constant phenomenon that makes *Anti-Memoirs* as different from memoirs as a poem is different from the most brilliant narrative. Where memoirs would explain and describe the author through the settings in which he appears, through his voice, his actions, antimemoirs refashion memories to the shape of his mental contours, and deflect the meaning of words in accordance with his inner rules. He does not write about a reality remembered; it is rather that reality, filtered by his mind, becomes the symbol of that mind.

THOMAS JEFFERSON KLINE

Le Temps du mépris *Recaptured*

*The greatest mystery is not that we have been flung at
random between the profusion of the earth and the galaxy
of the stars, but that in this prison we can fashion
images of ourselves sufficiently powerful to deny our
nothingness.*

—*Les Noyers de l'Altenburg*

Every major character in Malraux's fiction up to Kassner in *Le Temps du
mépris* illustrates his thesis that the modern novel represents "the development
of a personal problem through images." Each novel elicits its successor, for
each protagonist encounters a final philosophical dilemma to which he is
incapable of providing an answer. All Malraux's heroes prior to *Le Temps du
mépris* clearly present what George Lukács and Lucien Goldmann termed
the problematical character.

Kassner, however, has been interpreted as Malraux's paradigm of the
true revolutionary, whose absolute faith in the *fraternité virile* of the Comintern enables him to undertake any sacrifice. No matter how shattering the
physical discomfort and isolation, his faith in the massive solidarity of the
Party remains unshaken. His integration into the greater fraternity of the
Party and his devotion to its cause appear to provide neither the occasion
nor the excuse for the agonizing ontological and existential doubts of his
predecessors. Goldmann thus considered Kassner Malraux's unique nonproblematical character, within the context of a community which is itself
nonproblematical. Even death, which had stymied the earlier characters,
would appear, therefore, to present no intolerable enigma for Kassner, who

From *André Malraux and the Metamorphosis of Death.* © 1973 by Columbia University
Press.

sees his own life as an integral part of an independent collectivity which will continue to function without him.

This interpretation, then, considers Kassner's problems to be practical rather than philosophical, more concerned with the prison's limitations on his political activity than with the imperative to justify his existence, with what Comte Rabaud, in *Les Noyers de l'Altenburg*, calls the "eternal . . . in man . . . his divine quality . . . his ability to call the world in question."

With this view of the novel, questions raised by the earlier novels would appear to be circumvented. The only solution apparently proposed to man's confrontation with death and the absurdity of life would involve a total loss of self within the ideology of a larger group, a solution, it must be borne in mind, which the author himself never embraced. Even more disconcerting than the nature of the particular doctrine is the presence of *one* overriding ideology which, as Irving Howe has observed, "reflects a hardening of commitment, the freezing of opinion into system."

This interpretation, however, is undermined by one overpowering consideration: one entire stratum of the work, the level of metaphorical language, belies the protagonist's nonproblematical status just as significantly as this level established the problematicity of Malraux's earlier works. The most compelling indictment of the nonproblematical interpretation is to be seen in Malraux's decision to situate nearly two-thirds of the novel in prison, rather than in scenes either actively depicting the corruption or society or extolling the achievements and fraternity of the Party. This in itself would not necessarily require a critical about-face had the prison not proved such a pregnant metaphor in Malraux's earlier works. Although Kassner never explicitly questions the human condition, although his values and beliefs preclude the anguish of a Garine, the central situation of the novel once again revolves around the quintessential Pascalian image. Kassner's prison inevitably evokes incidents and metaphors of imprisonment from *Les Conquérants*, *La Voie royale*, and *La Condition humaine*, in the last of which the scene of the execution of Kyo and Katow so obviously derives from Pascal's image of the human condition as prison.

Three key passages in rapid succession elaborate on this Pascalian theme. As Kassner falls prey to a flood of associative thoughts threatening to dissolve his will and carry him over the frontier of sanity, Malraux compares the loss of reason to the prescribed movement of the heavens: "His youth, his suffering, his very will, all was vanishing, revolving in the motionless cadence of a constellation." This preliminary identification of the enslavement of the mind to overpowering forces with the unvarying rhythm of the constellations is soon developed. Moments after Kassner's first panic, Malraux amplifies the comparison with two additional metaphysical themes: man's own insignificance in the universe, and an overwhelming sense of *destin:*

> Beyond time, there was a world . . . in which all that had made up his life glided with the invincible movement of a cosmos in eternity. . . . He now felt his lean body mingling, little by little, with the boundless fatality of the stars, his whole being held spellbound by the army of the night careening towards eternity through the silence.

Kassner's prison is invested with a double significance; the passage first recalls Pascal's "this little dungeon . . . I mean the universe." When Kassner compares his life (destiny) to the boundless fatality of the stars, he moves from a sense of his own meaninglessness to one of enslavement and finally to a kind of universal determinism. These two aspects of the prison image, together with the fact of physical imprisonment, are united in the novel's most powerful image:

> The fervor of life and death just now united in the musical harmony was swallowed up in the world's limitless servitude: the stars would always follow the same course in that sky spangled with fatality, and those captive planets would forever turn in their captive immensity, like the prisoners in this court, like himself in his cell.

Here the centrifugal expansion of Kassner's awareness outward toward the constellations is reversed in a dramatic series of references to enslavement telescoping centripetally, starting from a universal vision, moving to the specific group of stars, converging on the tiny group of prisoners, focusing finally on the smallest element, assaulting Kassner with Pascal's realization that he is "no more than the tiniest point compared to that described by the stars revolving in the firmament." The centripetal movement strongly insists upon Kassner as a more metaphorical and metaphysical than merely physical prisoner. By so obviously re-creating Pascal's image of the human condition, Malraux suggests that even the militant Kassner, faced with the possibility of a solitary death, is recast into the problematical world of his predecessors Garine, Perken, and Kyo. In thus resurrecting the existential questions so crucial in his first three novels, Malraux intimates that the answers of the militant may finally prove inadequate in certain critical contexts. An analysis of other image patterns in *Le Temps du mépris* will clarify this observation. When Kyo is imprisoned in *La Condition humaine*, he experiences a gradual, then accelerated metaphorical regression from man, to beast bound for slaughter, to tortoise, and finally to worm. The overwhelming impact of these seriated metaphors communicates the loss of dignity incurred through imprisonment. Robbed of liberty and constantly forced to submit to physical brutality, the prisoner is stripped of his fundamental virility and humanity. In 1935 Malraux declared, "It is not at all certain that confidence raises man up from the dust, but it is sure that scorn will trample man in the dust for ever," a statement which casts doubt upon the novelist's belief in the un-problematical nature of the Party and its militant adherents.

As a result, it is much more logical to view Kassner, as Malraux viewed Ernst Thälmann (undoubtedly the model on which Kassner is based) as one of "those few intellectuals who mean to recover for the abused word *dignity* its most profound meaning." The novel's imagery repeatedly insists that the most heinous aspect of the prison consists not in its interference with political activity (which is put aside for two-thirds of the work) but rather in its encroachment on human dignity. Throughout the novel, each prison reference carries the metaphorical weight of such an impairment of dignity, implemented, as in so many other passages of Malraux's previous fiction and especially *La Voie royale*, by the insect.

Kassner quickly descends metaphorically to the level of the insect when the prison is described as "a seething nest (*une fourmillière*) of tiny sounds." The prisoner reacts not so much to the entry of guards themselves as to their shadows "like enormous spiders" cast by a small lantern onto the low ceiling. The implication is clear: if the prisoners themselves are reduced to "tireless centipedes" by the "life-like quality of a creature's shell" of this "black termite's nest," the guards who enforce this dehumanization become degraded into mere abstractions, shadows once removed of one of the lowest forms of life.

Throughout the novel, then, the insect metaphor becomes an objective correlative of the defeat of dignity. When Kassner, fearing that his tumultuous and uncontrollable thoughts verge on insanity, decides to take his life,

> he began to pace the floor. . . . The hour that was approaching
> would be the same as this; the thousand smothered sounds that
> teem like lice beneath the silence of the prison would repeat to
> infinity the pattern of their crushed life; and suffering, like dust,
> would cover the immutable domain of nothingness.

The element of submission, compellingly communicated by the insect metaphor, is deliberately reinforced by the existentially affective phrase "the immutable domain of nothingness," which insists once again upon the prison as human condition.

Aside from symbolizing the humiliation so destructive to the militant, the insect also communicates the frustration of the prisoner's attempt to impose a vital order on his thought. For the militant, the insect would signify only the inhumanity of other men, an exterior infliction of suffering. Yet for Kassner the insect embodies the demon within, the subconscious which threatens to cast him irretrievably into mental chaos. The insect, a particularly appropriate image of such self-alienation, has always carried in Malraux's work a connotation of the unknowable and incomprehensible *other*, the content of hallucinations and childhood traumas.

The demon of self-alienation—one for which even the militant can provide no answer—emerges with the ebbing of Kassner's former strength: "His strength, grown parasitic, was gnawing him relentlessly."

Of the factors which constantly threaten Kassner's sanity, one of the most obsessive is time, without a clear sense of which order in impossible. Kassner, threatened less by political realities than by the subtle invasion of both past and future into his sense of the present, slides into a perpetual sense of "forever" which destroys perspective and coherent thinking. Time metamorphoses into a dreadful black spider driving Kassner to the level of the subhuman:

> Only a sly submissive kind of sub-human creature grown utterly indifferent to time could adapt itself to the stone. Time, that black spider, swung back and forth in the cells of all the prisoners as horrible and fascinating for them as it was for their comrades who were sentenced to die.

If sleep represents momentary escape, insomnia promises certain insanity: "He knew the world of insomnia, and had been haunted by sensations of distress inexhaustibly reiterated, with an insect's precision."

At moments when Kassner is in greatest danger of losing his lucidity, *le destin* is presented through the metaphor of the insect. Such an image hovers hauntingly over his difficulty in concentrating on the coded tapping from a neighboring cell: "He could not drive from his mind the image of a hand vainly trying to catch a fly on the wing."

Recovering sufficient control to apply his mind to deciphering the code, Kassner encounters the frustration of succeeding in retaining the order of the numbers only to face their incomprehensibility, of coming close enough to hope but not close enough to succeed. This renewed frustration illuminates the growing dichotomy between the former assurance of the unproblematical militant and the submissive weakness of the problematical prisoner. Faced with this impasse Kassner undergoes a Kafkaesque metamorphosis: "He felt like an insect squeezed in its hollow stone, avariciously contracting its legs over its accumulated wealth—just as his fingers against his chest at this moment were contracted over those numbers, which were tokens of friendship." Tantalizingly close to meaning and yet resisting interpretation, the numbers themselves behave like spiders: "Hanging by some imperceptible and precarious thread in back of his eyes, they nevertheless flooded the darkness, flowed over him as though he should have to hold on to them to save himself, and his hands were repeatedly missing them."

Hours later, with the code still undeciphered, the problematical Kassner is "eaten away by the ant-like numbers." Only when he overcomes his mental chaos long enough to unravel the cryptic message does he regain his lost will, finding dignity in a sense of fraternity which momentarily overrides the sense of submission. But the victory proves illusory; with the removal of the comrade in the neighboring cell, Kassner is immediately replunged into his solitary battle against insanity. The lesson is clear: fraternity is a valid defense against the power of the existential milieu only as long as the militant is in direct contact with another. The entire decoding exercise constitutes merely a form of Pascalian "diversion," nothing more than a delay in Kassner's ultimate confrontation with himself. Alone, Kassner will be forced to search *within himself* for answers at variance with the notions of solidarity which had sustained him in the political world.

It should be evident from the discussion of this persistent metaphor that the practical problems of the militant as militant have been eclipsed by more difficult problems specific to the prisoner. Protected by the Marxist values of his Party from existential anguish and reflection, Kassner the militant never considers his mortality a threat to the meaning of his life. Death, for the militant, is problematic only in so far as it obstructs his further contributions to the revolution.

As we have just seen, however, Kassner, in the metaphorically charged prison, confronts not simply death but rather the necessity of maintaining his sanity in the face of death, the problem of "diversion." Kassner realizes, once his neighbor disappears, the awful proportions of the problem that "man . . . does not know how to stay quietly in his room."

It is here that we witness the emergence of Malraux's new hero, the artist. The adventurer and militant proving unable to resolve the problem of man face to face with this solitary destiny, it is left to the potential artist in man to reach within himself to find a solution to the crisis.

The appearance of the artist figure is revealed through the series of metaphors whose vehicle is water. Malraux underlines the presence of water the moment Kassner enters his cell: "the wall exuded (*suait*) human destinies," as though it had dissolved many before Kassner who were now being slowly exuded through the wall's subterranean pores. Kassner himself soon feels the effect of this dissolution: "While he remained motionless his limbs and his flesh seemed to dissolve in the darkness." All sounds are perceived as "something confused and distant, like sounds under water." These metaphors create the impression of suspension in a pool, and, though the sexual interpretation is not developed, the implications of a return to the womb are enormous for Kassner the militant; such a powerless and dependent state again suggests the denial of manhood and virility imposed by the prison. To a militant, containment and constraint amount to death and confront him with a problematical situation in which his militancy is no longer relevant.

Representing the stream of consciousness, the image is even more prevalent and refers consistently to the emerging artist. Close upon Kassner's first suspicion of his own insanity, music, although initially presented as a salvation, inspires a series of increasingly chaotic apocalyptic visions:

> Uneasy waves, torpid like his wounds, began to stir in the depth
> of his consciousness, and little by little the solemnity of the deep
> began to settle over them . . . the chant fell and suddenly rose
> again . . . lifting him like a ship to the very crest of suffering.

The torrent of images oriented toward a Rimbaldien apocalypse flows into a vision of "life and death merged in the immobility of the starry sky" before being "submerged beneath a flooding death chant." This cosmic vision of destiny subsides before a calmer indifferent oblivion: "All memory was dissolving in an endless rain which fell over things as though it were sweeping them into the remotest reaches of the past."

This vision of destiny as an eternally dissolving rain gradually cascades into an ocean of aimless images threatening to drown the life of the mind: "his life . . . wholly submerged in solemnity as his body was now enveloped by the darkness, as these shreds of memories were flooded by these sacred harmonies." Kassner, totally subsumed by the flow of his mind, is abandoned by the music which had originally carried him away, "all this music born of his mind which now gradually was withdrawing, ebbing away with the very sound of human happiness, leaving him stranded on the shore (*comme un poisson mort*)."

Recapitulating Kassner's experience, the author resorts to more water imagery to suggest the involuntary dissolution of the will:

> Ikons, stoles, chasubles, dalmatics and crosses . . . finally dis-
> solved into nothingness. This struggle against stupor and the slow

hours went on relentlessly, at a tempo which was gradually de-
creasing, and Kassner would live through it here to infinity, with
those orthodox ornaments in the depth of his obsession as if in
the hold of a sunken galley, to a slower and slower rhythm, more
and more drawn out, like circles in the water, until all was nul-
lified in the silence of complete mindlessness.

Kassner, though momentarily shaken from his stupor by insistent tapping from the neighboring cell, is soon plunged anew into "a jumble of
images," every one of which ends in dissolution. Although Kassner's sense
of hearing registers the tapping on the wall, his mind incorporates these
sounds into the memories of the revolution, each of which in turn becomes
a literal correlative of the dissolving fluidity of Kassner's stream of consciousness. Thus, the "Trans-Siberian grounded like an ocean liner in the
forest"; "the convent . . . [which] drifts with the dreary clouds like a phantom
ship, far from its dead crew"; "the muffled pounding, its hurried beat gradually slowing down to the rhythm of a steamboat engine"; "the long wave-
like gallop of creatures . . . carried away by their own momentum like sails
before the wind"; "this convulsed fleet whose motion rose and fell; both fleet
and sea filled the street from end to end"; and "the earth that was as living
as the rivers and the sea." Although initiated by several similes whose tenor
recapitulates the sound of tapping ("steamboat engine," "muffled pounding,"
"gallop"), this series of comparisons is gradually emancipated from any non-
fluid association, suggesting that Kassner's mind has been set adrift and is
now cut off from outside stimuli, subject only to its own flow.

Once the destructiveness of the uncontrollable stream of consciousness
has been so closely identified with the image of water, anguish itself is
transposed into water imagery: "it was the tide of anguish rising at each peal
of the bells in his temples."

Time, Kassner's most dangerous and elusive enemy in the prison, is
both compressed and expanded into an amorphous sense of perpetuity. When
this timelessness is sporadically interrupted by specific sounds, the floodgates
of the present seem to open; with the sudden steps of a guard "time was
rushing like a boiling torrent towards Kassner, was tearing out the tiniest
fibres of his nerves." Finally, all the various elements eroding his mental
stability culminate in vast and sweeping "waves of madness."

Water images, the most extensive and complicated pattern in the novel,
thus point up Kassner's temporary inability to control the direction of his
thoughts. He discovers the imperative of channeling the tides of his subconscious in order to resist the invidious temptation to surrender to the

comforable prison of insanity, submitting to the "world's limitless servitude" under "that sky spangled with fatality." Just as Montaigne had reined in the "runaway horse" of his mental chaos by composing the *Essais*, so Kassner decides to compose a speech, not for the purpose of communication, since it cannot be heard, but rather to channel and manipulate his thoughts into a coherent structure:

> Deprived (*vidé*) of brotherhood as he had been of dreams and hope, Kassner waited in the silence which hung over the desires of hundreds of men in that black termite's nest. . . .
> "Comrades in the darkness around me. . . ."
> For as many hours, as many days as were needed, he would prepare what could be told to the darkness.

The only means of salvation lies in creativity. Kassner discovers what Walter would express ten years later in *Les Noyers de l'Altenburg:*

> In the prison which Pascal describes, men manage to drag out of themselves an answer which . . . cloaks those who are worthy of it with immortality. . . . The greatest mystery is not that we have been flung at random between the profusion of the earth and the galaxy of the stars, but that in this prison we can fashion images of ourselves sufficiently powerful to deny our nothingness.

It is the artist who redeems the militant when the latter, like Perken, Garine, and Kyo before him, is thrown face to face with death and destiny. Kassner's composition of his speech constitutes what Berger will call "a rectification, a humanisation of the world."

With freedom, Kassner's world is radically transformed. As darkness yields to light and mental chaos is replaced by resolute assurance, the artist once again accedes to the militant. This transformation entails a reversal of the previous symbolic patterns. As mental turmoil subsides, its metaphorical expression as a rushing stream of consciousness is superseded by the image of water as purification. As the door opens, "the full light of the corridor . . . streamed over his whole body, washed away the darkness which glued his eyelids." He proceeds from cell to guardroom "through great yellow waves of light," where "a ray of sunlight full of motes glittered like a canal in the wind." Once outside, Kassner is ritualistically purified of the darkness of the prison: he finds himself "in the clear air washed by great blue streams."

The last insect image in the novel parallels the more optimistic outlook of these later water images. Waiting for his eyes to reaccustom themselves to light, Kassner realizes that "his mind remained attached to the cell by a thousand delicate spider-webs." The metaphor is brilliant; imprinted on Kassner's memory are the brutal affronts to the dignity and mental stability of the prisoner. Yet, with his freedom, these memories begin to fade before the new duties; they have become mere spider-webs, the fragile reminder of a once all-consuming danger.

The artist-militant duality in the character reflects Malraux's interests and activities at the time he was writing the novel. While politically maneuvering to free Thälmann and Dimitrov, Malraux simultaneously and passionately pursued his notion of the artist as final defender of culture in the West. His speeches of the period extol the heroism of the artist daring to defy the hypocrisy and corruption of Western society. He proclaimed, for example, that

> the important thing is to possess *the world of solitude*, to transform what had been suffered into conquest for the artist. . . . Art lives in as much as it permits men to escape from their human condition, not by evasion but by possession. All art is a means of possession of destiny. . . . Like imprisoned or free men, imprisoned or free civilizations reorder the past which they have undergone. [Italics mine.]

In his world of solitude, the prison, Kassner transforms submission into conquest not by a futile attempt to escape destiny but rather by confronting and possessing it. In Malraux's eyes, the possession of destiny through art comes to assume an equal importance with revolution: "From day to day and thought to thought, men re-create the world in the image of their greatest destiny. Revolution gives them only the possibility of their dignity; it is for the individual to make of this possibility a possession."

Through his discovery of the creative act as a response to ontological despair, Kassner emerges as a correlative of the novelist himself, and indeed of all creative artists. Camus was to write of Proust's *Le Temps retrouvé:*

> He has demonstrated that the art of the novel can reconstruct creation itself, in the form that it is imposed on us and in the form in which we reject it. . . . But still more profoundly, it is allied to the beauty of the world or of its inhabitants against the powers of death and oblivion. It is in this way that his rebellion is creative.

The passage would apply equally well to the novel under consideration. Kassner's metaphysical revolt, no longer simply political reaction, leads inevitably to the proposal of the creative act as a positive assertion of man's control over his world.

Despite a discovery as fundamental as that of art, Malraux was as yet unwilling to abandon his philosophy of action and virile fraternity. The last third of the novel contains a structurally identical retranscription of the prison experience. Aloft in a tiny plane piloted by a comilitant, Kassner is resubjected to a confrontation with "destiny." Again a flood of water imagery suggests a menacing tide of destiny which threatens to sweep Kassner away to death in the tiny enclosed cell of the cockpit. The sky, a "mist-covered sea," contains "tidal waves" which threaten to "submerge" the plane, become "battleship" or "sperm-whale." In this tiny prison, Kassner again executes the circles of destiny, as "in the center of the cyclone the plane was spinning on its own axis," and it is natural for Kassner to discover other links with his recent imprisonment: "The inscriptions in the cells, the screams, the knocks on the wall, the craving for revenge were with them in the fuselage against the hurricane." Once again, Kassner is confronted with a Pascalian sense of his own finitude:

> Only the memory of the prison darkness enabled Kassner to realize the surrounding immensity. . . . The silent throngs of his comrades who had filled the darkness of the prison seemed to people this region of fog, the immense gray universe. . . . In the midst of the fog, which was now constant, time was disappearing in the strange sleep-like struggle. . . . Before the immense black cloud . . . Kassner became once more acutely conscious of his infinite smallness.

And again the lesson is double: Kassner discovers anew the fraternity of combat ("It occurred to Kassner that only the proximity of death entitles one to get sufficiently close to a man to know that child-like look which he had just seen, and that this man too was about to die for him"): but he also senses a much deeper lesson, the "simple consciousness" necessary to perceive life and capture it in art. Having reaffirmed his sense of militant fraternity and artistic consciousness, Kassner is at last ready for his discovery of the earth, of its "rhythm of life and death," and for his return to his people and reunion with Anna.

It should be evident that the two natures of the protagonist of *Le Temps du mépris*, the revolutionary and the artist, are necessary and complementary. Unable to survive within the solitary confines of the prison, the militant calls from within himself the artist. Yet once having come to grips through art with the existential problems raised by the prison, the militant and the revolution regain the foreground. It is no artistic accident that Kassner is ultimately freed through the selfless fraternal act of a coworker.

This artist-militant dichotomy is clearly visible in the distribution of the tensive language, the bulk of which occurs in the prison scenes and throws into relief the previously unrecognized problematical artist. But neither artist nor militant is ultimately rejected. When the artist has dealt with the anguish of a solitary destiny, the militant must again take up the arms of the political arena. Man must come to grips with his existential situation before he can fearlessly enter the world of action. Though the novel ends with the reunification of the militant with Anna, and the realization that he must renew his political activity, it is the artist, more representative of Malraux as novelist, who was forced to question the world's meaning, and to transform his destiny into consciousness. It is the artist in Kassner who can claim, "I have refused the beast in me and have become a man without the help of the gods."

Le Temps du mépris, therefore, stands as an eloquent fictional transcription of Malraux's words to the International Congress for the Defense of Culture in 1935:

> Every work of art is created to satisfy a need, but only a need passionate enough to give birth to it. . . . Each of us must re-create in his own domain and through his own quest the heritage of the phantoms which surround us . . . and to create out of the hopes and wills . . . a human consciousness with the age-old suffering of men.

Kassner the prisoner becomes, however briefly, this artist. Led to a confrontation with destiny by the militant, this Promethean figure, capable of denying the nothingness of the universe through creativity, has exemplified Malraux's most eloquent statement of man's objective. "The entire destiny of what men call culture can be summed up in one idea: to transform destiny into *conscience* (conscience *and* consciousness)." This phrase from 1935 would become the slogan of the protagonists of *L'Espoir* and *Les Noyers de l'Altenburg*, just as the duality of art and action inherent in Kassner would become the basis of Malraux's subsequent thought.

LUCIEN GOLDMANN

The Structure of La Condition humaine

Appearing after *Les Conquérants* and *La Voie royale*, this third novel [*La Condition humaine*] was to have an enormous impact and made Malraux famous throughout the world.

Although it is still what I have called one of the "transitional" novels (between the novel with a problematic hero and the novel without character), and although the subject is still, as in *Les Conquérants*, the Chinese revolution, the world of *La Condition humaine* is, in relation to the two preceding novels, entirely different.

Was the author influenced by his discussion with Trotsky? It is, of course, impossible to establish this with any certainty. Nevertheless, the work is in certain respects—but *only in certain respects*—fairly close to the Trotskyist point of view.

But however important an element the "chronicle of the revelation" is (and it is much more important in *La Condition humaine* than in *Les Conquérants*), it remains, in the final resort, of secondary importance for a structuralist or even a merely literary analysis. The true novelty of the book lies in the fact that, in relation to the worlds of *La Voie royale* and *Les Conquérants*, which were governed by the problem of the hero's individual realization, the world of *La Condition humaine* is governed by quite other laws and above all by a different value: *that of the revolutionary community*.

Let us approach the essential point at once: as a novel in the strictest sense of the word, *La Condition humaine* has a problematic hero, but, as a

---

From *Toward a Sociology of the Novel*, translated by Alan Sheridan. © 1975 by Tavistock Publications Ltd.

novel of transition, it describes for us, not an individual but a *collective problematic character:* the community of Shanghai revolutionaries represented in the narrative primarily by three individual characters, Kyo, Katow, and May, but also Hemmelrich and by all the anonymous militants by whom we know they are surrounded.

A *collective* and *problematic* hero; this characteristic, which makes *La Condition humaine* a true novel, derives from the fact that the Shanghai revolutionaries are attached to the essential and, in the world of the novel, contradictory requirements: on the one hand, the deepening and development of the revolution and, on the other hand, discipline towards the Party and the International.

But the Party and the International are engaged in a purely defensive policy. They are strictly opposed to any revolutionary action in the city, withdraw the troops that are faithful to them, and demand the handing back of arms to Chiang Kai-shek, although, quite plainly, Chiang is planning to assassinate the Communist leaders and militants.

In these conditions, it is inevitable that the Shanghai militants should turn to defeat and massacre.

In so far as the book is *also* a "chronicle of the revolution," one sees why its point of view is *fairly close* to the thinking of the Communist opposition. It is written from the point of view of Kyo, May, Katow, and their comrades and implicitly stresses the sabotage of their struggle by the leadership of the Party and the responsibility of this leadership for the defeat, massacre, and torture of the militants.

In this framework, the value that governs the world of *La Condition humaine* is that of the *community*, which is, of course, the *community of the revolutionary struggle*.

Since the world in which the action unfolds is the same as that of *Les Conquérants*, the characters—with a few minor exceptions—are necessarily the same, though they are seen from a quite different point of view. So, in order to illuminate them more clearly, it might be useful to analyse them in turn, situating each of them in relation to the corresponding character of the preceding novel.

We will begin, of course, with the main character: the group of revolutionaries. In *Les Conquérants*, it was personified by Borodin. The difference is obvious enough, but it is justified by the difference of perspective.

As seen by the individualist Garine, the revolutionary can only be *an individual* whose distinctive feature is the fact that he is not only closely linked to the proletariat and to the organization that directs the revolution, but also that he goes so far as to identify himself with this proletariat and this revolution, whereas, *seen from the inside*, this distinctive feature is specifically what transforms the individual into a community. So the story related in *La Condition humaine* is not only that of the action carried out by Kyo, May, Katow, and their comrades, the history of their defeat and death, but also, closely bound up with this action, the history of their community, which is a living dynamic psychical reality.

Around them, if we leave to one side certain incidental figures, we will meet four characters who belong to no community and who remain more or less isolated individuals: an ally, the Chinese terrorist Chen, an enemy, Ferral, and two intermediary characters, Clappique and Gisors.

I have just written "an *ally*, the Chinese terrorist Chen," whereas in *Les Conquérants*, Hong remained in spite of everything an *enemy* whom Garine— in spite of all his sympathy—was finally to execute. The difference derives from the fact that, far from being Hong's homologue, Chen is a mixture of Hong and Garine, a mixture in which the elements related to those that made up the personality of Garine are predominant. This is explained and, indeed, justified by the same difference of perspective. Seen with Garine's eyes, the difference between him and Hong was considerable. Hong, in effect, has an abstract attitude, alien to any concern for efficacity, whereas Garine could find meaning—however precarious and provisional—in his existence only in revolutionary action entirely subordinated to the *efficacity* of the struggle.

From Borodin's point of view, however, this difference loses much of its importance. Hong and Garine resemble one another in so far as they are both individuals who, though declared and active enemies of the bourgeoisie, nevertheless do not identify themselves with the revolution.

On the side of the enemies of the revolution, only one character is really present in the novel: Ferral, who directs an industrial consortium, helps to overthrow Chiang Kai-shek's alliances and organizes the agreement between Chiang and the Shanghai bourgeoisie. He is a character of the *conqueror* type but, of course, a much more superficial conqueror than Garine and Perken, since instead of rallying to the revolution he has committed himself to the side of false values, to what, in the novel, embodies evil and lies. In fact, he really represents one of the risks to which this human type is exposed, a risk that had been touched on in *Les Conquérants* by Nikolaieff when he suggested to the narrator that Garine might have become a "Mussolinian."

Lastly, between the revolutionaries and reaction, two characters in the novel occupy a fairly important position: Gisors, Kyo's father, and Clappique. Clappique is an old acquaintance who had disappeared from Malraux's two preceding novels. He personifies the aerostats and deadly sins of *Lunes*

en papier, the man who lived in imagination; the nonconformist artist, the
buffoon. It should be said, however, that at the time he was writing *La
Condition humaine*, Malraux had much more sympathy for him than at the
period of *Lunes en papier*. This, too, can be explained: *Lunes en papier* is an
attempt to unmask people who claimed to be [the] only valid revolutionaries
in a world in which there was no place for hope, whereas now Clappique,
between the revolutionaries on the one hand, and Chiang Kai-shek or Ferral
on the other, acts more or less as a sort of gadfly. Nevertheless, we must
admire a writer who, despite his sympathy for Clappique, is quite merciless
in showing that his attitude of detachment from reality, while useful at times,
may also be detrimental, even fatal, to the revolutionaries fighting for authentic values.

Gisors embodies the old Chinese culture, which is, in the last resort,
alien to all violence, whether reactionary or revolutionary. In relation to *Les
Conquérants*, he really corresponds to Chen-Dai. But he is a very real character
and this correspondence is more complex and more mediatized than in the
case of the other characters. Chen-Dai was opposed on principle to revolutionary violence. Gisors, on the contrary, is bound to the revolution not
directly—for ideological reasons—but out of affection for his son who is
committed to it body and soul. Now it seems to me that we have here two
complementary aspects of old China and it would be impossible to imagine
Gisors in *Les Conquérants* or Chen-Dai in *La Condition humaine*. Nevertheless,
there is a structural reason in favour of the solution adopted by Malraux: *Les
Conquérants* describes the victory of the revolution, *La Condition humaine* its
defeat. Now it is of the essence of the Gisors and Chen-Dais of this world
to be opposed to victorious violence and to find themselves, rather ineffec-
tively no doubt, on the side of the defeated.

The plot of the novel, although poignant and tragic, is simple enough:
faced with the advance of the Kuomintang army (which *still* comprises both
Chiang Kai-shek and the Chinese Communist Party) the clandestine organization of the Shanghai Communists, supported by the trade unions, is
planning an uprising intended both to facilitate the victory of the attackers
and, at the same time, to get control of the leadership of the movement *after*
victory. In fact, the conflict between Chiang Kai-shek and the Communists
became increasingly sharp as the victory of the Kuomintang became imminent. Having been united in a struggle between a common enemy, they
will now have to solve the problem of the social and political structures of
the new China that the defeat of its enemy will leave as the major problem.

An important section of the militants of the Chinese Party, and among
them, the Shanghai revolutionaries, organized the peasants and unions by

promising to the first agrarian reforms and to the second the seizure of power in the towns. In order to resist them and to maintain control of the Kuomintang, Chiang Kai-shek plans to form an alliance with his former enemies, break with the Communists, and massacre the militants. The leadership of the International and Chinese Communist Party decide that they are too weak to engage in the struggle and forbid any revolutionary action. They allow Chiang Kai-shek a free hand, in the hope that this timourous attitude will lead Chiang to think that repression of the Communists is pointless and to maintain his previous policy, or, at least, to postpone the break with them.

The Shanghai militants, who are already fully engaged in action, are rightly convinced of the contrary. For material as well as ideological reasons, however, they cannot act in isolation and in opposition to the Party leadership. So they are left with no option but to face defeat and massacre. The novel recounts their action just prior to the entry of the Kuomintang into Shanghai, their reactions on learning the decisions of the Party leadership, their defeat after Chiang Kai-shek's entry into the city and, lastly, the torture and massacre of the Communists by Chiang's men—a massacre in which, among many others, two of the novel's three heroes, Kyo and Katow, are killed.

The work begins with a famous scene: Chen's assassination of an arms dealer, or, to be more precise, an agent, in order to get from him a document that will enable the revolutionaries to gain possession of a number of pistols. This assassination reveals at once the difference between Chen and Hong: on the psychological plane, it is an act that will help Chen to become aware of his personal problems; on the material level, it is an act ordered by the revolutionary *organization* and therefore forms part of an *organized* action. There is a passage in the book that indicates both the importance of this assassination for the collective struggle and the particular meaning it has for Chen himself:

> The approaching attempt to place Shanghai in the hands of the revolutionaries would not have two hundred rifles behind it. If the short carbines (almost three hundred in number) which the dead entrepreneur had just arranged to sell the Government were thrown in too, the chances of the rebels would be doubled, for their first step would be to seize the arms of the police for their own troops. But during the last ten minutes, Chen had not once thought about that.

Having carried out the murder, Chen has to walk through the hotel, where life continues its usual way. The episode leads to a remarkable de-

scription of the opposition between two qualitatively different worlds: that
of revolutionary action and that of an everyday life indifferent to ideas and
politics. In *La Condition humaine*, this opposition serves to indicate Chen's
awareness of the difference between the world of terrorist action to which
he belongs and that of "the life of men who do not kill." Some years later,
in *Les Noyers de l'Altenburg*, Malraux was to use a similar description to indicate
Victor Berger's discovery, in Marseilles, at the time he was abandoning the
struggle for the fictory of *Ottomanism* (for which, I believe, one should read
Communism), of the existence of the world of everyday life that is indifferent
to ideas and action, in which however unattached he may be, he fails to
become integrated. Chen, meeting a "Burmese or Siamese by the look of
him, and rather drunk," who says to him "the little piece in red is an absolute
peach!" wanted "both to strike him, to make him hold his tongue, and to
embrace him because he was alive." In *Les Noyers de l'Altenburg*, only the
opposition between the two worlds, that of action and that of everyday life,
is emphasized. In *La Condition humaine*, on the other hand, there is added,
by way of opposition, to the everyday life that is indifferent to politics and
the world of terrorist action that isolates, a third world whose development
constitutes the essential subject of the novel: that of the revolutionary community, to which Chen's action partly belongs and whose function and aim
are precisely to integrate the two others. After the murder of the agent and
the walk through the hotel full of indifferent merrymakers, Chen returns to
his comrades:

> Their presence was breaking down Chen's ghastly feeling of iso-
> lation. It yielded gently, like an uprooted plant which still clings
> to the ground with a few slender threads. And as he gradually
> drew nearer to them it seemed to him that he suddenly knew
> them for the first time—as he had known his sister after his first
> visit to a brothel.

I have said that Chen corresponds much more to the character of Garine
than to that of Hong and that, in the last resort, he is a synthesis of the two.
As for Hong, his first assassination will be an intoxication, a decisive turning-
point in his life. Like Garine, however, he will return after the assassination
to the organization of revolutionary militants that Hong was never to see
again, and never at any point in the novel does he come into opposition with
that organization. Like Garine, too, he works within the collective struggle,
but does not identify himself with it.

Having returned, after the assassination, to the group of revolutionaries,
Chen meets among his comrades two characters who are at the centre of the

novel, not so much as individuals, but as representatives of the entire group, of the revolutionary community—Katow and Kyo.

What characterizes each of them is their total commitment to action. In the book, Katow will be seen only as a militant in the struggle, at the moment of his arrest, then of his execution. Kyo, on the other hand, will be seen also in his private life, in his relations with May. But this does not represent the addition of a new, different sphere, for May and Kyo are characterized by the organic synthesis of their public and private lives, or, to use Lukács's expression, by the total synthesis of the individual and the citizen; and precisely because, in everyday life, this synthesis—which did not exist in Malraux's earlier writings either—is extremely rare, it is important to stress the extent to which Kyo's thinking and consciousness are *entirely* engaged in action. Moreover, Malraux will tell us on several occasions that Kyo's entire thinking was organically structured by the imminent struggle.

One such moment is when he is entering the Chinese quarter, after deciding to attack the boat and take the pistols:

> "A good quarter," thought Kyo. For more than a month he had gone from one meeting to another, organizing the rising, oblivious of the existence of streets: what was mud to him beside his plans? . . .
>
> As he turned out of a narrow passage he suddenly found himself looking down one of the main streets, wide and well-lit. Despite the rain beating down, which half obscured its outlines, he never for a moment saw it save as something flat which would have to be attacked in the face of rifles and machine-guns, firing hoirizontally.

Another moment occurs when he has crossed the Chinese quarter and reached the gates of the Concession:

> Two Annamese troopers and a sergeant from the Colonial army came and examined his papers. He had his French passport. As a temptation to the guards, hopeful Chinamen had stuck little pies all over the barbs of the wire. ("Good way of poisoning a station, if need be," thought Kyo.)

Once inside the Concession, he looks for Clappique. As I have already remarked, Clappique lives not in reality, but in imagination. This is expressed among other things by his external appearance: whatever he was wearing—tonight he was in evening clothes—Baron Clappique looked as if he were in disguise.

He finds him drawing an imaginary picture of Chiang Kai-shek for the benefit of two dancing-girls. How does he see himself in this picture?:

> "And what'll *you* find to do?"
>
> He whimpered: "Can't you guess, dear girl, do you mean to say you can't guess? I shall be Court astrologer, and one night when I am drunk—can it be tonight?—I shall meet my death digging for the moon in a pond!"

I shall come back later to the two other characters to be examined here—Gisors and Ferral.

What defines *La Condition humaine* in relation to the previous novels is first of all the absence of the element that was the most important in those works, the principal characteristic of Garine, Perken, and even Borodin—illness. Illness does exist, of course, in *La Condition humaine*, but only to the extent that the work *also* is in part a social chronicle: illness among the children of the poor, the consequences of an unsuccessful suicide attempt by a woman who wanted to die in order to avoid being married to a rich old man, etc. As revolutionary militants, the heroes themselves may be massacred and tortured, but they remain nevertheless essentially healthy; one might even go so far as to say that they define, by their existence, the summit of the human condition and, therefore, the summit of health. If there is disease, it concerns, not the individuals, but the revolutionary collectivity that is the true hero of the novel and whose problematic character I have already re-marked on. It would not be possible here to study the psychology of this community step by step, so we shall approach it from two particularly important points of view: love and death, the relations between Kyo and May on the one hand, and, on the other, the torture and execution of the revolutionaries after Chiang Kai-shek's victory.

Love and death are, in effect, two important elements in characterizing fictional characters in general and particularly those of Malraux. In *La Condition humaine*, however, they have a different nature and function from those that they had in the previous works. I have already said that, in Malraux's world, relations between men and women always reflect the over-all relation between men and the world. That is why, in the world of Perken and Garine, we met only eroticism and relations of domination, whereas in *La Condition humaine*, a novel of the authentic revolutionary community, eroticism is, like the individual, integrated and superseded in an authentic, higher community: that of love.

In *La Voie royale* one sentence alone hinted at the possibility of the relation that was to be at the centre of *La Condition humaine*. I have already quoted it: at the moment when Perken, learning of his imminent death, takes refuge in a final erotic fling, at the moment he becomes aware of the impossibility of any lasting erotic possession, he also realizes that "one possesses only what one loves."

These words, *which have no meaning in the world of La Voie royale, where love is non-existent*, prefigure *La Condition humaine*, in which Malraux was to create with Kyo and May the first pair of lovers in his oeuvre and one of the most beautiful, purest love stories in major twentieth-century fiction.

Eroticism and domination are not, of course, totally absent from the work—there are even justly famous scenes of this kind, but they involve, not Kyo and May, the heroes of the novel, but the subsidiary character of Ferral, who as I have already said, corresponds in certain respects to Garine/Perken. In addition, though in a more human context, we also find in the character of Chen, who is also to a large degree reminiscent of Garine, the same pure erotic relationship with women.

However, between the eroticism and domination of the previous novels and the same relations in *La Condition humaine*, there is an important difference—one that is essential for the understanding of the characters. In the earlier novels, eroticism and domination constituted precarious, but positive values, whereas they are entirely modified, even devalued by the very presence of love in this novel of the revolutionary community. I shall return to this. Let us begin however with the love of Kyo and May which is, in *La Condition humaine*, a story of love in the twentieth century, a period in which such a feeling is no longer accessible to every man or woman. That is why it can be successful only in so far as it is organically linked to the revolutionary action of the two partners.

The story of this love is that of an entirely new feeling that comes into conflict with the relics that still exist in each of them of a type of feeling and eroticism that they have in fact superseded. In other words, Kyo and May cannot always live up to their own existence and the weakness that survives in each of them will finally be overcome only through action and imminent death, which help them and force them to rediscover their own levels.

The facts are well known: knowing that their relationship allows each of them both to preserve his own freedom and to respect the freedom of the other, May in a moment of exhaustion—and, partly also, moved by the pity and solidarity that binds her to a man who she knows will run the risk of being killed in a few hours—has slept with a comrade, even though she did not love him. Convinced that this is of no importance in her relations with Kyo, which on the contrary would be affected by the slightest lie, she tells Kyo about it. Kyo feels intense pain and an acute feeling of jealousy:

Kyo felt pain in its most degrading form; pain which his self-respect dare not admit. In point of fact she was free to sleep with whoever she wished. What then was the cause of his suffering for which he could find no justification, but which held him in such complete subjection? . . .

"Kyo, I'm going to tell you something strange, but true. Until five minutes ago, I thought you wouldn't mind. Perhaps it suited me to think so. There are some things people ask of one, above all when death is as near as this (it's other people's death that I've had to face till now, Kyo . . .) which have no connexion with love. . . ."

Jealousy there was, notwithstanding; all the less clearly perceived in that the desire which she awoke in him was based upon affection. His eyes closed, and, still leaning on his elbow, he set himself the painful task of understanding. He could hear nothing but May's laboured breathing and the scratching of the puppy's paws. The principal cause of his suffering (he would inevitably find others: he could feel them lying in ambush, like his comrades who still waited behind their closed doors) lay in his idea that that man who had just slept with May ("I can't after all call him her lover") despised her. The man in question was an old friend of hers, whom he hardly knew; but he knew well enough the contempt in which women were ultimately held by almost all men. "The idea that having slept with her, as a result of having slept with her, he may be thinking: 'That little tart'; I could kill him for that. Are we always only jealous of what we imagine the other person is thinking? Men are pretty hopeless creatures. . . ." As far as May was concerned, sexual relations implied no kind of contract. That ought to be made clear to this man. If he slept with her, well and good; but don't let him start thinking he possessed her. ("This is becoming pitiable. . . .") But that was something out of his control—and he knew that, in any case, it wasn't the vital thing. The vital thing, the thing which was torturing him almost beyond endurance, was the barrier which had suddenly cut him off from her: it wasn't hatred which had done it, though there was hatred in him: it wasn't jealousy (or perhaps that was just what jealousy was?): it was a feeling to which he could give no name, as destructive as Time or Death: he could not recapture her.

And Kyo leaves without relations between them returning to normal:

May offered him her lips. In his heart Kyo wanted to kiss her; not her mouth, though—as if there alone bitterness still lingered. He kissed her at last, clumsily. She looked at him sadly, with listless eyes which suddenly filled with animation as the muscles regained control. He left her.

It is only when he is alone in the street again, involved once more in action, that he realizes how deep their love is:

> "What have other men in common with me? Just so many entities who look at me and criticize. My real fellow-creatures love me unreflectingly, love me in spite of everything, love me so that no corruption, vileness or betrayal has any power to alter it: love me for myself and not for what I have done or will do; whose love for me goes as far as my own—embracing suicide. . . . With her alone do I share a love like that, whatever batterings it may have undergone, as others share the sickness of their children, their risk of death. . . ." It certainly wasn't a feeling of happiness, it was something primeval, in tune with the darkness, which set him tingling till he stood there locked in an embrace, as if his cheek were laid against another—the only part of him which was stronger than death.
> On the roof-tops, vague shapes were already at their posts.

The crisis is overcome only at the moment of defeat, when Kyo sets out for the meeting of the Central Committee; he knows, as does May, that he will probably be arrested and executed. At first, however, the tension seems to accumulate:

> "Where are you going?"
> "With you, Kyo."
> "What for?"
> There was no reply.
> "We shall be more easily recognized together than separately," he said.
> "I don't see why. If you're on their list, nothing is going to make any difference. . . ."
> "You can't do any good."
> "What good should I do waiting here? Men don't know what waiting is like."
> He walked a few steps, then stopped and turned towards her.
> "Listen, May: when it was a question of your freedom, I gave it you."

She knew what he was alluding to, and it frightened her: she had forgotten it. She was right, for he went on, dully this time:

". . . and you took advantage of it all right. Now it's mine that is involved."

"But, Kyo, what has that got to do with it?"

"To recognize someone else's right to liberty is to acknowledge that that is more important than one's own suffering: I know that from experience."

"Am I just 'someone else,' Kyo?"

He remained silent. Yes, at that moment, she was. A change had taken place in their relations.

"You mean that because I . . . well, because of that, in future we can't even face danger together? Think, Kyo: one would almost imagine this was a kind of revenge."

"Not to be able to any more and to try to when it's useless are quite different things."

"But if it rankled as much as that, you could perfectly well have taken a mistress. At least, no: that's not true. Why do I say that? I didn't take a lover, I just went to bed with somebody. It's not the same thing, and you know quite well that you can sleep with anyone you want."

"I'm satisfied with you," he answered bitterly.

May was rather puzzled by the way he looked at her. Every possible feeling seemed to enter into his expression. What made her feel really uneasy was the quite unconscious lust which was apparent in his face.

"As far as that goes," he went on, "my feelings are the same now as they were a fortnight ago: I just don't want to. I'm not saying that you are wrong, but that I want to go alone. You acknowledge my liberty; you possess the same degree of liberty yourself. Liberty to do what *you* please. Liberty isn't a bargain, it's just liberty."

"It's a desertion."

Silence.

"What is it that brings people who love each other to face death, unless it is that they can face it together?"

She guessed that he was going to leave without further argument, and placed herself in front of the door.

"You shouldn't have given me this liberty, if we have to be separated now as a result."

"You certainly didn't ask for it."

"You had already given it me."

"You shouldn't have believed me," he thought. It was true, he had always given it. But that she should discuss rights now, that widened the gulf between them.

"There are some rights which one only grants," she said bitterly, "so that they shall not be used."

"If they had been granted so that you could hang on to them at this moment it wouldn't be so bad. . . ."

In that second they were drawing even farther apart than in death. Eyelids, mouth, temples, a dead woman's face still shows the site of every caress, whereas those high cheekbones and elongated eyelids which confronted him then belonged to a foreign world. The wounds of the deepest love suffice to create a thorough hatred. Was she so near death that she was recoiling from the animosity which she had seen preparing? She said:

"I'm not hanging on to anything, Kyo. Say I am making a mistake if you like, that I've already made one; say what you please, but just at this moment I want to go with you, at once. I beg you."

He didn't answer.

"If you didn't love me," she went on, "you wouldn't think twice about letting me come. Well then? Why cause us unnecessary suffering?"

"As if this were a good time to choose," she added wearily. . . .

"Are we going?" she asked.

"No."

Too honest to hide her impulses, she reiterated her desires with a cat-like persistence which often exasperated Kyo. She had moved away from the door, but he realized that all the time he had wanted to pass through he had been sure that he wouldn't really do it.

"May, are we just going to leave each other quite suddenly like this?"

"Have I behaved like a woman who expects protection?"

They stood there face to face, not knowing what else to say, and not content to remain silent, conscious at once that that moment was one of the most solemn of their lives, and that it could not endure—that time was already corrupting it: Kyo's place was not there, but with the Committee, and a certain impatience lurked all the time at the back of his mind.

She nodded towards the door.

He looked at her, took her head between his hands and drew it gently towards him, without kissing her; as though in that firm embrace he had somehow projected all the mingled tenderness and ardour of which masculine love is capable. At last he withdrew his hands.

The doors shut, one after the other. May continued to listen, as if she were expecting to hear a third one close, brought into existence by her imagination. Her mouth hanging limply open, wild with grief, she was beginning to realize that if she had signed to him to leave, it was because she saw in that movement the one final hope of persuading him to take her with him.

But, once in the street, Kyo again feels the strength that unites him to May:

> Parting had not relieved Kyo's distress. The reverse was the case: May seemed all the stronger in this deserted street—after yielding to him—than when she had been fighting him face-to-face. He entered the Chinese town, aware of the fact, but quite indifferent to it. "Have I behaved like a woman who needs protection?" What right had he to extend his pitiable protection to this woman who had submitted even to his leaving her? *Why* was he leaving her? Was it perhaps a kind of vengeance? No doubt May was still sitting on the bed, broken by despair which no reasoning could alleviate.
>
> He turned and ran back.
>
> The phoenix-room was empty: his father had gone out, May was still where he had left her. He stopped in front of the door, overwhelmed by a feeling of the friendliness of death, and yet conscious of how, despite its fascination, his body recoiled grimly before the unnaturalness of the contact. He understood now that to be willing to lead the woman he loved to her death was perhaps love in its most complete form, the love beyond which nothing can go.
>
> He opened the door.
>
> Without a word she hurriedly threw her cloak around her shoulders, and followed him out.

When they arrive at the meeting-place, May is knocked unconscious and Kyo arrested. Later, when he's about to be executed, he swallows the cyanide that most of the revolutionary leaders carried with them for just such an eventuality, thus killing himself in order to avoid torture. At the moment of death, he rediscovers unreservedly, and in their entirety, both May and all his comrades in the struggle:

> Kyo shut his eyes. . . . He had witnessed death on many occasions and, aided in this by his Japanese upbringing, he had always felt that it would be beautiful to die a death that is one's own, a death appropriate to the life it closes. And to die is passive, but to kill oneself is to turn passivity into action. As soon as they came to fetch the first of his lot, he would kill himself in full consciousness of what he was doing. He remembered the gramophone records and his heart dropped a beat: in those days hope still had meaning. He would never see May again, and the only hurt he felt was the hurt that she would feel—as if he were doing something unkind, and wrong, in dying. "Death brings remorse," he thought, with a twinge of irony. He felt no such qualms for his father, who had always given him an impression not of weakness, but of strength. For more than a year now May had protected him from all loneliness, though not from every sorrow. There sprang into his mind, alas, as soon as he thought of her, the remembrance of that swift refuge in tenderness of body joined to body. Now that he was no longer to be numbered among the living . . . "She will have to forget me now." Could he have written to tell her so, he would only have been torturing her and tying her closer to him. "And it would mean telling her to love another. . . ." Oh, this prison—a place where time stops still, while elsewhere it runs on.

Compared with this total union between Kyo and May, in which one can dissociate in no way the private relationship from the revolutionary activity, compared with this *realized totality*, the other relationship between man and woman described in the novel, that between Ferral and Valérie (there are only a few references to Chen's erotic relations with prostitutes) is naturally devalued and degraded; and it is hardly surprising if this devaluation necessarily involves in *La Condition humaine* a change of nature. There is no longer any domination, any predominance on the part of the man. Valérie revolts and, in order to humiliate Ferral, arranges to meet him in the hotel lounge at the same time as another meeting she has arranged with a character of the same world—each man having been instructed to bring a canary. Valérie does not turn up at the rendez-vous and the two men find themselves face to face, ridiculous, accompanied by their servants carrying the cages with the birds.

By way of revenge, Ferral fills Valérie's room with birds. We do not know what happens afterwards—and we hardly care. The relationship has lost all interest.

And yet, in *Les Conquérants* and *La Voie royale*, this relationship of erotic domination was, on the level of the private life, the very value that enabled Garine and Perken to assert themselves and to feel their own existence.

In addition to love, death is the other event that constitutes the existence of the main characters in the novel. In my comments on the moment when Kyo swallows the cyanide and feels May's presence in an unusually intense way, I pointed out the significance and function that death has for the revolutionaries of *La Condition humaine*, a significance and function different and even opposed to those that it had for Garine and Perken in the earlier novels. In *Les Conquérants* and *La Voie royale*, death was the inevitable reality that rendered precarious and provisional all social values bound up with action, which annihilated them *retroactively* and brought the hero back to the formless, to absolute solitude, whereas in *La Condition humaine* it is, on the contrary, the moment that realizes in its entirety an organic union with action and a community with the other comrades. In the preceding novels death broke all links between the individual and the community. In *La Condition humaine* it ensures the final supersession of solitude. Among the characters embodying the revolutionary group itself, two deaths have already been described for us, those of Katow and Kyo. I have already spoken of the latter: Kyo is to die, reunited not only with May, but also with Katow, his comrades, and above all the very meaning of his struggle and his existence. That is why his death is not an end: his life and his struggle will be taken up again by all those who continue the action after him:

> He would die having fought for what in his own day would have possessed the strongest meaning and inspired the most splendid hope; die, too, among those whom he would wish to have seen live; die, like each of these recumbent forms, so as to give significance to his own life. What would have been the value of a life for which he would not have accepted death? It is less hard to die when one is not alone in dying. This death of his was hallowed by a touch of common brotherhood, by contact with a gathering of broken men whom future multitudes would recognize as martyrs, whose bloody memory would bring forth a golden hope! How, already staring into the eyes of death, should he fail to hear the murmur of human sacrifice calling aloud to him that the heart of man is a resting-place for the dead, well worth the loss of life itself? . . .

No, dying could become an action, an exalted deed, the supreme expression of a life to which this death was itself so similar; it meant, too, escape from these two soldiers who now uncertainly approached him. He jerked the poison between his teeth, as he would have barked an order, heard anguished Katow still asking him something, felt him stir and touch him; then just as, gasping for breath, he tried to clutch him, he felt his whole strength slip, fading from him, giving way before the onrush of an overwhelming convulsion.

Similarly, Katow's death is the moment at which he is reunited in the most intense way with the revolutionary community. Beside him, two Chinese militants are lying full length, terrified by the whistle of the locomotive into which Chiang Kai-shek has the prisoners thrown alive. Katow, in an act of supreme fraternity, gives them his cyanide. Unfortunately, one of the Chinese is wounded in the hand and drops it. For a few moments it might be thought that Katow's act had no efficacity. But beyond the material reality, fraternity is stronger and more present than ever. His two Chinese comrades no longer feel alone:

> Their hands brushed against his. Then suddenly one of these hands seized his hand, clutched it, held it fast.
> "Even if we don't find anything," said one of the voices, "still. . . ."

But the cyanide is found again, and his two comrades escape torture. Katow is led to the train. It is perhaps the most intense and solemn moment in the novel. He goes through the scene surrounded by the fraternity of all the other prisoners, wounded, bound to the ground, and destined to the same fate:

> The torch-flare now showed him in even blacker silhouette against the windows that looked out on to the night. He walked heavily, slumping first on one leg, then the other, hampered by his wounds; as he staggered towards the glare of the torch, the shadowed outline of his head merged into the roof. The entire darkness of the hall had come to life and watched him step by step. The silence now was such that the ground rang at each heavy tread of his foot. Nodding up and down, every head followed the rhythm of his walk, tenderly, in terror, in resignation, as if, although all the movements were the same, each man would himself have struggled to follow these faltering footsteps. No head fell back as the door closed.

> A sound of deep breathing, like the sound of sleep, came up
> from the ground; breathing through the nose, jaws clenched in
> anguish, not stirring now, quite still, all those who were not yet
> dead waited to hear the shriek of a distant whistle.

It becomes obvious that the subject of *La Condition humaine* is not only a chronicle of the events in Shanghai; it is also, indeed primarily, this extraordinary realization of the revolutionary community in the defeat of the militants and their survival in the revolutionary struggle that continues after their death. And, of course, it is in relation to this struggle that the later destiny of the other characters is situated. Two of them, Hemmelrich and Chen, will be brought back into the struggle. The former had hesitated all his life between his duties to his wife and child, passive victims, incapable of defending themselves in a barbarous and unjust world, and his revolutionary aspirations; he will be freed by the repression which, murdering those dearest to him, gives him back the freedom he had always dreamed of and enables him to commit himself entirely to action.

Chen, who was supported unofficially by the group of revolutionaries, tried twice to organize an assassination attempt on Chiang Kai-shek. He is cut to shreds during the second attempt and kills himself. At the moment he throws the bomb, he finds himself entirely alone and when he dies he is aware that in this world "even the death of Chiang Kai-shek can no longer affect him." This is, on the immediate level, the death of Garine and Perken, but at the end of the novel we learn that his disciple Pei, through whom he had hoped to ensure the continuity of his anarchist action, has set out for Russia and joined the communists. Thus Chen's very act and total solitude into which he found himself thrown back at the moment of death have been superseded and integrated by historical action.

Three characters leave the orbit of action: Gisors, for whom Kyo's death broke all links with the revolution, returns to the passive pantheism of traditional Chinese culture; Ferral is ousted from action by a consortium of bankers and civil servants who take over his work; Clappique is forced to hide from the repression that is directed at him in so far as he helped Kyo and disguises himself as a sailor—a disguise in which he finds the true meaning of his life.

There remain the combatants, May, and, behind her, Pei and Hemmelrich, about whom something more should be said. The novel tells us simply that all three went to the USSR, where they continue the struggle, and that they will later come back to China, the construction of the USSR, the realization of the five-year plan having become "the main weapon of the class struggle" for the moment.

Malraux's ideological position at the time he wrote the novel, therefore, was not Trotskyist, but, on the contrary, fairly close to the Stalinist positions. Nevertheless, the two chapters that express his position, namely the twenty odd pages of part 3 that take place in Hankow, and the last six pages of the book, are much more abstract and schematic than the rest of the novel, and appear to some extent as an afterthought or foreign body.

If the unity of the novel does not suffer from this, and if *La Condition humaine* remains a powerful coherent and unified novel, it is above all because these fragments scarcely add up to a tenth of the work; moreover this tenth is not entirely devoted to expressing this ideological position.

In fact, Malraux's explicit ideology has an insignificant place in *La Condition humaine*, whereas the unorthodox point of view of the Shanghai revolutionaries constitutes the unifying point of view from which the novel is written. Nevertheless, in each of these two passages, Malraux is forced to make the transition between two almost irreconcilable positions. He does this in the chapter that takes place in Hankow by referring to "all the hesitations" of Vologuin, the representative of the International. These doubts are expressed in the fact that, while declaring himself to be opposed to any assassination attempt on individuals, and in particular against the attempt on Chiang Kai-shek proposed by Chen, Vologuin nevertheless lets Chen go, thus encouraging his terrorist action.

Malraux also makes this transition at the end of the work in the psychology of May who, going over to the side of the Party and the International, becomes integrated in a struggle that must in principle absorb and integrate that of the Shanghai revolutionaries. May is going, we are led to believe, to begin a new life, but she does so "without enthusiasm," with a heavy heart and, quite obviously, without having resolved her problems: " 'I hardly ever weep now, any more,' she said with bitter pride."

In *Les Conquérants* and *La Condition humaine*, Malraux wrote the first two French novels of the proletarian revolution of the twentieth century. He did not identify himself however with the Communist Party that directed this revolution. Indeed, we have seen that the fundamental values that structure the worlds of these two works are different from those of the Party, although the Party represented, in each case, a positive value and, quite obviously the transition from the novel of Garine to that of the community of the Shanghai revolutionaries constitutes an important step towards a revolutionary perspective.

C. J. GRESHOFF

Les Noyers de l'Altenburg

André Malraux took part in the Flanders Campaign in 1940 in the Tank Corps. He was made prisoner in June and was sent to a POW camp in Sens. He escaped in November and reached the so-called Free Zone. According to Hoffmann's Chronology, *Les Noyers de l'Altenburg* was written between 1940 and 1943. It was published in Switzerland as part 1 of a series of novels entitled *La Lutte avec l'ange*. The same title appears in the Skira edition of the *Oeuvres complètes* but in the French edition of 1948 the book is published under the sole title *Les Noyers de l'Altenburg*. This edition is preceded by a note by André Malraux which says: "La suite de *La Lutte avec l'ange* a été détruite par la Gestapo. On ne récrit pas un roman. Lorsque celui-ci paraîtra sous sa forme définitive, la forme des *Noyers* sera sans doute fondamentalement modifiée." However, *La Lutte avec l'ange*, like *Les Puissances du désert* of which *La Voie royale* was part, will never be written. It is also possible that the destruction of the sequel of *Les Noyers* by the Gestapo never really took place. Boak suggests as much in his article on Malraux and T. E. Lawrence. "The parallels in the two legends are equalled by parallels in attitudes: Lawrence lost, or claimed to lose, the manuscript of *The Seven Pillars of Wisdom* while changing trains (a story disbelieved by various acquaintances and critics) while Malraux's sequel of *Les Noyers* was seized by the Gestapo during a raid. Or was it?" Malraux's *mythomanie* might well be at play here. It is also possible that Malraux used (or invented) this raid as an alibi for his

From *An Introduction to the Novels of Malraux*. © 1975 by C. J. Greshoff. A. A. Balkema, 1975.

inability to complete the projected series of novels. It is unlikely we shall ever know the truth about this matter. Nor is it ultimately important.

Les Noyers de l'Altenburg opens with a prologue which takes place in 1940 and which is written in the first person. Here we meet the narrator who is a writer and a POW. This narrator who remains, as it were, faceless, like the narrator of *Les Conquérants*, proceeds in the following sections to tell three episodes of the life of his father, Vincent Berger, an Alsatian. In the first of these episodes we see him in the service of Enver Pacha, leader of the Young Turks who dreams of creating the Touran, "l'unité de tous les peuples turcs depuis Adrianople jusqu'aux oasis chinoises." Disillusioned, Berger returns to Europe. The second episode describes a colloquium of intellectuals in which Vincent Berger participates and which takes place at Altenburg in a disaffected Romanesque priory owned by Walter Berger, Vincent's uncle. The third episode, dated June 11, 1915, describes a German experimental gas attack against the Russians on the Vistula front. This attack is being witnessed by Vincent Berger who will die, at least this is implied and not shown, of gas poisoning. The novel ends with an epilogue in which the narrator, in the first person, describes a tank battle during the 1940 campaign.

As can be seen from this brief résumé, *Les Noyers* is the most disjointed of all Malraux's novels which, although broken up in "sequences," nevertheless retained some kind of unity. But here, in *Les Noyers*, we have five wholly independent episodes, in fact five separate short stories, three of which—the most important ones—are held together only by the presence in each of them of Vincent Berger. This central character, however, partly because of the discontinuity, never emerges strongly or clearly. What also binds these episodes together is the underlying idea which these five episodes illustrate.

Now the extreme disjointedness of this novel might well be a symptom of creative exhaustion, as well as a sign of Malraux's inability to create a coherent whole, for we should not forget that *Les Noyers* is Malraux's last novel. Whether he himself knew this at the time of its writing is immaterial. We, with a quarter of a century hindsight, might well see in it the characteristics of a last novel, written by a novelist who has had his say and is no longer able to renew himself. The novel might be considered as consisting of the novelist's leftovers which somehow had to be used up. This would also explain the fragmentary nature of *Les Noyers*. Obviously the haunting episode of the gas attack had to be written before Malraux put an end to his career as a novelist, also the return of Vincent Berger to Europe—an episode which has obvious autobiographical roots and the experience on which it is based seeming to have made a deep impression on Malraux. It was equally necessary that he had to "write out" his war experiences, just as he had to "write out" his Spanish Civil war. The presence of the colloquium episode is less necessary and it is also the least successful of all the episodes. One other thing which our hindsight makes very clear is that *Les Noyers* looks back to a very much earlier inspiration while at the same time it looks forward to *Les Voix du silence*.

Les Noyers de l'Altenburg, although different from the preceding novels, bears a very close resemblance to *La Voie royale*. This return at the end of his career to his earliest inspiration might also be seen as a symptom of exhaustion. The autobiographical background of both novels is the same. There is also a clear resemblance between Vincent Berger as agent of the Touran in the first episode and Perken, and behind both we find the shadow of T. E. Lawrence. Vincent Berger's need for action has the same roots as that of Perken. Perken's "je veux laisser une cicatrice sur cette carte" is exactly echoed by Vincent Berger's "désir fanatique de laisser sur la terre une cicatrice." Also Perken's vision of man as an ant living its life in an antheap, finds its direct echo in Möllberg's pessimism: "Depuis que derrière l'homme . . . nous ne voyons plus le singe que commençons-nous à voir apparaître? Une sorte de fourmi." And again: "Rien de meilleur que de regarder longtemps les termitières pour être fixé sur l'homme."

At the same time, the ideas expressed by Walter Berger on the nature of art, which we quoted [elsewhere], will form the basic idea of Malraux's work on art. More particularly, Vincent Berger's ideas on art and some of those of Möllberg will find their way word for word into *La Psychologie de l'art*. It would appear then that when writing *Les Noyers*, Malraux was at a crossroad. He was writing his last novel (which resembles one of his first) and he is at the same time writing his *Psychologie de l'art*.

Yet, in spite of its drawing on an earlier inspiration, *Les Noyers* is nevertheless a very different novel from Malraux's other books. Firstly the key in which it is written is very different and secondly, Malraux's vision of Man's fate, which forms still the core of this novel, has undergone some significant changes.

To begin with, in *Les Noyers* Malraux abandons the contemporary urban scene which, with the exception of *La Voie royale*, forms the décor of all his novels. The action is set in pre-1914–18 days (except the gas attack) and takes place in Reichbach, a small village in Alsace, in the deserts of Tripolitania and Afghanistan and on the banks of the Vistula.

The prologue and the episodes set in Alsace have a curious medieval aura surrounding them. The prisoners, in the prologue, are herded together under the majestic *ogives* of the cathedral of Chartres and the prisoners, as

their beards grow, acquire "des visages gothiques." The Berger family is
deeply rooted in this region "toute couverte des vestiges de la 'Sainte Forêt'
du moyen âge." The Berger clan itself with its hierarchical structure, has a
feudal air about it and old Dietrich, the formidable head of the clan, who
sets off on foot for a pilgrimage to Rome, suggests the image of a medieval
patriarch. The colloquium takes place in an old priory in a room decorated
with gothic sculptures and outside "des hommes chargeaient des troncs
semblables à ceux que mon grand-père avait pendant quarante ans fait empiler
devant la mairie de Reichbach, semblables à ceux qu'empilaient les bûcherons
de la Sainte Forêt du moyen âge."

This all-prevading presence of the Middle Ages tends to suggest a sense
of continuity and gives a concrete image of the permanence of Man. The
gothic-looking soldiers are not merely the descendants of their medieval
forefathers, they *are* these forefathers:

> Celui-là a un de ces visages gothiques de plus en plus nombreux
> depuis que les barbes poussent. La mémoire séculaire de fléau.
> Le fléau devait venir, et voici qu'il est là. Je me souviens des
> mobilisés silencieux de septembre, en marche à travers la pous-
> sière blanche des routes et les dahlias de fin d'été, et qui me
> semblaient partir contre l'inondation, contre l'incendie; mais au-
> dessous de cette familiarité séculaire avec le malheur, pointe la
> ruse non moins séculaire de l'homme, sa foi clandestine dans une
> patience pourtant gorgée de désastres, la même peut-être que,
> jadis, devant la famine des cavernes. "J'attends que ça s'use. . . ."
> Dans notre tanière engourdie sous le grand soleil de toujours,
> murmure une voix préhistorique.

It is, no doubt, in order to accentuate this permanence of the fundamental man that Malraux has housed his prisoners in a cathedral. Like
Proust's church of St Hilaire, the cathedral has a fifth dimension, that of
Time. It is both present now and in a very distant past, which is thus made
contemporary with us. What is more, "le moyen âge n'a pas de temps, le
moyen âge est un présent éternel," one of the speakers at the colloquium
points out. We, through these "visages gothiques," through the cathedral
and the gestures of the woodcutters, are linked to this eternal present.

The need for permanence and continuity which this "medievalism" of
Les Noyers seems to reflect, is something new in the world of Malraux and
might well be, at least in part, a reflection of the mood of the time. *Les Noyers*
was written during one of the darkest periods of recent French history, when
the very texture of France and of Europe seemed to disintegrate. We find a

similar kind of harking after a feeling of permanence reflected in St Exupéry's *Pilote de guerre* which was written at the same time.

What also differentiates *Les Noyers* from Malraux's other novels is the absence of violence. Instead, we find in *Les Noyers* a much more effective, almost Goyaesque horror, especially in the description of the gas attack. For example:

> Le sentier obliqua davantage vers les positions allemandes. Au milieu, un homme bondissait à quatre pattes, d'un mouvement si spasmodique qu'il semblait projeté. Nu. A deux mètres l'apparition leva son visage gris aux yeux sans blanc, ouvrit comme pour hurler sa bouche d'épileptique: mon père s'effaça. Folle de douleur avec les mouvements de tous les fous, comme si son corps n'eût plus été habité que par un supplice, en quelques sauts de grenouille, elle s'enfonça dans la purulence.

Finally, again with *La Voie royale* as a significant exception, politics, contemporary revolutionary politics, play no part in *Les Noyers*. The activities of Vincent Berger in Turkey and Afghanistan are, as it were, sterilised by time and space and Malraux takes no sides. This apolitical nature of *Les Noyers*, especially when seen in comparison with the preceding novel *L'Espoir*, reflects a dramatic change. The partisan, deeply engaged novelist seems to have disengaged himself in *Les Noyers*. A possible explanation for this change might be found in the traumatic experience of the Left, and more especially of the fellow-travelling or committed intelligentsia: the signing of the Russo-German pact in 1939. We have no records of Malraux's reaction but it is safe to surmise that he who had seen in Soviet civilisation a total renewal, must have been profoundly shocked and disillusioned. This might well explain the importance of the theme of disillusionment in *Les Noyers*. The ideal of the Touran to which Vincent Berger was wholly devoted, dies on his hands. He discovers that "le Touran n'existait pas." The anthropologist Möllberg loses faith in his own ideas and destroys his book, the result of fifteen years of work. The shattering of the belief in "L'Homme nouveau" might also have brought Malraux to revise his ideas: man cannot be reborn, his nature is constant and unchanged; hence the discovery of the permanence of man which informs the whole of *Les Noyers*.

The lack of partisanship and politics in *Les Noyers* results in, what might be termed, a broadening and mellowing of Malraux's attitude. *Les Noyers* is the only book in which the ordinary man, the peasant and worker, *le petit peuple* are really present. In *Les Conquérants* we see an anonymous and amorphous mass which for Garine has no real existence except as a political force.

In *La Condition humaine* we catch a fleeting glimpse of a few members of the workers' militia but they are mere shadows. In *Le Temps du mépris* we only see the intellectual Kassner. Finally in *L'Espoir* we do meet a number of ordinary members of the International Brigades and a few anonymous peasants. In all his books the centre of the stage is held by articulate intellectuals. This is undoubtedly still the case of *Les Noyers* but it contains other elements as well. The whole of the prologue is dominated by ordinary men who are no longer seen as anonymous man, but as alive and real. We see them as prisoners listening to and believing in rumours ("Pétain a tué Weygand en plein conseil des ministres"), we see them painstakingly writing letters home: "Les doigts crispés sur le papier comme s'il allait leur être arraché." Before this common humanity, the narrator who at this point can be wholly identified with Malraux himself, exclaims: "Ecrivain par quoi suis-je obsédé depuis dix ans sinon par l'homme. Me voici devant la matière originelle." There is an unmistakable feeling of discovery behind this exclamation. As if after ten years of writing about Man, the narrator only now discovers the humble, tough, persistent reality that exists independently of the abstraction Man. This discovery might well be, in part, that of Malraux himself. During his days of militancy he had, no doubt, more dealings with the leaders and the intelligentsia than with the rank and file. He fought the war in Spain in a *corps d'élite* of which moreover he was the commander, but during the campaign of 1940 he was, if Hoffmann is correct, a *simple deuxième classe* and it is then, no doubt, that he came into real, living, intimate contact with the ageless humanity of which he writes in *Les Noyers*. Yet in spite of this identification the narrator realises the distance which remains between him, the bourgeois (Malraux is very much *un grand bourgeois*) intellectual and "them." Describing the prisoners writing home, the narrator reflects:

> Combien de jours les ai-je vus ainsi dans la chambrée, emplissant
> page après page. . . . Redisent-ils une fois de plus qu'il faut reviser
> la lieuse, profiter du temps entre la moisson et le battage pour
> réparer les gouttières,—avec les répétitions sans fin qui sont leur
> mode instinctif d'expression?

The distance here is clearly indicated by "*leur* mode instinctif d'expression." Later on, in what is, no doubt, an oblique reference to the days when he thought he could identify himself with "the masses," the narrator underlines what separates him from them.

> J'ai cru connaître plus que ma culture parce que j'avais rencontré
> les foules militantes d'une foi, religieuses ou politiques; je sais

maintenant qu'un intellectuel n'est pas seulement celui à qui les livres sont nécessaires, mais tout homme dont une idée, si élémentaire soit-elle, engage et ordonne la vie. Ceux qui m'entourent, eux, vivent au jour le jour depuis des millénaires.

At the same time this awareness of difference is, paradoxically perhaps, accompanied by a greater awareness of the existence of these men and also by a feeling of sympathy for them. When Malraux describes the soldiers looking at the photographs of each other's wives, the description is tinged by a kind of protective tenderness:

Lequel tira le premier de son portefeuille la photo de sa femme, pour la regarder à la lueur clandestine d'une lampe de poche? Cinq minutes plus tard, entre petits groupes, les images circulaient, quatre ou cinq calots autour d'une sourde lumière, les photos d'amateur tombant des gros doigts dans la paille sous les engueulades. Chacun d'ailleurs se fichait des femmes des autres, ne les regardait que pour montrer la sienne. Et pourtant, dans cette lumière de confidence, elles apparaissaient comme des secrets, les robes suggérant tout à coup la vie des maris mieux que ne l'eussent fait leurs photos en civils. La femme de Pradé est une ménagère en bois dur, aux bandeaux plats; Bonneau, seul entre tous, possédait quatre photos, plus putains l'une que l'autre. Et le petit Léonard au nez de betterave,—notre radio,—réticent et se faisant prier, finit par tirer une carte postale, une très belle fille en éblouissant costume de plumes. Quelques lignes étaient écrites au bas. Et les copains, têtes collées l'une à l'autre sous le nez de Léonard fantastiquement éclairé par dessous, déchiffraient en approchant l'ampoule: "A mon petit minet Louis," et la signature d'une des gloires du music-hall.

The same tenderness, mingled perhaps with pity, gives its poignancy to the passage which shows the German soldiers, whose conversations Vincent has just overheard, going into battle:

Les compagnies reconstituées cessèrent d'avancer.

Mineur pour qui la lampe était le Bon Dieu, sous-officier qui allait au temple pour se souvenir, fossoyeur dont l'enfant n'avait appris le prénom qu'à cause du chien, ajusteur, comptable, coiffeur, tueur de cochons, cantonnier, lecteur de "Trois Boys-Scouts," et celui qui n'avait pas épousé sa femme pour sa beauté et celui dont la femme n'était pas bien jolie non plus, hommes

semblables à tant d'autres, entre tous les hommes morts et tous
les hommes tués. Et avec eux seraient tués leurs sentiments impersonnels et poignants, leur destin qui avait cherché son sens
dans ces tarots sur quoi maintenant cheminait un rayon de soleil
bienvaillant; leur résignation toute d'expérience comme si tant de
fosses communes n'eussent été crées et dispersées que pour abou-
tir au timbre d'une pauvre sagesse: . . . Très haut, la grande
migration des oiseaux continuait; et sous elle, l'espèce humaine
plaquée sur ces prés livides dans l'attente du pilonnement russe
avait l'unité complexe des nuits d'été, cette unité de cris lointains,
de rêves, de présences, d'odeur profonde d'arbres et de blés
coupés, de sommeils inquiets à la surface de la terre sous l'immense nuit immobile.

We come here across an attitude and a tone which are wholly new. Perhaps
it was to give expression of this discovery of the reality of man that Malraux
wrote *Les Noyers de l'Altenburg*.

II

While a POW, the narrator, in the prologue, thinks of his father and
of his memoirs which his death from gas poisoning prevents him from
writing:

A quel point je retrouve mon père, depuis que certains instants
de sa vie semblent préfigurer la mienne! J'ai été blessé le 14,
prisonnier le 18; son sort dans l'autre guerre—de l'autre côté
. . .—a été décidé le 12 juin 1915. Il y a vingt-cinq ans, presque
jour pour jour. . . . Il n'était pas beaucoup plus vieux que moi
lorsqu'a commencé de s'imposer à lui ce mystère de l'homme qui
m'obsède aujourd'hui, et qui me fait commencer, peut-être, à le
comprendre. Ses "Mémoires," que quelques-uns attendent encore
et qui ne paraîtront jamais—ils n'ont jamais été rédigés—n'étaient
qu'une masse de notes sur ce qu'il appelait "ses rencontres avec
l'homme."

The three episodes that follow are, in fact, the memoirs of Vincent Berger
but written by his son and each episode shows, perhaps a little mechanically,
a "rencontre avec l'homme."

Vincent Berger, then, is Malraux's last hero and he seems almost a
résumé of all the previous Malrauvian heroes: like Garine and Claude he

feels the need to leave Europe; like Perken he wants to leave a scar on the world and like Kyo he seeks the warm comradeship born from communal action; his last action, the attempt to carry back to the German lines a gassed Russian soldier, resembles Katow's last, generous and fraternal gesture. The composite nature of Vincent Berger is undoubtedly due to the failing of Malraux's creative and imaginative powers.

Let us now look more closely at the three episodes which make up the body of *Les Noyers*. The first one is rather peculiar in structure and different from the other two which are straightforward narratives. It begins with the suicide of Dietrich Berger a few days after the arrival of his son Vincent from the East and ends with these words: "cinq jours après mon père se suicidait." Let us remark in passing that this suicide has no real function in the novel, since it is the suicide of a character who plays no part in the action. It is there because it happened to Malraux's father, and it also gives a starting point to the very important conversation between Walter Berger and his nephew Vincent. The first episode, then, beginning and ending with Dietrich Berger's suicide, has a circular structure. Inside this circle we find a description of the Berger clan dominated by the formidable patriarch Dietrich; we find too the story of Vincent Berger's activities in the Middle East for the formation of the Touran. In the building of this dream Berger also participates with passion, not for the Touran itself, but because it would enable him to leave *his* mark on history:

> Sa passion, mon père n'en avait guère mis en question l'origine.
> En elle se mêlaient son besoin de s'écarter de l'Europe, l'appel de
> l'histoire, le désir fanatique de laisser sur la terre une cicatrice,
> la fascination d'un dessein qu'il n'avait pas peu contribué à pré-
> ciser, la camaraderie de combat, l'amitié.

We see Vincent Berger setting out to win over to this ideal the Turks of Central Asia, the Kurds, the Turks of Bokhara and of Afghanistan. He wanders through the bleak, barren Afghanistan desert talking to chiefs. In the bazaar of Ghazin a madman, sensing a European beneath the Eastern clothes, beats him up:

> Mon père regagna sa maison furieux, rompu et inexplicablement
> délivré d'un charme: tout à coup la vérité était là, abrupte: le
> Touran qui animait les nouvelles passions turques, qui avait peut-
> être sauvé Constantinople, le Touran n'existait pas.

One does not see quite the link between this beating and the discovery that the Touran does not exist. The fact remains that Vincent Berger now returns to Europe. He is later described as "ruiné" (morally) or as "battu à ses propres yeux." But one is not convinced because we are merely *told* about his being "à ce point intéressé personnellement dans le touranisme," "passionné," etc, but we are not shown, we are not made to feel the involvement of Vincent as we are made to feel Kyo's, Tchen's and even Ferral's *engagement*; and it is therefore hard to see that the discovery of the emptiness of the Touran ideal has such profound repercussions on Berger's life. Now, if Kyo had discovered that Communism was a false god. . . .

When Vincent Berger returns to Europe, after so many years in the East, he has an experience which will deeply affect him and which will echo throughout *Les Noyers*. In Marseilles, where he lands, through the shock of this *dépaysement*, he suddenly sees Man. The experience is akin to the one described in both *Le Temps du mépris* and the *Antimémoires* and which Malraux called "le retour à la terre"; in the case of Vincent Berger it is rather a return to Man:

> Jeté à quelque rive de néant ou d'éternité, il en contemplait la confuse coulée—aussi séparé d'elle que de ceux qui avaient passé, avec leurs angoisses oubliées et leurs contes perdus, dans les rues des premières dynasties de Bactres et de Babylone, dans les oasis dominées par les Tours du Silence. A travers la musique et l'odeur de pain chaud, des ménagères se hâtaient, un filet sous le bras; un marchand de couleurs posait ses volets arlequins où s'attardait un dernier rayon, la sirène d'un paquebot appelait; un commis en calotte rapportait un mannequin sur son dos, à l'intérieur d'un étroit magasin plein d'ombres,—sur la terre, vers la fin du second millénaire de l'ère chrétienne.

There is something very *pascalien* about this passage and especially about the idea expressed a little further on that man can only live in "un état de distraction tout-puissant," which comes very close to the notion of the divertissement. "Les hommes n'ayant pu guérir la mort ont résolu de ne plus y penser." Later, Vincent Berger's mind will return again and again to this experience, elucidating and deepening it:

> L'aventure humaine, la terre. Et tout cela, comme le destin achevé de son père, eût pu être autre. . . . Il se sentait peu à peu envahi par un sentiment inconnu, comme il l'avait été, sur les hauts lieux nocturnes d'Asie, par la présence du sacré, tandis qu'autour de lui les ailes feutrées des petites chouettes des sables battaient en silence. . . . C'était beaucoup plus profonde, l'angoissante liberté

de ce soir de Marseille où il regardait glisser les ombres dans une
odeur ténue de cigarettes et d'absinthe,—où l'Europe lui était si
étrangère; où il la regardait comme, libéré du temps, il eût regardé
glisser lentement une heure d'un lointain passé, avec tout son
cortège insolite. Ainsi sentait-il maintenant devenir insolite la vie
tout entière; et il s'en trouvait tout à coup délivré,—mystérieuse-
ment étranger à la terre et surpris par elle, comme il l'avait été
par cette rue où les hommes de sa race retrouvée glissaient dans
l'heure verte.

During the colloquium, as he listens to the ethnologist Möllberg describing
the prehistoric civilisation ("Nous sommes ici dans le domaine antérieur
même à la mythologie"), Vincent Berger "retrouvait sous ces phrases une
expérience qu'il connaissait lui aussi, celle où l'homme cesse d'être privilégié,
l'angoissante virginité de regarder l'humanité comme une espèce parmi
d'autres." In Marseilles, then, takes place the first of these "rencontres avec
l'homme" which is the main theme of the novel.

After his father's suicide which takes place five days after his return to
Reichbach, Vincent goes to Altenburg to attend the colloquium organised
by his uncle Walter on the subject: "Permanence et métamorphose de
l'homme." In this episode there is no action and a great deal of talk. It is
obvious that the "philosophical" centre of gravity of the novel lies in these
debates of which Roger Caillois writes rather haughtily, but rightly nevertheless: "les discussions abstraites ont l'air d'avoir été introduites par l'auteur
pour satisfaire on ne sait quel goût de philosophie." In these scenes lies also
the great flaw of the novel. The philosophical pretentions of Malraux are
not so much at fault as the fact that these ideas are formulated separately
from the action. This has always been a weakness of Malraux's novels, for
example the dialogue of Ferral and Gisors in *La Condition humaine*, or the
dialogues in *L'Espoir* which, as we have noted, could be lifted out of the main
body of the book. But these dialogues were nevertheless, however tenuously,
linked to the action; they were to some extent woven into the texture of the
novel. In *Les Noyers* however, we find in the middle of the novel an episode
which has, so to speak, no links with the preceding and following episodes
and which consists solely of abstract ideas. In a very sharp critical note on
Les Noyers, André Gide makes this very acute remark: "L'emploi abusif des
termes abstraits nuit souvent beaucoup au réel d'une action. Il ne faut pas
chercher à la fois à faire voir et à faire comprendre." Here Gide touches on
Malraux's greatest weakness as a novelist. In not one of this novels does
Malraux succeed in wholly fusing into one organic whole thought and action.

Perhaps he did not in his life either: the squadron leader in Spain was not Malraux, the writer; and the author of *L'Espoir* was not the leader of the squadron "España."

The central episode of the colloquium is divided into three parts of which the third is undoubtedly the most important, since it is here that we will find the ideas which inform the novel. The first part consists of a discussion between Walter Berger and his nephew Vincent. This discussion deals mainly with the suicide of Dietrich and its motives. We have here not only a clash of ideas but also a clash of two types of men, the dyed-in-the-wool bourgeois intellectual, Walter, who believes that "pour l'essentiel l'homme est ce qu'il cache . . . , un misérable petit tas de secrets," and the intellectual man of action, Vincent, who replies "presque avec brutalité: l'homme est ce qu'il fait." This is clearly an echo of the clash between Malraux and Léon Brunschvicg during the colloquium on *Les Conquérants* at the "Union pour la vérité." Moreover, during this discussion Malraux expresses, through Walter, the ideas on art which will form the basis of his *Voix du silence*.

The second part is a kind of interlude which gives us, through a vaguely Clappique-like character Hermann Müller ("gigolo vieilli à cravate frivolette") an ironic picture of Walter and of life at Altenburg and of the kind of discussion Vincent is to expect:

> Tu as été surpris qu'il (Walter) t'accompagne à pied: c'était pour te contraindre à marcher à son pas. Ce colloque-ci, c'est la même chose. . . .
>
> Les autres, bien entendu, lui font le coup de l'éléphant: "La métamorphose, l'art, le haricot germé? L'art et le haricot germé, Messieurs, se distinguent de l'éléphant en ceci: l'éléphant est un animal de grande taille, lourd de poids, etc." Discours sur l'éléphant.
>
> —Alors pourquoi des hommes éminents viennent-ils ici?
>
> —Et pourquoi ailleurs? Ils vont bien à l'hôtel: ici, les gens sont plus intelligents! Ils vont bien au café: ici, les fauteuils sont meilleurs!

This ironic detachment from the high-powered intellectual *phalanstère* is, of course, also that of Malraux himself and of Vincent Berger; hence the kind of complicity which exists between the ironic, caustic Müller and Vincent. This second part also serves to introduce the ethnologist Möllberg who will dominate the colloquium.

The colloquium itself is the subject of the third section. Here we find a number of earnest and conventional intellectuals who are debating the theme "*permanence ou métamorphose de l'homme*." Vincent Berger's position in their gathering is an ambiguous one: he is and he is not one of them. He is looked upon by the sedate intellectuals with awe: "les intellectuels sont comme les femmes, mon cher bon," says Müller, "les militaires les font rêver." He is also the object of great curiosity: "Les intellectuels n'aiment pas qu'un des leurs touche à l'action, mais s'il y réussit ils en sont plus curieux que les autres." Vincent has no intention of entering the debate. He is determined to keep his distance from this world which rejects the world of action, and where "une idée ne naissait jamais d'un fait: toujours d'une autre idée." But slowly, almost instinctively, he is drawn back into this world of the intellectuals of which, in spite of his years of action, he is nevertheless part: "Mon père s'était cru amputé de la culture: il la retrouvait aussi familière que lors de son premier cours à Constantinople." Vincent Berger, the prodigal son of the intellectual family, has come back.

This ambiguous attitude of Vincent Berger is also that of Malraux towards the gathering he describes. His intentions are partly, but unmistakably, satirical: the intellectuals are all a little grotesque or at least ridiculous, yet their ideas are not. These are, in fact, to a great extent the ideas of Malraux himself. Some contributions to the colloquium come straight from earlier writings of Malraux himself. Thus Thirard's idea that "trois livres tiennent en face de la prison: Robinson Crusoe, Don Quichotte, L'Idiot" comes from Malraux's speech to the "Secrétariat de l'Association Internationale des Ecrivains pour la Défense de la Culture" (June 21, 1936), and Möllburg's ideas on "le double" can be found in Malraux's closing speech of the Congress of 1935. So that, if the participants of the colloquium should not be taken seriously, the ideas they express should.

The colloquium itself is in reality one long Malrauvian monologue broken up, for the sake of the novel, into a series of dialogues and short monologues punctuated by interruptions. Like a Malrauvian monologue, it follows no logical, systematic sequence but goes from insight to insight according to the laws of a mysterious chain reaction. Time and again, the original theme is lost out of sight and the arguments go off at a tangent. It is true also that in discussions of this kind this tends to happen.

The debate seems to turn around three unrelated questions or assertions, all three of which shock the participants. It is this which creates in the debate a kind of dramatic tension. The first one is put by Thirard:

> Mon fils avait à peu près quinze ans, et je venais de lui dire, imprudemment, à propos de je ne sais quoi: "Ce n'est pas comme ça qu'on connaît les hommes!" A quoi il m'a répondu: "—Ah? c'est comment? . . ."
> —La question, avait repris Thirard, n'est pas de celles à quoi

l'on répond en cinq minutes? Tout de même, elle avait la force
de l'innocence: imaginez que vous soyez en face d'elle. . . .

Il parcourut la salle de son regard ironique derrière ses gros
sourcils:

—Allons, je vous la pose!

Une protestation générale monta jusqu'au bruit de la pluie sur
les hautes vitres, dans un envol de mains et de carnets. Tous les
noms illustres, Molière, La Rochefoucauld et Pascal, Hegel et
Goethe, Bacon et Shakespeare, Cervantes et les autres, se mêlaient
sous la passion fanatique de gens qui défendaient ce à quoi ils
avaient donné leur vie. La culture est une religion. Mais beaucoup
reprenaient conscience du banal mystère humain, tel qu'ils l'a-
vaient rencontré dans les cliniques, les maternités et les chambres
de mourants.

There is clearly a satirical edge to the description of the reaction, yet at the
same time Thirard's question upsets age-old habits of thinking which are so
ingrained as to appear natural: Western civilisation is so rooted in a psychological conception of Man that it seems a law of nature that we know man
through introspection and psychology. The debate now turns to art: "on
conçoit tout de même mal un art . . . à quoi toute psychologie serait
étrangère." At this point Vincent Berger decides to enter the debate. His
arguments, on the one hand, hark back to Malraux's ideas expressed in *La
Tentation;* for example:

Il n'y a de psychologie valable qu'en Occident, vient-on de nous
dire? mais, d'abord, il n'y a de *besoin* de psychologie qu'en Occident. Parce que l'Occident s'oppose au cosmos, à la fatalité, au
lieu de s'accorder à eux.

On the other hand, his ideas on art are those of *Les Voix du silence:*

Notre art me paraît une rectification du monde, un moyen d'é-
chapper à la condition d'homme. La confusion capitale me paraît
venir de ce qu'on a cru—dans l'idée que nous nous faisons de la
tragédie grecque c'est éclatant!—que représenter une fatalité était
la subir. Mais mon! C'est presque la posséder. Le seul fait de
pouvoir la représenter, de la concevoir, la fait échapper au vrai
destin, à l'implacable échelle divine; la réduit à l'échelle humaine.
Dans ce qu'il a d'essentiel, notre art est une humanisation du
monde.

Finally, after a break, the discussion is resumed and the main speaker now is Möllberg who is a character parallel to Vincent Berger. Like him, he is an intellectual and a man of action. He was at work on an immense Spengler-like synthesis:

> servi par un style massif, aux répétitions empilées, il semblait devoir fonder, sur la saisissante documentation qu'il avait découverte, une synthèse d'une ampleur hégélienne. Et c'était précisément à l'époque où le pluralisme des civilisations touchait déjà nombre d'esprits (et en particulier mon père, qui vivait dans l'Islam), que Möllberg, obsédé d'ordre et d'unité, commençait à tirer du domaine le plus fertile en différences: l'ethnologie, une notion de l'homme d'une rigoureuse continuité, une structure de l'aventure humaine.

At the basis of this work lies then "une notion de l'homme d'une rigoureuse continuité." However, a long contact with primeval Africa makes him lose faith in the fundamental idea of his entreprise and destroys his lifework:

> Ses feuillets pendent aux basses branches d'arbres d'espèces diverses, entre le Sahara et Zanzibar. Parfait. Selon l'usage, le vainqueur porte les dépouilles du vaincu.

To Vincent Berger's Asia corresponds Möllberg's Africa. Like Vincent, Möllberg has only recently returned and both return defeated.

Möllberg now raises the fundamental question:

> La notion d'homme a-t-elle un sens?
>
> Autrement dit: sous les croyances, les mythes, et surtout sous la multiplicité des structures mentales, peut-on isoler une donnée permanente, valable à travers les lieux, valable à travers l'histoire, sur quoi puisse se fonder la notion d'homme?

After having posed the question, Möllberg begins a series of haunting evocations of ancient civilisations ("nous sommes dans un domaine cosmique") which show "des civilisations qui ignorent: la première, notre sentiment du destin; la deuxième, notre sentiment de la naissance; la troisième, notre sentiment de l'échange; la dernière, notre sentiment de la mort." What Möllberg wants to show is that what we might consider as some of man's most natural fundamental feelings, have been unknown to some men and have been foreign to some civilisations. There is, therefore, not a permanent notion of Man. Human civilisations are born and die and are impermeable to one another:

> Les états psychiques successifs de l'humanité sont irréductible-
> ment différents, parce qu'ils n'affectent pas, ne cultivent pas,
> n'engagent pas la même *part* de l'homme. Sur l'essentiel, Platon
> et Saint-Paul ne peuvent ni s'accorder ni se convaincre: ils ne
> peuvent que se convertir. Un roi chrétien et un roi proto-histo-
> rique lié aux astres n'ont pas deux *idées* du destin: pour que le roi
> chrétien ressente, conçoive le destin, il faut que le monde psy-
> chique de l'autre ait disparu. Je doute qu'il y ait un dialogue de
> la chenille et du papillon. Même entre l'Hindou qui croit à l'absolu
> et à la métempsychose, et l'Occidental qui croit à la patrie et à
> la mort, le dialogue est postiche.

Eventually, Möllberg can "concevoir une permanence de l'homme, mais c'est
une permanence dans le néant."

It is obvious that some of the ideas of Möllberg are Malraux's but one
should be careful here. The identification of Möllberg with Malraux is only
partial. What Möllberg represents is the most extreme point of Malraux's
thought to its ultimate and desperate conclusions. He travels much further
than Malraux and arrives at a sterile, haughty and stoic pessimism.

When Möllberg says that the permanency of man is in nothingness,
Vincent Berger counters by suggesting "une permanence dans le fondamen-
tal." On this question Möllberg and Berger are clearly divided. Vincent
Berger believes in man, in a fundamental man, the nihilist Möllberg believes,
if that were possible, in nothingness. The faith of Berger in man and in his
ability to draw out of nothingness the protest against it, his man-made art,
are expressed in the description of the walnut trees of Altenburg, which
Berger goes to contemplate after the colloquium:

> La plénitude des arbres séculaires émanait de leur masse, mais
> l'effort par quoi sortaient de leurs énormes troncs les branches
> tordues, l'épanouissement en feuilles sombres de ce bois, si vieux
> et si lourd qu'il semblait s'enfoncer dans la terre et non s'en
> arracher, imposaient à la fois l'idée d'une volonté et d'une méta-
> morphose sans fin. Entre eux les collines dévalaient jusqu'au Rhin;
> ils encadraient la cathédrale de Strasbourg très loin dans le cré-
> puscule heureux, comme tant d'autres troncs encadraient d'autres
> cathédrales dans des champs d'Occident. Et cette tour dressée
> dans son oraison d'amputé, toute la patience et le travail humains
> développés en vagues de vignes jusqu'au fleuve n'étaient qu'un
> décor du soir autour de la séculaire poussée du bois vivant, des
> deux jets drus et noueux qui arrachaient les forces de la terre
> pour les déployer en ramures.

Here we have the central image from which the novel derives its title. Here we find expressed, for the trees are Man, the ideas of will and of endless metamorphosis. And the trees frame another "tree," this one made by man, the cathedral of Strasbourg.

The last episode of *Les Noyers* should be seen as an answer to Möllberg's nihilism. Vincent Berger, now an intelligence officer in the German army, is an observer of the first experiments with gas on the Vistula Front. The experiment is being conducted by the inventor, Professor Hoffmann. We find here another form of the intellectual, the intellectual dehumanized by his discipline. For him, man does not exist (another form of nihilism), or rather exists only as far as he reacts to his gas:

> —On a essayé d'employer des poisons. Mais c'est parfaitement idiot! L'acide cyanhydrique, l'oxyde de carbone sont des poisons parfaits, qu'est-ce qu'ils ont donné? L'acide cyanhydrique demande un demi-gramme au mètre cube d'air: le sujet entre en convulsions et tombe mort dans une rigidité tétanique. C'est parfait. En lieu clos . . . Mais qu'est-ce que ça veut dire? Le champ de bataille, figurez-vous, se permet d'être à l'air libre! . . .
>
> —Ensuite, quoi? On a essayé de l'oxyde de carbone. En laboratoire. Toxique redoutable, présentant toutes les qualités requises, facile à préparer, bon marché. Il fixe l'hemoglobine du sang, l'empêche de s'unir à l'oxygène de l'air. Mais il y a toujours le problème de l'air libre!

While there is here a touch of the "mad scientist," nevertheless Hoffmann's scientific inhumanity is made perfectly clear. Some thirty years later, another "Hoffmann" will invent *Zyklon B*.

The attack takes place the day after Hoffmann's arrival. While waiting for the attack to begin, Vincent listens to the soldiers talking in the trenches. Here Berger finds an answer to Möllberg. The soldiers talk of the age-old obsession of unfaithful wives, then talk of the gas which, they believe, will freeze men in whatever position they were at the time: man's ancient dream, embodied in "The Sleeping Beauty." This scene should be read together with the POW scene of the prologue of which it is the counterpart. Vincent Berger, like his son twenty-five years later at Chartres, finds himself before "la matière originelle," before prehistoric, but fundamental and indestructible man:

> —Quand même, vous voyez ça, le maréchal-ferrant avec son marteau au-dessus de l'enclume, qui bouge plus! Des trucs comme ça, c'est des blagues, le marteau tomberait, vu qu'il est trop lourd.—L'électricité, elle, a' doit rester allumée. . . .

Mon père se souvint de la ville des Mille et une nuits où tous les gestes humains, la vie des fleurs, la flamme des lampes ont été suspendus par l'Ange de la Mort. . . . Il était là tout près, avec ses têtes de bonhommes. Mais la coulée du temps mène si bien à la mort, elle aussi, que le vieux rêve du destin suspendu reparaissait comme s'il eût été le secret de la terre, tapi dans ces hommes aux casques à pointe recouverts de toile grise, comme il l'avait été sous les heaumes des soldats de Saladin. . . . L'obscurité était de nouveau tout habitée de voix, voix d'indifférences et de rêves séculaires, voix de métiers—comme si les métiers seuls eussent vécu, sous les hommes impersonnels et provisoires. Les timbres changeaient, mais les tons restaient les mêmes, très anciens, enrobés dans le passé comme l'ombre de cette sape—la même résignation, la même fausse autorité, la même absurde science et la même expérience, la même inusable gaîté, et ces discussions qui ne connaissaient que l'affirmation de plus en plus brutale, comme si ces voix de l'obscurité ne fussent jamais parvenus à individualiser même leur colère.

The description of the gas attack is undoubtedly one of the great scenes written by Malraux. After the gas has been released and the wind has pushed it to the Russian lines, the German soldiers go in to mop up the trenches. Vincent Berger follows. The gas not only killed men, it rotted and putrified all it touched:

Mon père avançait lourdement, mais il avançait. Isolé dans la solitude comme pour veiller le cheval gazé, était un arbre mort; non pas moisi de gaz, mais toutes ses branches nettes, anguleuses, ossifiées, avec la poussée tragique de tous les arbres morts de la terre. Et cet arbre pétrifié depuis tant d'années semblait, dans cet univers de pourriture, le dernier vestige de la vie. Une pie passa d'un vol ralenti, ses plumes blanches découpées dans ses ailes noires; et tomba comme un oiseau de chiffon. Mon père atteignit enfin l'autre rive de la forêt. Il ne s'agissait plus de marcher dans le dégoût, mais d'y plonger. Le taillis des ronces et des aubépines doubles était fauché, gluant lui aussi, de ce roux livide de bête crevée qui devenait noir à vingt mètres. Mais les ronces ne s'accrochaient plus: avec la troublante sensation d'avoir retrouvé sa force, mon père avançait sans résistance à travers une barrière épineuse en déliquescence sous ses genous, sous son épaule, sous son ventre. Seules piquaient encore less longues épines des acacias, dont les branches ne se rompaient pas au premier contact; leurs feuilles semblaient seulement commencer à se flétrir, touchées par un début d'automne. Au-dessus de sa tête, toutes les autres feuilles devenues semblables—chêne, bouleau, mélèze, peuplier—pendaient comme des salades cuites, avec çà et là une araignée morte au centre de sa toile où perlait une rosée verdâtre. Le lierre agglutiné pendait aux troncs suppurants. A chaque pas, des buissons écrasés montait une odeur amère et douceâtre, celle des gaz sans doute.

The gas is not merely a gas, it attacks the very spring of life, it becomes in fact Death. This is where the achievement of Malraux in *Les Noyers* lies. A writer can without difficulty show the death of an individual (of *La Mort du père* in *Les Thibault* or *The Death of Ivan Illitch*); death itself cannot so easily be represented without falling into allegory. In the novels of Malraux, as obsessed with death as they are, we have up to now found only individual deaths (Perken, Tchen, Kyo, Hernandez). But here, in the form of the lethal gas, we have death itself as an inescapable plague that kills everything that lives.

Soon Vincent Berger sees the German soldiers running back towards their lines. Overcome by horror and pity, they carry the horribly suffering Russian soldiers on their backs and try to bring them to the German ambulances. There is no trace of sentimentality in this description, no trace of the usual Malrauvian flamboyance and heroics. In fact, the writing is rather flat and therefore all the more effective:

Le Russe allongé sur le does entre eux, fit un effort pour se retourner sur le ventre, y parvint enfin. Les deux Allemands se redressaient lentement, les jambes encore à demi ployées, stupéfaits comme mon père de retrouver cette vallée de Terre Promise. Le sous-officier dit entre ses dents quelque chose que couvrit le bruit de ses bottes pompant des feuilles.

—Quoi! demanda mon père. Son compagnon grogna de nouveau. Il eût voulu montrer du doigt, mais ses doigts étaient enfoncés dans la capote de celui qu'il portait.

—Il se débine, leur gars! répéta-t-il enfin.

Le grand vent s'engouffrait dans les chemises des porteurs que le repos abrutissait; derrière eux, le gazé essayait de ramper vers les lignes russes. Plus de cent mètres le séparaient du bois; à chaque effort, il avançait dérisoirement de vingt centimètres, retombait; remontait vers sa tranchée, vers l'étroite fosse à gaz où se décomposaient les siens. Et le plus inhumain n'était pas ce mourant qui rampait, les bras dans la boue jusqu'au-dessus des coudes, et les yeux en face des bouillons-blancs gainés d'essaims morts, c'était le silence.

Les porteurs avaient enfin vu le mouvement du Russe. Ils firent les deux pas qui les séparaient de lui; l'un lui botta les fesses, puis tous deux le hissèrent de nouveau sur leurs bras, et ils repartirent.

Vincent Berger, terrified by this evidence of evil ("sans doute les croyants appellent-ils présence du démon une semblable visitation de l'épouvante"), also feels he must act against it:

L'Esprit du Mal ici était plus fort encore que la mort, si fort, qu'il fallait trouver un Russe qui ne fût pas tué, n'importe lequel, le mettre sur ses épaules et le sauver.

Cinqu ou six étaient épars dans les buissons, au-dessous d'une capote accrochée par le col, et qui oscillait sur ce délire comme un pendu; mon père se jeta sous le premier, s'arcbouta dans les ronces molles et se releva avec lui. . . . Mon père, paupières serrées, tout son corps collé à ce cadavre fraternel qui le protégeait comme un bouclier contre tout ce qu'il fuyait, marmonnait sans arrêt: "Vite, vite," sans savoir ce qu'il voulait dire par là, et n'avait même plus conscience de marcher.

Later on he reflects on what lay behind this spontaneous action of the men saving their enemies:

La pitié? pensa-t-il confusément, comme lorsqu'il avait vu revenir les compagnies; il s'agissait d'un élan bien autrement profund, où l'angoisse et la fraternité se rejoignaient inextricablement, d'un élan venu de très loin dans les temps—comme si la nappe des gaz n'eût abandonné, au lieu de ces Russes, que des cadavres amis d'hommes du quaternaire. . . . Jusqu'au ciel miroitant et bleu, le coteau montait avec son odeur retrouvée d'arbres, l'odeur des buis et des sapins qui ruissellent sous l'averse. Tout à coup le souvenir de l'Altenburg traversa l'obsession de mon père: il était en face de vastes bouquets de noyers.

Here we find the final answer to Möllberg. What is fundamental in man is this "élan où l'angoisse et la fraternité se rejoignent," this solidarity of man against death. Here lies the true meaning of Malraux's last novel and not, as some critics have thought, in Vincent Berger's wild longing for happiness as he is dying.

And so, Vincent Berger, the last of Malraux's heroes, dies a death which we shall not witness—not any more than we witnessed Katow's death—both sharing the stubborn conviction that this *fraternité* (or love) can justify a human life which means nothing but which we must live to the end with all its despair and happiness.

E. H. GOMBRICH

Malraux's Philosophy of Art in Historical Perspective

In the third part of Malraux's *Les Voix du silence*— to my mind the most persuasive and important section of the book—the conclusion is put forward that "the artist builds up his forms from other forms; the raw material of an art that is emerging is never life, but an art preceding it." What Malraux here says of art also applies to other manifestations of human life. Civilization is composed of a web of traditions which reach back into the distant past. It is one of the paradoxes of Malraux's position that he would not seem to have drawn this inference from his study of art. Nurtured, as he is, on the extremist philosophies of Nietzsche and Spengler, he likes to dramatize the discontinuities of human culture, the revolutionary ruptures with the past which separate one culture from another and leave us no choice but to contemplate their radical otherness in the guise of a myth that is really of our own making.

It is difficult for a professional historian to follow him here. For why should that continuity of forms which Malraux likes to celebrate not also extend to intellectual as well as artistic creations? Indeed it is tempting to make this point by a *demonstratio ad hominem*. In trying to place Malraux's philosophy of art in its historical perspective I am not out to belittle its status. On the contrary, I hope that his "Museum of the mind"—as I should like to render his *Musée imaginaire*—will become both more intelligible and more accessible once its historical background has been sketched in.

Surveying the library of the mind, the literary heritage of Rome, that

From *Malraux: Life and Work*, edited by Martine de Courcel. © 1976 by George Weidenfeld & Nicolson Ltd. Harcourt Brace Jovanovich, 1976.

great and humane teacher of Latin oratory, Quintilian, who wrote in the
first century A.D. comes to speak of Ennius, the earliest of the great national
poets of the Roman world who lived some three hundred years before him:
"We worship Ennius as we worship those groves which have become sacred
through their very age, where the grand and ancient oaks are not so much
beautiful as numinous."

The reaction of the Roman critic from a sophisticated age to the rugged
grandeur of what had become the archaic diction of Ennius illustrates a
response to the art of remote periods which has recurred quite frequently
in the Western tradition. Seen in this perspective, André Malraux stands as
the most recent in a long line of critics who are captivated by that numinous
quality which ancient utterances or creations so frequently assume in our
civilization. Quintilian, like Malraux, might have conceded that there was
nothing sacred in a knobbly old oak tree; in other words, and again like
Malraux, he might have said that the awe inspired by vegetation really sprang
from a myth, just as he realized that his response to Ennius was due to
distance. But neither he nor, as we know, Malraux, would have wanted for
this reason to forgo the experience which archaic poetry or nature can arouse.

Indeed it is tempting at this point to recall the pages of *Les Noyers de
l'Altenburg* which describe the narrator's father entering just such a grove
after the end of the great *colloque* on the Concept of Man:

> The richness of these age-old trees came from their bulk. But the
> effort with which their twisted branches sprang from their huge
> trunks, the way in which this heavy old timber burst into dark
> leaves so that it seemed rather to be sinking deep into the earth
> than tearing itself out of it, all this suggested the idea of endless
> strivings, and endless metamorphosis. . . .
>
> . . . the tortured trees with their burnished leaves and their
> ripening nuts silhouetted against the sky, burgeoned into eternal
> life in all their solemn mass, overhanging the young branches and
> the dead nuts of winter.

At another time Malraux has told us explicitly how open he is to that
suggestion of divinity that emanates from old trees. In the *Antimémoires* we
read of a sacred tree he visited with an African queen:

> The Queen's fetish was a tree like a giant plane. They had cleared
> the ground around it, which made one realize that it dominated
> the forest. From the writhing ganglions of its roots there rose
> tree trunks, straight as walls, together forming a colossal shaft
> which, some thirty metres above, curved royally outwards. . . .

What I was looking at was not a marvellous tree, a King of
trees—although it was that—but a tree that conjured up a whole
world into which it magically compelled the living as the Gods
of Egypt compelled the dead.

As if to confirm the fusion in Malraux's thoughts, as in those of the
cultivated Roman, of ancient trees and ancient art, we encounter the same
link in *La Tête d'obsidienne*, where the author is meditating on an elongated
fetish "which resembles a branch, like the angels of the Autun tympanum."

Those subtle critics of language, the ancient teachers of oratory, had a
word for that cluster of emotions—the word we translate as "the sublime."
The unknown Greek author of a treatise on the sublime which goes under
the name of Longinus characteristically finds this precious and elusive quality
in the words of power uttered by the creator in the Hebrew scriptures: "Let
there be light and there was light." This numinous quality which is thus
attributed to the sacred texts of an alien cult cannot be achieved at will. If
you try to make your speech sublime you will only make it bombastic. For
the sublime is not so much an aesthetic as a psychological category. It is, in
the famous formulation of Longinus, "the echo of a noble soul." We relish
the sublime precisely for that reason. It brings us face to face with great
minds. It will satisfy those who seek not beauty and contrivance but an
encounter with greatness. In fact Longinus is emphatic on the point that
polish and flawless perfection counteracts sublimity. He thus sowed another
seed which produced a rich critical harvest, particularly after the rediscovery
of Longinus and the various translations of his treatise in the late seventeenth
and eighteenth centuries. A certain suspicion began to cling to the idea of
beauty in art. Was there not a higher and less accessible value—the value
of sublime? Malraux has no doubts on this score. He sees the significance
of modern art starting from Goya in its rejection of beauty and pleasure,
and he connects the rediscovery of earlier exotic styles with this revaluation
of old values.

I believe we can still learn something about this momentous development
by following up the clues offered by the sublime. Perhaps the most pene-
trating psychological analysis of human aesthetic reaction is to be found in
Edmund Burke's *Philosophical Enquiry into the origin of our ideas of the Sublime
and Beautiful*, of 1756. The boldness of Burke's conceptions commands respect even though we may find him overambitious. What he attempts is no
more and no less than a system of aesthetics based entirely on naturalistic
premises. Briefly he proposes the hypothesis that the sentiment of beauty is
rooted in the instinct of the propagation of the species, in other words in

sex, while the sentiment of the sublime is rooted in the instinct of self-preservation, in other words in anxiety. It may well be argued that the identification of our enjoyment of beauty with the erotic response, so natural for a critic writing during the age of the Rococo, contributed to that conscious or unconscious devaluation of beauty of which I have spoken. The eighteenth century was a century of guilt feelings, whose spokesman was Jean-Jacques Rousseau. The charge of corruption, of decadence, of the debasing influence of an art pandering to the superficial pleasure of a licentious public, could only serve to raise the stock of the sublime, for there was no guilt in feeling dread and awe.

It is true that Edmund Burke looked for this experience primarily in nature rather than in art, but even so his analysis affords sufficient parallels both backwards to Quintilian and forwards to André Malraux. Discussing the sublime effects of obscurity in the second part of his treatise (section 3), he writes: "Almost all the heathen temples were dark. Even in the barbarous temples of the Americans at this day, they keep their idol in a dark part of the hut, which is consecrated to his worship. For this purpose too the Druids performed all their ceremonies in the bosom of the darkest woods, and in the shade of the old and most spreading oaks."

Once more a transition suggests itself from here to a revealing passage in Malraux's *Antimémoires* where he traces his ideas about art back to his first sight of the Great Sphinx of Gizeh before the site was tidied up and sterilized by archaeologists and thus still spoke "the solemn language of ruins." He had asked himself what there was in common "between the message of the medieval half-light filling the naves and the imprint the Egyptians left on their vast creations, in short between all the shapes which embody something of the ineffable." We know Burke's answer to this question. Obscurity arouses fear and is therefore sublime. Malraux's intuition was less psychological. He suddenly conceived of two contrasting languages, the language of everyday appearances and the language of Truth, of the Eternal and the Sacred. The Sphinx as an embodiment of mystery also embodies that unknowable truth that is revealed through her very metamorphosis. It is that intimation of the supernatural that the eighteenth century sought in nature.

Not only in nature, though, but also in the manifestations of the human mind. Malraux writes in *Le Musée imaginaire* that the idea of interpreting a style as the expression of a civilization belongs entirely to the twentieth century. He is right that as far as the visual arts are concerned the idea has only recently become a cliché. But after all it was the great proto-Romantic Johann Gottfried Herder who, in 1773, published a collection of folk songs under the programmatic title *Stimmen der Völker in Liedern* (The Voices of People in Song).

Why folk songs? Because in the creations of the untutored "folk" we hear the voice of natural man, uncorrupted by reason and artifice. The German langauge identifies the primitive or savage with the *wild*, and Herder seized on this usage to expound this theory of poetry:

> The *wilder*, that is the more vital, the more spontaneous a nation is (for the word means no more than that), the wilder, also, that is the more vital, more spontaneous, more sensuous, more lyrically active will be their songs if it has any songs at all. The further removed their modes of thought, their language and their literature remains from artifice and logic, the less their songs will have been composed for paper and become dead literary exercises . . . the longer a song is to last, the stronger, the more sensuous must these arousers of soul be to defy the power of time and the changes of centuries.

The pamphlet in which Herder published these subversive thoughts also contained an essay by a young student of law he had befriended in Strasbourg, Goethe's prose hymn on the Strasbourg Minister. It is in this essay that we find the first impatient denunciations of the "effeminate" "beauty mongering" which blinded people to the greatness of medieval architecture, and a first intimation of the cult of primitive art which Malraux, like others, regards as a twentieth-century novelty:

> In this way the savage may use weird lines, horrible shapes, strident colours on a coconut, on feathers or on his own body. However arbitrary these forms, they will harmonize without his knowing anything about the laws of proportion, since it was one single emotion that fused them into one significant whole. This significant art is the only true one.

Though Goethe probably spoke without actual knowledge of the work of American Red Indians, knowledge of the arts of the globe was expanding in the eighteenth century, and lovers of art were beginning to reflect on that widening of horizons which Malraux also wants to locate in our own era.

Before the end of the eighteenth century there appeared that embarrassingly named collection of essays on art, the *Outpourings from the Heart of an Art-loving Monk* from the pen of W. H. Wackenroder. A much lesser mind than either Goethe or Herder, Wackenroder was, for all his sentimentality, more radical than either. In his essay "On two miraculous languages and their mysterious power," he thrusts aside the "benefaction" of human speech to celebrate the message of "the invisible that hovers around us," conveyed by the two languages of Nature and of Art. Inevitably we hear again of the rustling of the trees in the woods and other natural events which arouse in us dark intimations inaccessible to well-weighed words. And in another essay he drives to the conclusion that foreshadows the claims of the *Musée imaginaire:*

> We, the sons of this century, have been granted the advantage to be standing on the summit of a high mountain, with many countries and many ages lying quite open before our eyes and at our feet. Let us, then, make use of this good fortune, and let our eyes serenely roam over all ages and nations, endeavouring all the while to sense in these manifold works and emotions only what is *human.*

Almost the only word in this passage which immediately betrays that Malraux cannot have been its author is the word "serenely." Wackenroder's pieties makes him trust in the deity, while Malraux's heroic despair has no room for serenity in his view of man's changing destiny.

Even so, it is important to note that Wackenroder's acknowledgment of global art should not be considered an isolated freak. Throughout the nineteenth century artistic horizons were widening, but this process first affected two arts which happen to interest Malraux very little and have not found admission to his Museum of the Mind—architecture and decoration. Nobody who remembers the variety of styles exemplified in our nineteenth-century cities will doubt the worldwide eclecticism prevalent at the time.

But the real breakthrough to a global viewpoint first happened in the art of ornament and decoration, and here, as so often, it was triggered by a nagging dissatisfaction with the state of European design. The Industrial Revolution had debased the standards of craftmanship and created a deep-seated malaise that first found its expression in England. The Great Exhibition of 1851 was both the result and the cause of thoroughgoing heart-searching, for it looked as if the decorative instinct of savage nations were far superior to the taste of Western manufacturers. Indeed, if the *Musée imaginarie* has a real predecessor it is Caxton's Glass Palace in South Kensington, with its dazzling display of the products of India, Africa and America, which deeply impressed the crowd of visitors. It impressed precisely because it enforced the conclusions that artistic talent had nothing to do with representational skill. On the contrary, the very dexterity of Europeans in imitating natural objects, flowers or animals, appeared to militate against the effectiveness of their design which, as it was increasingly emphasized, should lack all illusionist features and rather emphasize the flat surface. Here, indeed, is an important root of that revaluation of nonillusionistic art which Malraux has overlooked. One quotation must suffice. It comes from an essay on "The Critic as Artist" by that influential spokesman of the fin de siècle, Oscar Wilde: "By its deliberate rejection of Nature as the ideal of beauty, as well as of the imitative method of the ordinary painter, decorative art not merely prepares the soul for the true imaginative work, but develops in it that sense of form which is the basis of creative no less than of critical achievement."

It was in this way, I believe, that the ground was prepared for that reversal of values that Malraux celebrates in his writings: the rejection not only of beauty but of truth to appearance. Nor is he concerned with decoration or indeed with "abstract" art: what interests him is the acceptance of nonillusionistic representations, particularly of the human figure.

It is only natural that in his accounts of that revolution Malraux concentrates on its French antecedents, notably on the contribution of painters such as Cézanne, who accustomed the public to a different scale of values. It may be worthwhile therefore to redress the balance a little and to draw attention to other sources.

Characteristically it was a student of decorative art, the Austrian Alois Riegl, who first explicitly rejected the notion that changes of style could be described in terms of progress and decline. He wrote for specialists, but his doctrine was spread among artists and critics by Wilhelm Worringer, whose *Abstraction and Empathy* came out in 1908.

As far as this doctrine is remembered at all, it lives on in Bernard Berenson's glorification of the "life enhancing ideated sensations of tactile values" which the sensitive observer is supposed to experience in front of a Renaissance painting. Worringer did not deny the possibility of such aesthetic enjoyment, but he rejected any attempt to judge all styles by this standard. A positive relation to nature, such as it is expressed in classical and Renaissance art, he thought, could only develop in societies which felt safe in their existence. Most peoples lacked this sense of security. To them nature, reality, space itself was threatening. Their art, therefore, could not be an expression of love and confidence, but rather of an anxious withdrawal. It is this flight from reality that is manifested, according to Worringer, in the creation of abstract forms. Quoting the Latin tag that "fear created the Gods" Worringer wishes to add that fear also created art. We are back, on a different level, at Burke's identification of the sublime with dread. It is this dread or awe which Worringer sees expressed in all nonclassical styles, and since ours is said to be an "age of anxiety" his message was soon taken up by his contemporaries among German artists. Expressionism had found its ancestry in all styles of the globe founded on "abstraction."

It was in another of Worringer's books published before the First World

War, *Formprobleme der Gotik* (1911), that art lovers first encountered those impressive and expressive photographs of details of medieval works of art which dramatize their contemporary appeal. The technique caught on, as did Worringer's approach, and after the "latency period" of the war a spate of more or less scholarly art books began to flood the market which exploited this feeling of immediacy that could be achieved by cunningly lit and cleverly cut shots of medieval, exotic or primitive sculpture, particularly of heads.

When, in the early fifties, Malraux's *Psychologie de l'art* first came into my hands I therefore experienced something like a déjà vu sensation in turning its pages. While still a schoolboy in the Twenties I had been much impressed by books of this kind, which may well have had their share in propelling me towards the history of art. My studies had thoroughly weaned me of this approach, which now appeared to me somewhat hysterical and sensationalist. It was with considerable surprise that I discovered in reading Malraux that he shared the conviction at which I had arrived—the conviction that these photographic techniques falsified the works they purported to reproduce and imparted on them an "unjustified but aggressive modernity." Another surprise awaited me though when I saw that Malraux somehow accepted and even relished this falsification as part of that metamorphosis that turned the art of the past into an indispensable myth. In an age when man had begun to realize—if I can thus summarize Malraux's views—that God is dead, it is the art of the past which in this transformation preserves for him that sense of the numinous which is his birthright. Harking back to the earlier pages of the present essay we might say that the mysterious and unintelligible works of art of the past have joined the sublimities of nature in offering a screen for the projection of our deepest fears and longings. Communion with art, like communion with nature, is really a form of self-communion.

I have no doubt that we can learn a great deal from Malraux's diagnosis, but I do not think that we cannot go beyond it. The historian who is interested in the psychology of art is surely entitled to ask why it was that art assumed this function at a given period. More exactly perhaps, we should ask who it was who experienced this particular metamorphosis with such intensity. For one thing is clear—when Malraux uses the term "we" to characterize "our" response to the art of the past he is really talking of a tiny circle. It is to be feared that the overwhelming majority of people in our age never look at works of art in museums or in art books. Of those who do, again a large majority are quite unaffected by the attitudes described by Malraux. That rejection of beauty and sensual pleasure, that contempt for a faithful rendering of natural appearances, that worship of creative otherness which

Malraux attributes to "us" is—or should I say was?—the preserve of a mere handful of people. What were their motives?

In a paper on "Psychoanalysis and the History of Art," I once attempted to lay bare at least one hidden strand in this development which Malraux has not mentioned—I mean that tendency of the sophisticated to be repelled by what has come to appear to them as cloying, indulgent and emotionally cheap. We have seen how early the erotic sensualities of the Rococo became identified with the corruption of society and drove art-lovers into the arms of the sublime. There is a strong social element in this situation. The fear of sharing a debased taste with the despised bourgeois or petit bourgeois has put a premium on a preference for what is disturbing, shocking and difficult. True, in pursuing this type of analysis we must not fall into the trap of dismissing the modern revolution as mere snobbery. The *kitsch*, the sentimental trash of the department store, does indeed represent an unprecedented debasement of art precisely because it combines manual dexterity with meretriciousness. As a matter of fact the verdict of the rising generation on the art of the Salon and of the best parlour is much less severe than it was in my youth and in that of André Malraux. Even so, no historian of twentieth-century art can afford to neglect the forces of repulsion that drove the pioneers of the new movement towards new artistic explorations. Malraux is right when he links the emergence of his Museum of the Mind with this revolution, though he somewhat overdramatizes its novelty.

Perhaps it is only in one of his most recent books that he fully reveals who he means and has meant when he uses the term "we." *La Tête d'obsidienne* of 1974 combines a deeply felt tribute to Picasso with a restatement of Malraux's ideas about art occasioned by the great exhibition organized in Malraux's honor at Saint-Paul-de-Vence by the Maeght Foundation. Malraux's interpretation of art as a triumph over death finds much scope in these reminiscences and meditations, which open with an account of his visit to Picasso's home after his death. We must leave it to future historians to sort out how much in the "flashbacks" telling of conversations with Picasso is Malraux and how much may be authentic, but what these Platonic dialogues reveal is the degree to which Malraux made himself the spokesman of what he took to be Picasso's philosophy of art—a philosophy based on contempt for the purveyors of pleasure and on a constant striving for new transformations which are seen as the very essence of art.

Maybe this fusion of Malraux's interpretation of art with the oeuvre of the master of metamorphosis can also assist the historian to locate the source of Malraux's "myth." No artist in all history exhibited that range of styles and of skills that marks the fabulous oeuvre of Picasso. For him every new move was indeed also the rejection of an earlier manner of which he had grown tired. A virtuoso of the first order, he was able to evoke images of haunting beauty classical no less than of terrifying mystery and ugliness. Neither the rendering of natural appearances nor the creation of abstract structures presented any problem to him. If he did not cultivate a fully nonfigurative style it was, one may surmise, because what he was looking for in the images he created was precisely that expressive intensity that we experience most readily in front of a living organism, however distorted. When Malraux reports him as saying that what he was looking for was "the mask," it was perhaps an expression of that desire for a mysterious numinous physiognomy which his generation had discovered in the ritual masks of tribal Africa.

There are such heads and physiognomies in Picasso's oeuvre, sometimes achieved with the simplest of means, as in the *papiers déchirés* which appeared to look at us with haunting magic. But there is an old Latin proverb that tells us *si duo faciunt idem non est idem*. It is one thing for Picasso to reject his skill and to explore the expressive possibilities of chance formation, it is something very different for a tribal artist to carve a mask according to a strict tradition.

The myth Malraux distils from his Museum of the mind is really that mankind might be seen as a super-Picasso, ever creating new forms and rejecting others, each creation implying a negation of something else. It is this conception that permits Malraux to appreciate both the stark shapes of primitive idols and the stupendous virtuosity of masters such as Titian, Chardin and above all Goya and Manet. But this approach presupposes precisely that all artistic creations of the past are to be seen as the products of the same kind of choice which is inherent in all Picasso's creative whims.

Malraux tells us that Picasso remarked: "It is a good thing that nature exists, so that we can violate her," and though I cannot find this utterance very attractive it does throw light on his oeuvre. To look for the same kind of aggressive defiance in the nonnaturalistic styles of the past is to do violence, not to nature but to history. Yet Malraux cannot give up this interpretation, because he has made it the cornerstone of his philosophy. For him "the human power to which art testifies is man's eternal revenge on a hostile universe." We recognize echoes of Worringer's ideas, but now they have been absorbed into a wider vision of man, defiantly asserting himself in the face of blind "destiny."

The words "negation" and "refusal" punctuate his glorification of the hieratic styles of the past, and he is convinced that we all share this taste for negative virtues. "The rejection of the illusion," he writes, "rarely leaves us indifferent." If he is right in attributing this bias to us, it would do little credit to our sense of discrimination. Purely negative criteria are poor criteria in art. Anyone may like the device of rhyme in poetry, or abhor it as trivial jingling, but it really will not do to extol all rhymeless poetry of the world for its heroic refusal to indulge in an artifice that was not known.

It is at this point that Malraux's reading of the "message" of art impinges on the psychology of image making. It is strangely inconsistent for Malraux, who knows that images derive from images, to follow Riegl and Worringer in dismissing the idea that the remoteness from natural appearances which we find in most artistic styles of the globe can have anything to do with lack of skill in rendering the visible world. He is right in insisting that while there may be clumsy works of art there can be no clumsy style. But the issue of skill and will cannot be resolved by any facile formula. No doubt the master of the Lindisfarne Gospels had no longing to go out sketching and to paint the cloud formations which fascinated Constable. No doubt also Constable would have been unable to paint the crosspage of the Lindisfarne Gospel.

So much is trivial. What is not trivial is the question of what is involved in making an image that strikes the beholder as a faithful rendering of natural appearance. To assume that anyone could have done that but refrained, as Picasso refrained, because he wanted to "violate" reality is to fly in the face of all evidence. After all, the apprentices of the classical tradition spent years in the cast room and in the life class to master the human figure and the laws of perspective. Neither were the skills of landscape or still-life painting ever acquired overnight. Whether the toil was worthwhile is a matter of opinion. That it was a toil is not; and though there are no clumsy styles there are styles—as there are musical instruments—which demand a smaller repertoire of skills than others. The main reason why the rendering of nature has come to look trivial and even easy can be stated in Malraux's terms: we are constantly surrounded by images, photographic, painted or printed, in which three-dimensional reality has already been reduced to two dimensions, and those with a knack can pick up these formulas and reproduce them without too much trouble. It does not follow that all the image makers of the globe who practised different methods did so because they rejected appearances for the sake of a higher, invisible reality.

Once more I think that Malraux has seen an important point in the role of art in our civilization; he is right, no doubt, that far more people have come into contact with religion through works of art than in any other way. Temples and cathedrals, cult images and biblical illustrations keep alive a tradition that might otherwise be in danger of breaking off altogether. Naturally he is right again in insisting on the dominant role of religion in past societies, but once more he is turning a historical fact into a myth if he wants us to believe that men and women in the past were always cowed and overawed by the mystery of their existence. Anthropologists who have visited the tribes who carve these frightening masks tell us of much laughter and horseplay. Nor need we assume that all the art of these or other civilizations is really concerned with the "sacred" because it exhibits an unnaturalistic style. It has been suggested that some, at least, of the female figurines which have been called "mother goddesses" were really dolls, toys for children. The voice we have lent to their silence would have struck their owners as strange indeed. If we experience it as "sublime" and hear what Longinus called "the echo of a noble soul"—a collective soul, no doubt—we are certainly, as Malraux postulates, the victims of a myth.

But if we succumb, we do so precisely because we are questioning the work not for what it is but for what lies behind it, for the soul that we seek rather than the form that we see. The history of the "sublime" may here be particularly telling. For those who communed with the sublimities of nature certainly did so in the eighteenth century in the hope or belief that in nature they could find the echo of the Creator. And even when this hope was fading, the worship of nature offered the nearest substitute to religion. It is in the light of this development that we can appreciate Malraux's attitude to art. To him, remote and exotic images now speak with the voice of the forest, or of thunderclouds. The lover of art is like the child who holds the seashell at his ear to hear the sound of the sea. What he hears is the rush of his own blood, but is not the myth more poetic, more consoling than the knowledge that empty shells are nothing but empty shells?

One can sympathize with this dilemma and still think that it is an unreal one. It arises somehow from the basic assumption that what we must seek in nature or in art is some kind of message, that we must for ever look for a meaning in a universe devoid of meanings. I suspect that this expectation carries over into adult life an attitude that is natural to the child, for whom every object, every toy and every image has indeed an intense feeling tone, an intense personal physiognomy. It has been shown by the psychologist C. E. Osgood and his colleagues that we can make ourselves regress to this frame of mind at will and are ready to give an answer to any question about the feeling tone of any object or quality. In this frame of mind we will not be disposed to doubt that old oaktrees are not only stronger than birchtrees but also wiser, holier and perhaps more fatherly. We will be equally ready to respond in some such way to Easter Island idols or to a gingerbread figure. But are there no other ways to approach art and nature? Can we not appreciate the beauty and intricacy of the seashell instead of holding it to our ear? Granted that both the universe and the creations of man are mysterious, are they not also miraculous in a way that makes us transcend our puny selves? Do they not challenge our thirst for the knowledge rather than for communion?

One of the interlocutors of the colloquy that forms the core of *Les Noyers de l'Altenburg* is made to speak of this wish to understand, but Malraux has seen to it that the dice are heavily loaded against him: "We art historians, particularly if we are historians of German art, confront the Gothic or the Egyptian man with the disinterested intention of dragging him to the light. What is in question here is the honest will to knowledge: we interrogate him, and we interrogate ourselves."

It is not difficult to recognize in this art historian a disciple of someone like Worringer, who did indeed claim to have unriddled the psychologies of "Gothic man" and of "Egyptian man." One cannot but agree with Malraux that the claim is ridiculous, because there never were such creatures. But this insight need not throw doubt on the second part of the statement, the existence of an honest will to knowledge. After all it was this will that led to the information about the late Middle Ages and the ancient Egyptians which Malraux also uses. Without it the hieroglyphs would never have been deciphered and would still be regarded in the light of the myth that they embodied some portentous archetypal wisdom.

Maybe Malraux is right that it is not the most learned Egyptologist who can make us love Egyptian art best, but I for one would still entrust myself to his guidance rather than to anyone who wants to arouse my emotional response. Malraux makes much of Man in the abstract, but let us remember the opening words of Aristotle's *Metaphysics:* "All men naturally desire to know." True enough, what Aristotle took for knowledge has been partly consigned to the category of myth by science, that science which appears to play so little part in Malraux's image of man. If it did he would have to concede that we do know more about the universe than Aristotle did—and that rational inquiry has also increased our knowledge of man's past.

Not that Malraux is wrong in reminding us that the interpretation the historian imposes on the evidence also changes our perception of the main accents of developments. The historian who regards Mannerism as decadent will also select his facts differently from the one who sees in it a forerunner of modern art. And yet it is a fallacy to conclude that all is relative and that there are no facts to be discovered which would be of use to both historians. We have dispelled a good many myths about the past through our "honest will to knowledge." At any rate, what is the alternative? Should we not try to find the truth, should we close our research institutions and make do with those second-hand stereotypes about the "spirits" of past ages, the tired ghosts of Hegelian philosophies that have seeped into our art books including—regrettably—even into Malraux's own presentation of past cultures? Surely as a champion of change, of the search and the quest, he is the last man to advocate such a submission to mental inertia.

Maybe, however, he fails to see where his paradoxical glorification of the myth would lead: not to an initiation into the sacred, but to the cynicism of the hoax. Two years ago Cornell University in the State of New York organized an exhibition under the heading "The Civilization of Llhuros." Its guiding spirit was the American artist Normal Daly, who had picked up discarded machinery and other industrial detritus from rubbish heaps and cleverly transformed these pieces of metal into vaguely portentous objects suggesting implements of ritual and mysterious artefacts of a strange cult. The catalogue and labels expounded an elaborate interpretation based on the fiction that there once had been such a civilization which had been destroyed by an atomic explosion, and that archaeologists and anthropologists had succeeded in reading its script and reconstructing much of its creed and its mores—abounding in sexual practices of the more shocking kind. Needless to say, the whole thing was a transparent spoof; transparent in the sense that the visitor was not expected to be taken in for a moment. He was to look at these mounted screwdrivers or bent aerials "as if" they were the tragic relics of a vanished world of beliefs. In taking the small step from the sublime to the ridiculous, and back again, he was to be awed and amused in turn, playing the game and watching himself responding to these suggestive forms.

I am not sure that such a game can ever be worth the expensive candle, and I have only referred to it to reveal the danger inherent in Malraux's intellectual position. He himself has amply testified to his genuine love of art. Indeed the value of his writings on art seems to me to transcend his theories precisely because they reveal a man for whom the problems of art are ultimate problems of desperate seriousness. In a world where most academic study of art history has broken up into specialisms, he has challenged us to reflect on the totality of human artistic production and to incorporate it into our image of man. When the books by professionals are gathering dust in libraries he will be read, as we read Ruskin, as a witness to a civilization to which art still mattered.

VICTOR BROMBERT

Remembering Malraux: On Violence and the Image of Man

When an intellectual flirts with action, and throws himself into it with zest and commitment to the limits of his being, we are tempted to assume that he has achieved a harmony between action and thought, that he has resolved for himself the age-old conflict between thinking and doing, between singing the world and changing it. Or we may feel that somehow he has betrayed his true vocation. The matter appears more complex still when this involvement in action alternates with artistic activities that take as models not action, but other works of art. Our perplexity reveals perhaps something about our modern notion that art and life are separate realms, that art is fundamentally nonrepresentational, self-referential. For Malraux no such abstraction, no such separation is conceivable. Antagonism, yes; art as a struggle with the conditions of existence, art as a desperate engagement with that which unmans man, with all the forces of life and death that deny him. But such an agonistic relation to life is the very opposite of abstraction and separation: it implies a close combat from which man is able to emerge victorious only as he discovers in himself, through this confrontation, images and myths powerful enough to negate his nothingness. Art itself, at that level, becomes combat, war, ideology.

It is true of course that Malraux was present at all the crossroads of history-in-the-making: in the Orient when the wind of Revolution began to blow, in the anti-fascist rallies in Europe, in the Spanish Civil War where

---

From *Dialogues with the Unseen and the Unknown: Essays in memory of André Malraux*, edited by Lynne L. Gelber. (Proceedings of the Symposium in Honor of Malraux [April 15–16, 1977].) © 1978 by Skidmore College.

he organized and led an improvised air squadron against Franco, in the French army in 1940 when he was made prisoner, in the Resistance movement when he was captured and came close to being tortured, as a Colonel in the Free French Forces liberating Alsace, then as Minister of Information of de Gaulle, later as Minister of Cultural Affairs—and much of the time pursuing his interests in archaeology, cultural history, pursuing his work as creator of the most death-and-meaning obsessed fiction of our time.

In discussing Malraux it is easy to fall into two traps. The one is to consider him as an adventurer, a would-be French T. E. Lawrence (he in fact planned to write a study of him). That Malraux had a strong adventurous streak in him is borne out by many episodes in his life, some of which he himself has amplified, some of which he has dramatically left in the dark. But his opportunism—whether self-serving, political, or heroic—would not account for the obsessive quality of his thought that returns again and again to the same fundamental question of man's destiny and possible grandeur in the face of death.

The other trap is to reduce all of Malraux to ideological commitment, specifically in the cause of Revolutionary movements. But such a view evidently does not account for his allegiance to de Gaulle, and accounts even less for his notion of the *sacré* nature of Art ("sacré" is one of his favorite words): sacred not because of a participation in a given religious belief, but because of a confrontation with ultimate meanings, or rather a relentless search for ultimate meanings. "Tout art sacré s'oppose à la mort." No sentence of Malraux more tersely suggests how important the dialogue with death is for him, and how much he expects from art. But this dialogue with death is not merely that of individual works. Every civilization, he has said (perhaps it is even that which defines a civilization in his terms), is haunted, consciously or unconsciously, not so much by death itself, but by what to think of it. And every civilization finds and affirms itself through the meaning it bestows on suffering and death. Culture itself is both transcendence and resurrection. Malraux's imaginary museum is not an art historian's paradise: it is the tragic locus where the ultimate battle is constantly fought. We are far indeed from the notion of a common (or uncommon) adventure, far indeed also from any notion of a single political ideology.

Art and thought are not a hot-house affair; their pursuit is not a gratuitous *game*. If Malraux, evoking the loftiest or deepest texts of man, unerringly turns to the book of Job, to Dostoevsky, to Shakespeare, it is because in his view only that art can possibly be considered great that takes into account, and attempts to come to terms with, the mystery of suffering. Even the most admired philosophic stance can be condemned as inadequate if it does not articulate the basic question: "What are you doing on this earth where suffering reigns?" In his great novel about the Spanish Civil War, *L'Espoir*, Madrid in flames seems to be saying to the philosopher Unamuno "What good does your thinking do me, if it cannot cope with my tragedy?" And coping with tragedy implies lucidity in the face of man's incurable weakness; it implies King Lear's discovery that he is not "ague-proof" and that his hand "smells of mortality." One of the characters describes as follows man's noblest effort: "To translate into consciousness the widest experience possible." But it is consciousness of limits and fragility that makes for man's greatness. "Penser fait la grandeur de l'homme," says Pascal. And Malraux, though in a non-Christian perspective, shares Pascal's faith in man's grandeur—a grandeur rooted precisely in man's inherent weakness. The words of Pascall still echo: "Man is only a reed, the weakest in nature; but he is a thinking reed." Man is the only animal who knows that he must die. Weak, but aware of his weakness; mortal, but reading into this mortality a condition bigger by far than any individual fate: the fate of man. Not merely—as he puts it in *Antimémoires*—the *"condition de créature,"* but the "condition humaine." Hence the importance of the title Malraux chose almost half a century ago for what probably still is his most representative book.

La Condition humaine, though much read, is a book that is easily misread. The climate of violence is so pervasive, we are so brutally thrust into contact with murder, combat and torture, that one may hastily assume that violence is the subject of the novel. It seems to be a fiction of extreme situations. The violence of combat: grenades exploding in crowded rooms, bodies torn to shreds, blood-stained walls, mass executions—these are the striking images that remain with the reader. And there is worse violence. Man tortures and disfigures. Prisoners are skillfully martyrized, then burned alive. But here is the point. This kind of violence, this insistence on the "entreprise d'avilissement," corresponds not to a taste for the picturesqueness of war and revolution, or sheer sensationalism, but to Malraux's moral fervor. The sadistic will to reduce the other to the limits of his body, to reduce him to pain and degradation, is a concrete challenge to the dignity of man, and as such Evil in its pure, irreducible form. Again in *Antimémoires*, Malraux commented: "Hell is not horror, Hell is to be degraded unto death." And he concluded: "Satan is Degradation." König, the police chief in *La Condition humaine*, does not torture to exact information; he pretends to seek information so as to be able to torture. What he performs is a black mass that celebrates the death of the spirit.

Malraux's fictional techniques can also be misinterpreted. The brusk changes of scenes, the staccato of newspaper dispatches, seem designed to maintain suspense in a climate of revolutionary action. The narrative sequences propel the reader from the hotel room where Ch'en murders the sleeping man, to the Black Cat nightclub where Clappique drinks with prostitutes, to the street, to the port where the weapons are to be stolen from a boat, to the hotel room where Valérie and Ferral fight their erotic battle, to Hemmelrich's shop where a child cries in pain, to the street again, to Gisors's home, to an antiquarian shop, to the police station, to Communist headquarters, to a school yard and to death. The text imposes a succession of shots taken from different angles. Fadeouts, close-ups, ellipses, further suggest a cinematographic pace and vision. Malraux, who wrote an *Esquisse d'une psychologie du cinéma*, has said on various occasions that all art is a system of ellipses. Baroque art appeared to him as the distant ancestor of the cinema because it introduced the *succession* of images, prefigured the technique of *découpage*. "La voiture démarra à une allure de film" is an explicit image early in *La Condition humaine*. But these techniques in the service of action can be deceptive. On closer inspection, the meditative mode is installed into the tensest moments: dialogue and dialectics are often carried on, with action as mere background noise. And not only meditation, but mediation. For it is hard to remember who thought what. Malraux's characters are in the habit of quoting each other: they are mutually contaminated by each other's thought to the point of indifferentiation. And if the representational techniques confirm the climate of violence, they point less to action than to apocalypse. Explosions, sirens, the rattle of machine-guns, the cries of the wounded, are part of what Malraux himself calls the atmosphere of a "fin du monde," of a "nuit de jugement dernier."

From the outset, there are signals of the *revelatory* nature of violence. As Kyo and Katov walk together, early in the morning of the day of insurrection, low heavy clouds, now and then torn by the wind, give brief glimpses of fading stars. The Revolution begins under the sign of the end ("dernières étoiles"). And apocalypse means not only revelation but destruction. In *L'Espoir*, one entire section is entitled "L'Exercice de l'Apocalypse." The congregated intellectuals, who continue discussing while bombs explode and while Madrid burns, are perfectly aware of the self-destructive urges of Western culture; they lucidly assess the catastrophic nature of our times. Malraux's Orient is a pretext. Years ago, W. M. Frohock alerted us to the fact that when Malraux set his novel in Shanghai, he has not yet himself set foot in China. In fact, most of the participants in the novel's action are not Chinese: Hemmelrich, Katov, May, Clappique, Kyo, Gisors, Ferral—they are the protagonists in an extraterritorial drama, living out that moment in history when Western consciousness watches the beginning of the end of Europe as *mistress* of the world.

More complicated than this revelatory function of violence is the textual deconstruction of the notion of ideology. At face value, *La Condition humaine* may appear ideologically committed to the cause of Revolution. The world of the novel seems to be neatly divided. On the one hand, those who oppose the Revolution, or who are simply outside of it: the power-seeking eroto-maniac Ferral; Martial, the venal head of the police; König, the sadistic chief of Chang Kai Chek's secret service; the mythomaniacal, histrionic baron de Clappique, who literally gambles away the life of his friends. On the other, the revolutionary heroes: Ch'en, the terrorist, driven to a futile death; Kyo, the organizer of the insurrectional cells; his wife May; Hemmelrich who ends up as a factory worker in Russia; Pei, the young intellectual; above all, Katov who already once faced a firing squad and miraculously escaped, who already once, in Russia, sacrificed himself for solidarity's sake, and who, at the end of the novel, once again chooses "virile fraternity" when he gives his cyanide—the greatest gift he ever made—to two young comrades. But such a neat binary opposition leaves out Gisors, teacher of an entire gen-eration of revolutionaries, now symbol of the paralyzed intellect, unable to participate in revolutionary action, preferring the music of serenity. Nor does it account for the systematic discrediting of a party indifferent, for strategic reasons, to the plight of the Shanghai revolutionaries whom it decides to sacrifice. Vologin, the party official in Hankow, is in fact presented in a most unfavorable light. His short, plump silhouette, his unctuous im-personal manner of speaking, his cold-blooded references to party discipline and historic determinism, while the insurrectionists are in danger of being exterminated, make of him almost a caricature. Far from glorifying the party, the novel, it would seem, points rather to modalities of betrayal by a party line. If at all concerned with ideology in action, it would rather tend to show how ideology and action come into conflict. In such a perspective, *La Con-dition humaine* may well appear as a perverse text.

But ideologies are never an end for Malraux. As old Gisors thinks of his son's commitment to the Revolution, he understands that all for which men agree to sacrifice themselves tends to translate the otherwise unbearable human condition into dignity. Historically, it might have been Christianity for the slave, nationalism for the patriot, Communism for the worker of today—it may be something else tomorrow. Ideas or ideologies are only an opportunity for heroic commitment and a quest for meaning. What counts is the struggle with the angel, the attempt to raise man above the mere contingency. And this precisely is the function of art: not representational, but revelatory. In the important preface to *Le Temps du mépris*, Malraux very clearly states that the function of art is to give men a consciousness of their own potential grandeur ("la grandeur qu'ils ignorent en eux"), that the novel must therefore not limit itself to the analysis of a unique character, but rather show man-as-hero facing the meaning he chooses to bestow upon life.

The misreading of Malraux's work, and of *La Condition humaine* in particular, can be traced to ideological assumptions or ideological demands we make on the text, as well as to reader habits of fiction dealing with psychological individualization. A concrete example might help. At the beginning of the novel, in Hemmelrich's record shop, the assembled revolutionaries listen to coded messages they have prepared. Kyo, who has helped make these records, is present as they are tested, but surprised that he does not hear his voice. The truth is that he does not recognize his voice. The apparently insignificant incident disturbs him, and remains on his mind. He is haunted by this inability to recognize himself, or part of himself. A number of pages later, he remembers that already once, long ago, he felt a similar uneasiness when, as a child, he was shown his own tonsils which the surgeon had just removed. Throughout the novel, the memory of this nonrecogniton of his own voice accompanies him. When he sees his father, he cannot prevent himself from talking about it; and Gisors explains that he has had similar experiences, for instance that of unexpectedly seeing himself in a mirror and not recognizing himself. But in these thematic repetitions and modulations, the original combat purpose of the records is totally forgotten. What emerges and remains is what, in the 1930s and 1940s, one liked to call "existential anguish." Kyo is disturbed by the incident of the record because he realizes that we do not perceive the world as we perceive ourselves. Neither plot nor ideology determines the development of this motif. It is, moreover, not limited to the single character of Kyo. From the moment he tells his father, the principle of thematic contamination is at work. The obsession of the record invades and pervades the text, as it invades and pervades the consciousness of Kyo. It is wedded to the intimation of a fundamental solitude ("la solitude immuable derrière la multitude mortelle"); it is later relived by Gisors and linked to the impossibility of knowing the other, even in love. And it does reappear at the hour of Kyo's death. The result of these thematic *reprises* is the immobilization of a supposed novel of action in the spatial form of a lyric or meditative construct. The diachronically oriented novel of revolutionary participation in the historic process turns out to demand a synchronic reading that takes it out of time and movement.

The title, of course, already calls for such a reading. *La Condition humaine:* the definite article, the substantive "condition" both abstract and generalizing, the adjective "humaine" suggesting universality and permanence—all point to a time outside, or beyond, the linear time of events and of history, a time of a fundamental and durable truth placed in immediate opposition to the specific date (21 March 1927) and the specific hour (half past midnight) of the first page. The philosophical resonance and continuity of a cultural code inscribed into this title further stress the transhistorical, universalizing signal. For the expression "condition humaine" echoes Pascal, and beyond him Montaigne. We are engaged in a dialogue across time. Pascal's tragic image comes to mind. "Imagine a number of men in chains and all condemned to death; some of them each day are slaughtered in full view of the others; those who remain recognize their own condition in that of their fellow men, and, looking at each other with grief and without hope, wait for their turn. This is the image of the human condition." ("C'est l'image de la condition des hommes.")

Early signals reveal a great deal about the intentionality of a text. It is not a matter of indifference that the first two syntactic units of the novel are brief interrogative sentences, that the interrogation points to a projected action, that they suggest a consciousness through a mediational free indirect discourse that abolishes from the outset a clear line of demarcation between object and subject, between the character in action and a pervasive state of awareness. The novel opens under the sign of an anguished question mark. The word *angoisse*—one of the key terms of the novel—does in fact appear at the beginning of the third sentence. Other images in the first paragraph point, however, to a sharp demarcation between an inside and an outside. The hotel room where the murder is about to be committed is separated from the world of everyday life ("le monde des hommes") by window bars, introducing early into the text the prison imagery that is to play such an important role. This nocturnal world of artificial light and shadows locks Ch'en up in a solemn aloneness (the word "solennel" appears). He discovers in himself a "sacrifacteur" rather than a fighter—a term that seems out of place in the description of a brutal practical action, and rather points to a religious ceremonial. There are in fact strong suggestions of initiation and communion. The murder is viewed as a ritual comparable—Ch'en later explains—to the loss of virginity. Between the murderer and his victim a strange current is established. Not only is the blade, as Malraux writes, "sensitive to the very tip," but a current of unbearable anguish passes from the struck body to Ch'en's convulsive heart. Moreover, before he strikes, Ch'en performs a strange act: he directs the dagger against himself and stabs himself in the arm. A symbolic gesture, no doubt. But a symbol with what meaning? Return to reality? Solipsism (there are other suggestions of masturbatory determinants in his character)? Prefiguration of his own death in an act of futile terrorism? Blood pact with the victim? In any case, the thematic overture determines our own experience as we penetrate into the novel. Death and loneliness will remain concrete presences. At the moment Ch'en enters the room of the murder, he also enters a world of solitude. Even the traffic noises seem to come from another world. As Ch'en begins to tremble, Malraux explains: it was not fear, but "he was alone with death, alone in a place without men." The alley cat which suddenly appears seems like an obscene intrusion into the untamed region of silence and intoxication where solitude and death are revealed as the elemental facts of human existence.

Solitude, associated with death, thus comes into dialectical tension with action in the overture of the novel. The deconstruction of the activist mode seems further intensified by the position of centrality occupied by Kyo's father, old Gisors. At the time when the antihumanist stance implied a breach with the fathers, Malraux in a noteworthy fashion reinstalls the paternal figure, thereby retrieving a cultural continuity dear to him. This alone might explain Gisors's structural importance. Again the opening signals are determining: Ch'en's first impulse after the murder is to see Gisors, to whom the longest section of the First Part is devoted. And he is still the available interlocutor in the closing pages of the book. Father, teacher, midwife and mediator to everybody's ideas, he is, however, also the most radically separated from action. He is like a conscience in which all thought finds an echo and a prolongation, almost a symbol of absolute intelligence, as well as the depository of some important truths. Yet this opium smoker and art lover, though a Marxist mentor to a generation of revolutionists, is also the paralyzed intellectual, suffering from insomnia and the awareness of the irreducible tragedy of existence. He knows that the essence of man is anguish. He knows that despite his intelligence he can never penetrate another human being. Even love for his son cannot deliver him from his basic isolation. And so, just as Ch'en escapes to a wild region of terrorism, old Gisors seeks refuge in the realm of art and opium where he can contemplate his solitude.

The text plays out a series of counterpoints on intoxication and enclosure in the self. Eroticism in particular functions as a condemnation to self-entrapment. The power-obsessed, erotomaniac Ferral and his mistress Valérie may be well assorted partners for the games of the bed, but they remain strangers to each other and eventually become enemies. The sexual act turns out not to be a means of contact, but a lonely exercise performed by two people in close contact with each other, an exercise in which the body of the partner, and even the pleasure of the partner, is used for what is essentially like a "solitary vice." Ferral's sexual obsessions are directly linked to his need for power. Even his definition of intelligence (the "means to compel things and people") is like a program in rape. Pleasure itself is to be *inflicted*, like pain. The erotic obsession thus naturally gravitates toward sadism. The images are quite explicit. When Ferral, whose male ego has been bruised, dreams of avenging himself against Valérie, he has vision of his mistress strapped to a bed, being subjected to physical punishment. Ferral is moreover sexually doomed to solitude for the simple reason that eroticism is for him a means of humiliating the partner. Sex is for him what torture is for König. He takes pleasure in denying even a prostitute her dignity. Malraux explains that Ferral never went to bed with anyone but himself: "il ne couchait jamais qu'avec lui-même."

There are still other forms of solitude, as many it would seem as there are sinners and punishments in the circles of Dante's hell. Even compassion is doomed. Trying to console a comrade, himself helpless in the face of suffering, Katov cannot find the appropriate words and gestures, and discovers once again how few and how awkward the expressions of manly affection are. Perhaps the extreme manifestation of loneliness is provided by the mythomaniacal, fiction-making baron de Clappique, buffoonish amateur of Chinese antiques, émigré prostitutes, and especially dry martinis—a character who originally occupied an even larger place in the novel. Imaginative spinner of tales, sad clown traversing life as though he were eternally disguised, Clappique finds his intoxication in the identities he assumes, in the fictional universe into which he vanishes. He even indulges in dreams of suicide—but that too is a role he plays, as he stands in front of a mirror making gargoyle-like faces at himself, carnival grimaces for which the muscles of the face no longer suffice, and he uses his fingers, enlarging his mouth for toad-like effects, drawing out the corners of his eyes—grimaces through which he loses his identity. And no statement could be sadder and more profoundly true than the one this inveterate joker makes as he takes leave of one of the characters: "Goodbye my dear. The only man in Shanghai who does not exist . . . salutes you."

In the face of an inventory of loneliness that opium, sex, murder, pity, fiction-making cannot cure, but can only accentuate, what answers does the novel provide? There is of course the answer of art itself—not as Clappique understands it (as an attempt to introduce artifice into the act of living), but in the almost religious sense that the painter Kama bestows on his work. Kama's ideas are significantly brought out in a dialogue with Clappique—a dialogue whose symbolic meaning is stressed by the mediation of Kama's revelatory word through the offices of a disciple-interpreter. He literally and figuratively speaks another language. The presence of Kama in the context of revolutionary action is in itself a signal of deconstructive reading confirmed by the epilogue taking place in Kama's house, to the accompaniment of his serene music. The answer that Kama provides, in the exchange with Clappique, illuminates the function of art as a mystic and therefore passive acceptance of the world, a semiotic communion with all there is, a harmony found in art's ability to overcome solitude and to overcome even death, an infinitely regressive movement from sign to sign toward God. Malraux himself, in nonfictional texts, referred to art as an antisolitude and an antideath. Yet it is interesting to note that in *La Condition humaine*, in the context of activist commitment, such a view of art would seem to affirm, at face value, a spiritual escapism. Gisors, who is witness to this conversation between Kama and Clappique, finds such serenity almost an insult to those who have chosen political responsibility and political risks: "aujourd'hui la sérénité était presque une insulte." But of course Gisors himself is drawn toward the contemplative mode represented by Kama. At the end of the novel, he seeks refuge in his house in Kobe. The novel thus maintains an irresolvable tension between doing and thinking, between the desire to change the world and to meditate about it, between immanent violence and the yearning for transcendance.

That is why the other options—militant action and party discipline—are also seen as partial answers at best to the basic anguish of man's fate. When Ch'en, carrying in his briefcase the bomb with which he plans to kill Chang Kai Chek, meets his former teacher, the Lutheran minister Smithson, and is confronted with the question: "What political faith will account for the suffering in the world?" he has an answer ready. He does not wish to account for suffering, he wants to diminish it. But Smithson has a more searching question, "What political faith will destroy death?" And to this question Ch'en of course has no answer.

Solidarity, collective heroism, would seem to be means of retrieving a fundamental meaning. Malraux likes to sing the virtues of "virile fraternity." The word "dignity" is almost proposed as a magic formula. Such terms or notions may appear fuzzy if one pits them against realities measurable by political science. Malraux, however, treats them as transcendental values. And transcendence has little to do with a political message. It is crucially important to any interpretation of the novel that the most dramatic scene— the schoolyard assembly of the political prisoners who are to be executed, all staring into the unmasked face of their destiny—should be an unmistakable allusion to Pascal's famous "pensée"—the very image evoked by the title of the book: "Imagine a number of men in chains." Though God or the gods are dead or absent in the world of Malraux, the notion of the *sacré* remains. As Kyo and Katov lie side by side in the space reserved for those who will be burned alive, they feel tied to each other by that absolute friendship without reticence which, according to Malraux, death alone can give. They live their intense moments of communion. The schoolyard scene, like a volet in a diptych, is an answer to the opening scene of the novel, when solitude and death appeared as the very foundation of man's existence. This eventual destruction of loneliness through death (or love in death), Kyo already experienced when May wanted to accompany him on a dangerous mission and he realized that "the willingness to lead the being one loves to death itself is perhaps the complete expression of love, the one that cannot be surpassed."

These themes of religious communion and spiritual transcendence are textually verifiable. First, in the suggested mystery of the contact beyond words, in the undermining of the power of language, Malraux makes it clear, in *La Condition humaine* as elsewhere, that there exists for him a reality beyond verbal expression, that the truly fundamental experiences of man are not known but perceived. The bleeding body speaks a meaning that language cannot speak. At the tensest moment in the schoolyard scene, when the merciful poison is dropped to the ground, it is the hands, not the voice, that give the consolation and the love: hands brushing each other, taking hold of each other, clutching each other in a desperate fraternity. But more telling even are the semantic and metaphoric constructs: suggestions of apocalypse (the night of collective agony is called a "dernière nuit"); the doomed insurrectionists are compared to the martyrs of hagiographic legends ("légendes dorées"); their heroic association is termed a "mendicant order of the Revolution," metaphorizing it into a sacrificial religious community; the word "resurrection" appears twice. And there is little doubt that Malraux meant Katov, who sacrifices himself and takes upon himself the fear and the suffering of others, to loom as a Christ-like figure. Many pages earlier, he already appears to one of the characters with his "open hands like Jesus Christ, waiting to be pierced by nails." In his final moments, the words "human dignity" have an almost holy ring. Katov murmurs these words to himself as he is about to make the supreme sacrifice. He remembers what Kyo told him of his confrontation with the head of the secret police, and of König's irritated, angry question: "What do you call dignity? It doesn't mean anything." It is no doubt because Katov is about to give this negation the lie that Malraux has him approach death in a manner that suggests an apotheosis. As he slowly limps to the door, amongst the wounded comrades who follow his walk with love and awe, a religious silence falls in spite of the moans, the lantern projects Katov's shadow against the wall and the shadow grows until the outline of his head vanishes into the ceiling. Katov's love reaffirms the image of man in the face of the eternal torturer determined to deny this image. Malraux is explicit in *Antimémoires*. Degradation is Satan for Malraux.

Katov's stance, his self-sacrifice, have to be replaced in a larger context. The ritual of cruelty reenacts the derision of Christ, reenacts an eternal Passion.

Such redemptive images qualify the heroic strains in Malraux's work. Texts that follow *La Condition humaine* increasingly reach out to the pathos of universality as well as to an almost religious symbolization of violence. Again in *Antimémoires*, which often reads like a rereading of his own work, the long pages devoted to prison camps and torture illumine his life-long struggle to retrieve the image of man. "May God grant each of us the grace of consoling a companion." This is the theme of the sermon which the priest in the concentration camp delivers to the disease-ridden, beaten, crippled inmates. Characteristically, the subject of his sermon is not the Nativity, but the Calvary.

The retrieval of the image of man in a world of human violence bent on denying this image is perhaps nowhere more powerfully inscribed than into the most dramatic pages of *Les Noyers de l'Altenburg*—pages, in fact, that must be counted among the most haunting in all of twentieth century literature. This novel was to be part of a trilogy with a biblical title, "La Lutte avec l'ange." Malraux never completed the trilogy, but the book we have is one of the key texts in his corpus. The central section of it is given over to a symposium of anthropologists and ethnographers gathered to discuss the permanence of the concept of man. Is the dialogue between cultures possible, is there a valid notion of man transcending time and space? Or is man separated from himself by barriers of custom, ideology and ethnic difference? Is he to himself, in his changes and transformations, as the butterfly is to the caterpillar? The question involves not only the survival of the species, but the justification of man as possessed with a unique destiny. It is a central question not only in the novel, but in Malraux's entire intellectual adventure. The answer, however, does not come from the assembled intellectuals who engage in vain rhetoric. The answer, once again, comes from an experience of violence, is revealed through the frontline soldiers' reactions, whose voices seem to emerge from an "obscurité primitive." On the Eastern Front, during World War I, the German high command has decided to experiment with a new chemical weapon. It is already significant that the arrival of the scientist is greeted by frontline officers with dismay. It is he who appears as the enemy, an intellectual intruding into the world of war to destroy the notion of courage. But the real significance emerges when the German soldiers, after the gas has been released, advance through the scorched, lunar landscape, across the black grass and the dead wood, to penetrate into the defenseless enemy trenches, and to the surprise of the field officers watching from afar, fail to advance to the second line of trenches. Instead, they return to their own, each soldier carrying a gasping, choking, fatally wounded enemy. The horror has been too much for man to bear. Man is not made to be thus disintegrated and to watch it happen without a profound sense of rebellion. ("Non, l'homme n'est pas fait pour être moisi!") The assault wave has been metamorphosed into an assault of pity. Malraux's myth proposed the revelation of something fundamental in man that remains indestructible.

Since the literary account of the revelatory experience comes from an irrational depth ("élan venu de très loin dans les temps"), this questions the status of literature, the validity of the literary act. For Malraux, the immediate, unmediated event could even be betrayed by art. It is not the esthetic construct, least of all the "Wortkunstwerk," that brings about communion or even understanding. Passion, in the etymological sense of suffering, becomes the only possible silent language for a universal communion. Or rather: through silence and suffering, Malraux attempts to read a language behind language. Life for him is not, as it is for Proust, the servant of art. For Malraux, artistic symbols mediate a communication that exists because gesture itself and suffering are endowed with pathos and meaning. The implied truth of art suggests a paradox. Repeatedly, in *L'Espoir* for instance, Malraux has his characters worry about the meaning of art in the face of real blood and real suffering. "Que valent les mots en face d'un corps déchiqueté?" (What value have words in front of a torn up body?") Manuel's question, as he hears the screams of a wounded aviator, is echoed throughout *L'Espoir* in many registers: As Magnin visits another badly hurt aviator about to be amputated: "C'est peu, une idée, en face de deux jambes à couper." And more symbolically, this statement about large spots of blood in front of two paintings: "Art is of little weight in the face of suffering, and unhappily no painting holds up in the face of blood stains."

But old Alvear, in the same novel, chooses to believe that music and poetry are valid for life as well as for death, that only art can embrace the fundamental truths of both suffering and meaning. And so the dialogue continues. The meaning of art is bound up with art's struggle with meaning. And it is this struggle, as I suggested earlier, which is implied in Malraux's special, and so to speak nonreligious use of the word *sacré*. Just as Malraux explains, at the beginning of his *Antimémoires*, that he is not concerned with what only concerns him, so he is not concerned, in art, with what can only be accounted for in artistic terms. Neither formalist, nor structuralist, he conceives of *art sacré* as speaking to those who believe in the "mystery of the world" (a "secret du monde"). And all life becomes mystery when questioned by suffering. That is Malraux's formula at the end of *Antimémoires*: "toute

vie devient mystère lorsqu'elle est interrogée par la douleur." If masterpieces
are immortal, it is not only because they live in an "ungraspable time" (an
"insaisissable temps"), as he puts it in his book on Picasso, *La Tête d'obsidienne*,
but because they read into man's every gesture the grandeur of man's awareness of his mortality. And such awareness transcends political and cultural
differences. It is this attempt to read the "sacred" notion of art back into the
humblest manifestations of the human condition that explains why Malraux
has repeatedly been tempted by a very unorthodox kind of art history, or
rather by the fiction of an imaginary museum that brings into dialogue with
each other artifacts of different ages and civilizations—Renaissance paintings,
Celtic coins, Pompeian paving blocks, Byzantine mosaics—all revealing,
through the life of forms, a common struggle against solitude and death.
Early in his life, at a time Western thought was assailed by a post-war
Spenglerian pessimism, Malraux intuited that civilizations saved themselves
through the artistic forms they created, that man can overcome his own fear
of nonbeing. Increasingly, as he himself came closer to death that so obsessed
him, he felt that he was right in stating that the first man who sculpted a
human figure liberated man from the monsters, that every work of art was
a victory, a lasting defiance of man's inevitable undoing. Beyond the courage
of action, Malraux sings a more tragic courage: the courage of creating, in
the face of absurdity and despair, the concepts and the images that are the
only means of "negating our nothingness" and of humanizing the world.

NINA S. TUCCI

The Orient as Western Man's "Shadow" in Malraux's La Tentation de l'Occident

In his book *The Novelist as Philosopher*, John Cruickshank has explained the trend toward philosophical fiction in twentieth-century French literature as resulting from the almost total breakdown of metaphysical certainty in our time. He goes on to add that authors such as Sartre, Beckett, Simone de Beauvoir, Camus, Malraux and others, each in his own way, felt that they could no longer afford the luxury of creating works that merely "entertain." Rather, literary creation should offer as complete an overview as possible of the metaphysical status of man. For these authors and others, then, the process of writing can no longer fall into the category of a profession or "un métier" but becomes a creative spiritual adventure.

André Malraux, for one, who had espoused the Nietzschean idea that "God is dead" and who feared that Man, purported to have been created in his image and likeness, was also dead, sought not only to describe Western man's anguish at being left without an Absolute but also to explore new avenues to revalidate the individual and give new purpose to his existence. Beginning with *La Tentation de l'Occident*, which he followed with a series of fictional works, namely, the Asiatic trilogy (*La Voie royale*, *Les Conquérants*, *La Condition humaine*) and the Occidental trilogy (*Le Temps du mépris*, *L'Espoir*, *Les Noyers de l'Altenburg*), Malraux establishes a dialogue with the East which he actually pursued throughout his literary career. It is *La Tentation* which engages our interest here.

La Tentation de l'Occident (1926) is an epistolary work in which Malraux constructs a dialogue between the Westerner A.D. and the Chinaman Ling,

From *L'Esprit Createur* 22, no. 2 (Summer 1982). © 1982 by *L'Esprit Createur*.

in which each expresses his impressions of the other's culture. Now the immediate pressing question would seem to be this: What would a dialogue with the ever-mysterious East yield for the West? If we transpose the divergent philosophical attitudes of the Orient and the Occident to the realm of psychology, then perhaps the Jungian apperception would provide some far-reaching insights. On an individual level, Jungian psychology would explain the Ling-A.D. dialogue by means of the "shadow" principle, that is, that Ling represents the unlived side of A.D. and vice versa. Jung describes the shadow as being composed of the dark elements of the personality, those elements which have been repressed and have slipped into the unconscious.

The "shadow" or the "eastern" side of the personality, as it is sometimes called, has also been variously referred to as the Yin of Yang, being as opposed to doing, introversion versus extroversion. From this vantage point, Ling and A.D. can be viewed as two psychic figures which represent the East and West within Malraux's own psyche. However, from the Jungian optic, the shadow is not limited solely to the realm of the personal unconscious. It is also an archetype. An archetype, as Jung defines it, belongs to the collective unconscious, and, as such, is the matrix of a whole complex of attitudes and behavior. It is in this connection that we can speak of another culture. In his book *Turning East*, Harvey Cox sheds much light on this particular point. There he says that:

> Societies like individuals develop some traits at the expense of others. But the repressed elements never simply die. They lurk there in the psyche seeking some means of expression. Consequently, every people harbors a fretful fascination for its polar opposite, its "shadow self." As the Yin of the Western Yang, its power to fascinate the Western mind is infinite.

Cox's explanation of the "shadow" also greatly clarifies Malraux's investigation of a culture which does not repose on the concept of the individual as does the West.

Malraux looked to the Orient for the general base of thought developed by an essentially introverted culture that could be metamorphosed and assimilated into the Western psyche, thus creating a new man. In his attempt to create a synthesis between East and West, Malraux sought to rekindle the dormant Oriental shadow in each one of us. For, in essence, what do the terms Oriental-Occidental denote? Occidental has become synonymous with the material world, scientific progress, action, etc. The term Oriental has come to mean introspection, meditation, psychic proficiency on all levels. Yet the ability to be an introvert as well as an extrovert, as Jung has established, belongs to every individual and, through development, can affect an entire culture. Ling seems to be well aware of the ambivalent nature of the human psyche when he states that "un cerveau peut servir à des fins différentes." And it is also Ling who defines the fundamental lines of demarcation between the Orient and the Occident when he writes to A.D. that the Oriental wants "to be" and the Occidental wants "to do."

Though Ling is an affective part of Malraux himself, it would be inaccurate to say that Ling represents an emotionally assimilated part of Malraux's psyche. Actually, what Malraux is doing in this initial stage of his spiritual quest is to personify this "shadow" aspect of his being in order to conduct an objective study of how the Oriental (Ling) as opposed to the Occidental (A.D.) views the world. Let us now summarize Ling's observations as they reveal themselves, for example, in the domains of metaphysics, time, human relationships and art. Or, better still, let us allow the "shadow" to speak.

Ling teaches us that the basic Oriental tenet of "to be" consists in the ideal state of living in union with the Divine Principle. This mode of existence minimizes the ego (individuality) in favor of the Self, that particle of divinity which every man possesses, and which enables him, through sustained meditation, to contact and become one with the all-pervasive power that governs the cosmos. In this heightened state of awareness he knows himself to be but a fragment of the whole. This metaphysical orientation contrasts greatly with the Occidental concept of the supremacy of the individual in the order of the universe. This self-aggrandizement, as Ling points out, steeped in Greek and Christian traditions, led Occidental man to make himself master of the universe through the dialectic of action ("to do"). Through the gradual exteriorization of the Self, Occidental man became synonymous with his actions and lost contact with, or denied the presence of, a Supreme Power. "Vous vous confondez avec vos actions," asserts Ling.

The Occident literally exudes the attitudes of a civilization disposed "à l'action," a civilization that wants to impose order on the chaotic multiplicity of the world, that wants to systematize all planes of reality and to integrate them into the unity of a synthesis. Ling sees the Occident as "un pays dévoré par la géométrie." On the strength of his individuality, the Occidental aspires to what one of the characters of *Les Conquérants* will evoke later in these words: "laisser une cicatrice sur la carte." This same idea is expressed in other terms by A.D.: "Il y a en lui [l'Occidental] une tentative de conquérir le temps, d'en faire le prisonnier des formes." In short, the very nature of the Occident seems to be to reduce the world to human proportions. This is basically the attitude which Ling defines when he says that the Occident seeks to exercise control over the universe and when he labels the Occident as the land "où l'idée de la civilisation et celle de l'ordre sont chaque jour confondues."

One can deduce from the above that the Occidental, contrary to the Oriental, who does not consider himself a simple link in an established order, wants to endure. Ling concludes that "les méditations dont le moi a été en Occident l'objet, se sont attachées surtout à sa permanence." It is to this narrow metaphysical posture that Ling attributes "l'impossibilité où se trouve l'Europe de saisir une réalité quelconque," and he compares the Occidentals "à des savants forts sérieux qui noteraient avec soin les mouvements des poissons, mais qui n'auraient pas découvert que ces poissons vivent dans l'eau."

In the realm of relationship, A.D. defines Occidental as being "des existences emmurées." All communication between individuals is doomed to failure, for how can one know another when one does not have access to oneself? Ling exposes the Occidental problem of alienation in the domain of love. In the Orient there is no conflict. All that exists in a predestined order has its own intrinsic function. The role of the woman, explains Ling, is "d'être toujours passive. Comme une maladie mortelle, elle est constante et sans espoir. La possession, ni même la certitude de la réciprocité ne l'affaiblissent." She is void of any individual mark and the affective boundaries of sentiment of the partners never cross because "l'homme et la femme appartiennent à une espèce différente," and it is not "au pouvoir des hommes de fermer au flanc des destins les blessures éternelles."

In the Occident Love, which is also linked to metaphysical values, manifests itself otherwise. Ling sees in it the residue of the Christian heritage: conquest and unity. Although separated from God, the Occidental, haunted by the spectre of his individualism, refuses to be conquered because he is not successful in separating himself from the notion of the divine. He draws from his own resources and seeks to attribute a permanent value to his passion in order to transcend his finite condition. This attitude translates itself into conquest to assuage the omnipresent nostalgia of the Absolute. The Occidental wants to affirm himself: "Etre soi-même et l'autre, éprouver ses sensations propres et celles du partenaire. Tout le jeu érotique est là."

Ling carries these antinomic attitudes into the domain of art. He attests that the real artist is not one who "creates," as in the Occident, but the one who "feels." Oriental painting "n'imite pas, ne représente pas: elle signifie." The Occidental judges the merit of a work by comparing it with others. Ling complains that the museum teaches: "Les maîtres y sont enfermés; ils discutent. Ce n'est pas leur rôle, ni le nôtre de les écouter." Whereas the

Oriental artist seeks to be cognizant of the irreconcilable differences in the universe, the Occidental artist proceeds "d'analogies évidentes . . . à d'autres plus cachées" in the attempt to attain a knowledge of totality. The Oriental seeks an ordered sensibility; the Occidental, an ordered mind. Ling synthesizes his observations made during his sojourn in the Occident in these terms: "Vous avez fait à la puissance l'offrande de votre vie. . . . Votre pensée même . . . à peine comprenez-vous encore que pour être il ne soit pas nécessaire d'agir, et le monde vous transforme bien plus que vous ne le transformez."

Having briefly delineated the major differences between the Orient and the Occident in the real of metaphysics, time, human relationships and art as proposed by Ling and A.D., let us now return to the original question of how the West could profit from such an inquiry.

Earlier we suggested that according to the Jungian mode of thought, Ling represented a part of the human psyche that had fallen into disuse in the West. Here we should add that the Jungian concept of the "shadow" contains both negative and positive elements. Malraux responded to the Nietzschean cry that "God is dead" by "passing over" to the Orient to study how that culture participated in Being. He discovered that, for the Oriental, destiny unravels in the supra-human domain and is divorced from human contingency. Being expresses itself through the Oriental, and he is only a witness of the cosmic unfolding: "l'Oriental irresponsable s'efforce de se lever au-dessus d'un conflit dont il n'est pas l'enjeu." Destiny for the Occidental is relegated to the sphere of human activity ("to do"), something to be mastered and contained.

Given these divergent points of view, then, the solution to the West's metaphysical dilemma, concludes Malraux, cannot lie in a servile imitation of Oriental myths: "Traduire en mythes la pensée des hommes essentiellement différents de nous: former de ces mythes une expérience? . . . Non." And so, even though Malraux tolls the knell of Christianity, he refuses the Oriental solution. To the various postulations offered by Ling, A.D. has only one answer: "La plus belle proposition de mort n'est solution que pour la faiblesse." Clearly, the dialgoue of *La Tentation* is a dialogue between two condemned absolutes. C. G. Jung summed it up by explaining that "mankind could not stand the stress of this polarity, so it followed either the personal . . . or the impersonal; both, taken alone, are rational erroneous ways of religious thought, due to the too great strength of man's rational power."

On the other end of the spectrum, however, a confrontation with the "shadow" could prove very fruitful. Still persisting along Jungian lines, we shall say that, initially, one meets the "shadow" outside of oneself in another

individual. In a word, A.D.'s psychic possibilities for being became available
to him because they were mirrored in Ling, and vice versa. For although
Malraux focuses mainly on the West "passing over" to the East in *La Tentation*,
he also points out that, conversely, the East is moving West. A.D. writes
to Ling: "Voici presque deux ans que j'observe la Chine. Ce qu'elle a trans-
formé d'abord en moi, c'est l'idée occidentale de l'Homme. Je ne puis plus
concevoir l'Homme indépendant de son intensité." Ling, traveling in the
West, becomes poignantly aware of the fact that the Oriental propensity for
being all but stifled his ability to act ("to do"): "Hélas! j'aurai voulu trouver
là la force dont ma race a un si douleureux besoin."

Another essential aspect of the "shadow" that needs to be taken into
consideration is that all the potential qualities that remain dormant in the
unconscious, and have not yet entered an individual's character and his
actions, remain, understandably, undeveloped and infantile. Contact with
the East made Malraux keenly aware of the fact that an almost exclusive
concentration on the individual in the West had resulted in a loss of universal
consciousness of the ability "to be." Yet he also knew that a literal transposition of the Oriental ideal of a collective consciousness would be unac-
ceptable for the Westerner. The basic symbols that express a culture are not
transferable. What Malraux hoped for in facing his Eastern "shadow" was
to reactivate the archetypal spirit of "to be" which he felt belonged to the
psychic heritage of man both East and West. For as John Donne has so aptly
put it: "A man must have within him, somehow, what he finds in another"
(*The Way of all the Earth*). But then, after he has "passed over" to another
individual or another culture, he must return from his odyssey to his own
life, his own culture.

This treatment of the East as Western man's "shadow" also gives added
dimensions to the "God is dead" theory of the Western world. Harvey Cox
says that the "turn East" is the logical outcome of the death of God. Why?
Because, both on the individual and cultural levels, we could say that the
Western Yang ("to do") had exhausted all possibilities to heal the West's
metaphysical wounds. Therefore, Western man has no alternative but to
take upon himself the responsibility of bringing his "shadow" to consciousness and transforming it. Not a vicarious experience of Eastern spirituality,
"plutôt expérience de nos possibilités, de nos tendances encore larvaires, de
tout ce qui, en nous peut prendre forme et participer à notre vie profonde"
(Malraux, "Journal").

In *La Tentation de l'Occident*, which Henri Peyre characterized as "a
brilliant ideological debate between two poles of thought and sensibility,"
Malraux initiated an intellectual dialogue with the Orient. However, intel-

lectual awareness only constitutes the first step in the individuation process, as Jung would call it. Emotional assimilation of psychic content requires that one submit to a process of initiation. This means that purely Oriental concepts as they have been outlined by Ling must die in order to be reborn again in their Western form. This story of the assimilation of the shadow will unfold in the Oriental and Occidental trilogies to which we have alluded at the beginning of the present essay. The dialogue in these novels is no longer a clear-cut exchange of ideas, as in *La Tentation*, but rather a delicate absorption of Oriental-Occidental modes of thought brought to life by the heroes, each engaged in his own initiation process. For bringing the "shadow," both personal and archetypal, to light amounts to "forming the self-image, and initial expression of the self, or else, the representation of the self to be realized." For Malraux it is both. In *La Tentation*, Malraux's great fictional spiritual quest to create a balance between "to be" and "to do" has only just begun.

SUSAN RUBIN SULEIMAN

The Model Relativized: Malraux's L'Espoir

Despite a narrative technique that emphasizes fragmentation and the multiplicity of points of view (a technique that in principle acts against mon-
ologism), the primary structure of *L'Espoir* is that of a simple confrontation:
the Republican side is massively and unproblematically right and good in
its fight against Franco. No matter how confused and "embrouillés" the
details may be, the overall meaning of the war is clear. Every time one of
the Republican heroes expresses his views on why he is fighting (from the
simple peasant Barca, who states that "the opposite of humiliation is brotherhood" to the Catholic intellectual Guernico, who says: "I've *seen* the Spanish
people. This war is their war, whatever happens; and I shall stay with them"),
his words must be taken as a privileged interpretation. Indeed, over and
above individual and political differences (which I will get to in a moment),
there is virtual unanimity within the heroic group concerning the values for
whose triumph the struggle is being waged: human dignity, human brotherhood, social justice. The Republicans are on the side of the Spanish people.
Franco's forces hate the people (compare the bombardment of Madrid); the
values they represent are those of oppression and humiliation.

Insofar as its absolute division between the "good" and "bad" sides is
concerned, *L'Espoir* conforms, then, to the confrontation model in a quite
simple way. It also realizes the model through the collective hero and the
actantial configuration.

All this may seem too obvious to be worth mentioning. Yet, some of
the better known critical interpretations of the novel, by playing down the

From *Authoritarian Fictions.* © 1983 by Columbia University Press.

importance of this primary confrontation structure, end up curiously skewed. Lucien Goldmann, for example, places exclusive emphasis on what he calls Malraux's "Stalinist perspective"; W. M. Frohock [in *Malraux and the Tragic Imagination*] sees a conflict between Malraux's "intentions as artist" and his "intentions as propagandist." These interpretations focus on what I call a secondary, "relativized" confrontation—but, paradoxically, they treat this confrontation as an antagonistic one; and they underestimate the importance of the primary (antagonistic) confrontation that is its context.

The secondary, "relativized" version of the confrontation model is realized in the ongoing discussion that occurs within the Republican ranks, concerning the problem of means versus ends. This discussion takes place essentially between the Communists, who argue for the primacy of organization and discipline, and the anarchists and Catholics, who argue for the primacy of ethics and spontaneous human feeling. The fact that the discussion is given emphasis in the novel constitutes a perturbation in the primary antagonistic structure. As we saw, the antagonistic model requires a heroic group that is ideologically united. By recognizing the existence of serious divergences within the Republican ranks, *L'Espoir* yields to the pressure of historical fact: the Republicans *were* divided. For some observers like Orwell, the internal strife between anarchists, Trotskyists, and Communists became in a sense the primary event of the war. Malraux tries to minimize the internal strife by suggesting that everyone is in agreement about the ultimate values for which the war is being fought, and by emphasizing the necessary union of the rival factions in the face of the enemy.

The primary confrontation structure is perturbed, then, by a secondary confrontation between members of the heroic group. But this secondary confrontation is not at all simple nor antagonistic. Admittedly, the novel leaves no doubt that the defenders of organization and discipline are "right." That is why Goldmann accuses Malraux of having adopted, in this instance, a deplorably Stalinist perspective. According to Goldmann, the novel's thesis can be summed up as follows: "Everything that is immediately and spontaneously human must be banished and even abolished in the name of an exclusive concern for efficiency." In terms of such a reading, Manuel's gradual transformation into a hard-bitten military chief is a positive exemplary apprenticeship that proves the thesis of "efficiency (efficacité)": Manuel's troops are in large part responsible for the major victory at Guadalajara, with which the novel closes. Conversely, the Catholic officer Hernandez, who commands the Republican forces at the siege of Toledo and tries to put ethics before discipline (he allows the besieged Francoist general Moscardo to send a letter to his wife), pays for his lack of efficiency with his life. The defeat of the Republicans at Toledo shows that without disciplined and organized leadership, even a good cause is doomed to fail. Hernandez himself recognizes, on his way to the fascist firing squad, that "to be generous is to be the victor (la générosité, c'est d'être vainqueur)."

Goldmann cites a large number of statements by various characters as evidence that the "Stalinist" argument in favor of discipline ("organiser l'Apocalypse," "transformer la guérilla en armée," etc.) is massively supported and illustrated in the novel. What he does not sufficiently emphasize, however, is that this argument is itself only the minor premise of a larger argument whose major premise is as follows: "This is a war which *must* be won by the 'good' side." The necessity of discipline is presented as a necessity *of the moment*. It is the context and the pressure of the war—which is a "holy war"—that makes even certain non-Communist characters, whose profound values are not those of hierarchy and discipline, bow to that necessity. Goldmann, in other words, overlooks the importance of the primary confrontation in the novel. This leads him not only to place exclusive emphasis on what he considers a pernicious argument, but also to ignore the complex and altogether relative way in which it is presented.

If the novel presents a "Stalinist" thesis, one can only say that it does so reluctantly. It is significant that the most consistent spokesman for the thesis of efficiency, the commander Garcia, is not a Communist (Goldmann refers to him as "le communiste Garcia") and has only a grudging admiration for the Communists. In one of the major discussion scenes, when a Communist bureaucrat tells an anarchist that "concretely, there can be no politics with your ethics," Garcia intervenes: "The complication, and maybe the tragedy of the revolution is that there can be none without it either." At the end of the novel, after the "transformation of the guerilla into an army" promises an ultimate victory for the Republicans, the aviator Magnin, another non-Communist, asks Garcia what he thinks of the Communists. Garcia replies: "My friend Guernico says: 'They have all the virtues of action—and those alone!' But right now, it's action we are dealing with." Garcia is thus presented not as a Stalinist ideologue, but as a combatant in a just war who *must* choose efficiency and effectiveness ("efficacité" has both meanings) over generosity or nobility of heart, even while recognizing the moral superiority of the latter.

This choice, while affirmed as necessary, is also seen as tragic—not only by Garcia, but by others who defend the thesis of efficiency, including Manuel, who is a Communist. On his way to becoming an effective commander, Manuel becomes increasingly aware of the price he is obliged to pay. Toward the end of the novel, after having ordered the execution of two deserters, Manuel tells his former commander, the Catholic officer Ximénès: "I take responsibility for those executions: they were done in order to save the other men, our own. But listen here: every single step I've taken toward greater efficiency and better leadership has separated me more from my fellowmen." One of Garcia's earlier remarks, made during a lengthy discussion between him and the art historian Scali, can be seen as an anticipatory comment on Manuel's tragic self-perception. Garcia tells Scali:

> "Du moment que nous sommes d'accord sur le point décisif, la résistance de fait, cette résistance est un acte: elle vous engage, comme tout acte, comme tout choix. Elle porte en elle-même toutes ses fatalités. Dans certains cas, ce choix est un choix tragique, et pour l'intellectuel il l'est presque toujours, pour l'artiste surtout. Et après? Fallait-il ne pas résister?"

> ("As long as we agree about the crucial point, the fact of resistance, that resistance is an act: it commits you, like any act, like any choice. It carries in itself all of its necessary consequences. In certain cases, this is a tragic choice, and for an intellectual it is almost always a tragic choice, especially for the artist. So what? Does that mean we shouldn't have resisted?")

This comment strikes me as crucial, not only because it presents a highly self-conscious and relative justification for the thesis of efficiency (efficiency is not affirmed as a *value*), but also because it functions as an internal commentary on the simple articulations of the confrontation model itself, as it is realized in the novel. To the intellectual and the artist, the mythic oppositions of the confrontation model must appear simplistic. Yet, in a just war one cannot elude the necessity of making simple choices; one is obliged to act, and "all action is Manichean." Like the artist Lopez in the novel, whose frescoes speak "a language of man in battle," *L'Espoir* simplifies and perhaps mythifies historical reality; but it also suggests that there are times when such simplification is obligatory—and good.

The running dialogue between various members of the heroic group (and the important point is that it *is* a dialogue, despite the fact that under the circumstances one of the positions appears more "correct" than the others), as well as the internal dialogue that takes place within characters like Garcia and Manuel, who seek justifications for their own positions to themselves, suggests that Malraux was fully aware of the problems posed by the pro-Communist efficiency argument, but was willing to advance it as the only way to win the war. By ignoring the complexities of its presentation and the context of the primary confrontation which makes it justifiable,

Goldmann flattened out the argument into a straightforward apology for Stalinism.

W. M. Frohock's reading of *L'Espoir* is more subtle, but I think that he too tends to underplay the significance of the primary confrontation. According to Frohock, the novel presents a "propaganda thesis" which consists in negating ethical values in favor of efficiency (this is identical to Goldmann's reading); but this thesis is contradicted, Frohock claims, by Malraux's "art," since the most emotionally charged scenes in the novel suggest that it is the ethical values that really matter. Frohock's prime example is the famous "descent from the mountain," where the wounded aviators are carried down in an atmosphere of solemn communion with the population. According to Frohock, "this scene glorifies the fraternity of men, precisely the fraternity which, according to the propaganda thesis of the novel, will not and cannot win revolutions! . . . The emotional effect on the reader . . . is directly opposed to the conclusions to which, as a propaganda piece, *Man's Hope* should have led him."

This is a very subtle argument, and one could construct a similar one for many a *roman à thèse* (I myself present an argument along somewhat similar lines [elsewhere]). But as far as *L'Espoir* is concerned, the argument seems to me unjustified. The contradiction in this novel is not "between" Malraux's thesis and his art. It is not the art that affirms or "glorifies" the value of fraternity while the thesis affirms the value of efficiency. It is the thesis, indissociable from the "art," that affirms both—arguing that in order to make human fraternity triumph (fraternity is *the* value of the Republican side), one must first win the war. The descent from the mountain is a reminder of what the war is all about (significantly, it takes place just before the victory of Guadalajara); the story of Manuel's evolution and Garcia's arguments for efficiency are a reminder that the war must be won.

The relativized, dialogical confrontation within the Republican ranks appears, finally, as only a "local" perturbation in the primary confrontation structure. Malraux avoids the really vexing issues between the Communists and the other political groups, and suggests that all the differences between them can be subordinated to the cause of winning the war. They did not win the war, and according to historians one reason for their defeat was precisely their lack of cooperation. This fact, however, does not invalidate Malraux's argument, and it certainly does not imply, as Goldmann suggests, that the argument itself "led not to victory, but to defeat." The argument itself was a hope, a call for unity that did not materialize. *L'Espoir*, like any novel of confrontation, masks some contradictions and prevents some questions from being asked.

The dialogism (admittedly a limited one, for after all the defenders of efficiency have the last word) that characterizes the confrontation within the Republican ranks is due to the fact that the adversaries are all ultimately on the "right" side. That is why, in relation to the primary antagonistic confrontation, this secondary one is only a "local" perturbation. There exists, however, another perturbation in the novel's primary confrontation structure that is more than local; it is the presence of a muted suggestion that the "holy war" itself may not be all important. According to the confrontation model, nothing can take precedence over the fight for a just cause. That is why the confrontational hero must be subordinated to the heroic group. Malraux, however, allows the old art historian Alvear to affirm even in the midst of the bombardment of Madrid: "I want a man to be responsible to himself and not to a cause, even if the cause is that of the oppressed"—an idea that puts into question, or at least into an "other" perspective, the whole enterprise of confrontation. One of the most often quoted sentences in the novel, Garcia's statement that the best thing a man can do with his life is "to transform into consciousness the widest experience possible," has a similar effect, since it subordinates the holy war to individual experience. Even Manuel, who has totally accepted the necessities of military action and the price it costs him, is able to envisage a future where confrontation will no longer be a pertinent category ("One day there would be peace. And Manuel would become another man, unknown to himself"). Finally, the very discreet narrator himself suggests that there are certain things more important than even a just war. The novel closes with Manuel listening, during a momentary pause after the victory of Guadalajara, to Beethoven's music:

> Ces mouvements musicaux qui se succédaient, roulés dans son passé, parlaient comme eût pu parler cette ville qui jadis avait arrêté les Maures, et ce ciel et ces champs éternels; Manuel entendait pour la première fois la voix de ce qui est plus grave que le sang des hommes, plus inquiétant que leur présence sur la terre:—la possibilité infinie de leur destin: et il sentait en lui cette présence mêlée au bruit des ruisseaux et au pas des prisonniers, permanente et profonde comme la battement de son coeur.

> (Those musical movements that succeeded each other, rolled up in his past, spoke the way that city which long ago had stopped the Moors might have spoken, and that sky and those eternal fields; Manuel was hearing for the first time the voice of what is graver than the blood of men, more disquieting than their presence on earth:—the infinite possibility of their destiny; and he

felt in himself that presence joined to the sound of the running streams and to the march of the prisoners, permanent and deep like the beating of his heart.)

If the infinite possibility of human destiny is graver even than the blood of men (one section of *L'Espoir* is entitled "Sang de gauche"), then the open-endedness of this novel is *qualitatively* different from the potential open-endedness of any confrontation story: it is the difference between radical, unforeseeable change and mere repetition-with-variations.

To conclude: I think that *L'Espoir* is a *roman à thèses*, with the emphasis on the plural (it presents at least two theses: the necessity of fighting against fascism, and the necessity for discipline in order to win); at the same time, it is conscious of the difficulty of certain choices, and makes this difficulty one of the privileged subjects of the fiction. In less complex (or more simply monological) romans à thèse, the "right" choice is never problematic—even if some people are unable to make it—for the values involved are absolutes. In *L'Espoir*, the struggle against fascism is an absolute value; but after that the choices become more complicated, and even the "right" choice is affirmed as problematic—literally, it poses problems. Furthermore, this choice is not seen as a way of acceding to an authentic being or selfhood. Manuel's being remains open to the infinite possibility of his destiny—he is not defined as a "chief" once and for all. In its openness to the future and in its recognition of the complexity of certain choices, *L'Espoir* can be considered a roman à thèse that redefines, in a sense, the rules of the genre.

RHONDA K. GARELICK

La Voie royale *and the Double Time of Art*

Ce qui nous distinguait de nos maîtres, à vingt ans, c'était la presence de l'histoire. Pour eux, il ne s'était rien passé. Nous, nous commençons par des tués. Nous, nous sommes des gens dont' l'histoire a traversé le champs comme un char.

(What distinguished us from our masters, at the age of twenty, was the presence of history. For them, nothing had happened. As for us, we began with those who had been killed. We were those whose history rolled across the field like a chariot.)

These words are taken from an address by André Malraux, given during the summer of 1972 at Verrières-le-Buissons. I choose to quote them here because of the author's curious metaphor of the chariot of history. Like the one driven by Phoebus, the chariot that *moves across* is an obvious image of the cycle of time. And the standard conception of a generation is that of a group that travels together across a certain period of history. Here, however, Malraux detaches history from those who live it; history becomes a distinguishing presence for a particular generation—those who came of age during the First World War. A space, *le champs*, is affected by history, but, we can suppose, still exists even after the chariot has passed across it. Instead of moving through history, this generation is moved through *by* history. It is a generation detached then from its own history, just as it is detached from its predecessors—*les maîtres*—who are without history entirely, according to

Malraux. These masters, for whom nothing happened, are denied their place in the history of all generations. Malraux undercuts the generative, enchained structure implicit in the master/pupil relationship. He is not saying that his generation's history differs from that of its elders; he is saying that it is different by virtue of its very existence.

In another essay, Malraux expresses a similar sentiment. He writes, "A work of art survives by its own double time, the time of its author and our own." Here again, he subverts the notion of historical flow. The work of art bridges two separate temporal realities by existing in both, seemingly at once. The dual temporality of works of art can easily be placed in the context of Malraux's notion of temporal linearity. Going back to his metaphor of the chariot of history, one could compare the temporally transcendent artwork to a generational *champs* that is twice passed over by that chariot.

I have so far been dealing here with late texts of Malraux's, dating from the period of his life devoted almost exclusively to aesthetic theory. But these ideas have application to his earlier work as well. In fact, Malraux's later view of aesthetic time can illuminate very well a particular early novel of his, widely dismissed by critics: *The Royal Way*.

At play in this largely autobiographical novel are issues Malraux was to deal with in many of his subsequent works: temporality, history, aesthetic production, and the interpretation of cultural difference. In this essay I will look at the way in which these issues interact in *The Royal Way*. My intention is to give lie to the claim that this novel is the product of an unformed, apolitical Malraux.

Reading such an early work (it was published in 1930) side by side with texts written forty years later, one runs the risk of pushing too hard in an attempt to see correspondences where they do not exist, to overread the proximity of the later and earlier Malraux. At the same time, Malraux himself lends us critical license when he writes of that very "double time" of art. We read *The Royal Way* in our own time, informed by the oeuvre of Malraux in its entirety. Keeping in mind his later views on aesthetic temporality, we are only acknowledging the bridge between two realities, a bridge created by any work of art or literature.

Ironically, *The Royal Way* itself is a novel whose history enacts its own kind of dual temporality. Although it appeared in 1930, *The Royal Way* was conceived and most likely partially written *before* Malraux's first major novel, *Les Conquérants*, which was published in 1928. *The Royal Way* was intended to be the first volume of a series entitled *Les Puissances du désert*, commissioned by the publishing house of Grasset. The series was never completed and Malraux may have begun and then abandoned the novel, going back to it after several years only in order to satisfy part of his contract with Grasset. *The Royal Way* does not appear in the Pléiade edition of Malraux's writings, at the request of the author himself, and this fact has often been cited as proof of the novel's inferiority. Yet there is also something provocative in Malraux's exclusion of *The Royal Way* from the Pléiade; it lends the novel the status of a work cut off from a corpus, and denied a place in France's most institutional genealogy of any author's works. Similarly, the novel is a fragment of a series—*Les Puissances du désert*—written in a fragmented way. These facts surrounding the conception and execution of the novel seem less incidental once one begins an examination of the major issues of *The Royal Way*, which is, as I hope to show, largely concerned with dismantling traditional concepts of chronology and genealogy.

In an essay titled "Nietzsche, Genealogy and History," Foucault writes

> The search for descent is not the erecting of foundations, on the
> contrary, it disturbs what was previously considered immobile,
> it fragments what was thought unified, it shows the hetergeneity
> of what was imagined consistent with itself.

As its title implies, Malraux's novel concerns a "search for descent," the following of a path, the Royal Way, in a quest backward in time to discover a dead civilization through its art. It is a quest that will also attempt to enframe and record that past.

The Royal Way is the story of men who journey deep into the Indochinese jungle in the hope of unearthing its ancient monuments. Claude Vannec, like the young Malraux an archaeologist, is in the profession of uncovering the past, and decoding its language, Sanskrit. But this novel winds up subverting any archaeological concept of history in which one searches vertically through stratified layers in order to reach a past or an original point.

This subversion results primarily from Malraux's insistence upon the "double time" of art. Even early in the novel, Claude Vannec anticipates Malraux's ideas in the Anti-Critique, for he conceives of archaeology as *revivification* of art, "for me," he says to Rameges, "museums are places where works of an earlier epoch which have developed into myths lie sleeping, surviving on the historical plane alone, waiting for the day when artists will wake them to an active existence." The desire to resurrect is evident also in the most basic tenet of the plot. Inherent in tracing the Royal Way, is the idea that old travelers' legends can be brought to life: "several statements, which they dismiss as mere folk-tales," says Claude, "should be verified along the Royal Way itself." Dead cities are going to be resurrected, the past reactivated, and its artifacts sold on the European market.

But in setting out for the Royal Way, Claude and Perken do not move only in a direction away from legend and documents. By following this storied route of ancient travelers, they themselves will become characters in the same travel legends they seek to verify. In trying to defictionalize the jungle, they themselves will step directly into those fictions. Revivification and reaestheticization seem to occur simultaneously here, creating another example of the Malrauvian double time. The travelers' legends exist in their past but also in the present, as the reality of Claude and Perken.

The characters of Claude and Perken themselves are also affected by what could be called "legendization." The two constantly enact a drama in which myth meets "real" experience, aestheticized or enframed selves meet reality. Claude, as an intellectual, opposes his book knowledge to Perken's real-life adventures: "All he could set up against the other man's vast experience of life was a fairly wide acquaintance with books . . . perpetually countering actual experiences with booklore." Claude reads Sanskrit, but Perken *speaks* Siamese. And yet, Perken too—despite his "real-life" status— has a legendary quality. After discussing Perken's background at length with another shipmate, Claude begins to see Perkens's life in mythic proportions: "[It was] more potent than the menace of the jungle, that [ill-natured] 'Perken legend.' " Claude's friendship with him revivifies this legend, dispelling the aestheticized, bookish nature of Perken's character: "His companion's career had been so perfectly metabolized into experience, . . . that his 'biography' had ceased to matter." And here we see another oscillation of legend and experience.

Malraux's obsession and struggle with Nietzschean self-aestheticization is clear in the smaller details of the novel as well. Claude recalls his mother as a woman who "rouged and powdered for her daylong solitude, for the portraits of the dead owners of the house, for the stone emblems of the sea— but most of all to reassure the woman she confronted in the mirror." And like Claude's mother, Perken can seem to merge with his surroundings, as in this passage: "Nothing human remained, . . . outside—a sea of bestial faces, inside was Perken—a man of stone." The best example of the reversibility of the animate and the inanimate involves an animal skull. When Perken shoots a bullet, filled with his own blood, into a guar's skull, the skull appears to "bleed" human blood. Perken thus imposes upon a dead, inanimate object, the status of the supernaturally alive.

The oscillation between living and dead, legend and reality is, as I have tried to show, a constant subtheme of the novel. In the case of Claude and Perken, their relationship takes shape as Claude turns his highly aestheticized and literary conception of Perken into an emotional bond based on shared emotional experiences. Their rapport occupies a space between a tale narrated and an experience lived in the present. In this sense it is a rapport not unlike a pyschoanalytic transference. Claude transfers his oedipal admiration and resentment from the figure of his grandfather to Perken. The conflation of Perken with Claude's grandfather (whose tragic death in the novel echoes that of Malraux's own grandfather), is clear from the outset of the story: "Whenever Perken talked of himself, the picture of his grandfather always rose before Claude's eyes, his white imperial, his loathing for the world in general." Claude and Perken begin a relationship based on past stories, but move into the enactment of a present story: "It seemed that each of them expressed himself best indirectly, by parables; for it was under cover of their memories that they drew nearer to each other day by day." Theirs is a rapport that is at once part of a "legendized" past and part of a lived present, a rapport highly reminiscent of psychoanalytic transference.

The most self-consciously legendary character is, of course, Grabot. If Claude relies on his family tree to counter his companion's life experiences, Perken relies no less on a genealogy of his own. He clearly sees Grabot as his immediate predecessor, as someone upon whom to model his own career. His admiration for Grabot is not unlike Claude's for his Viking grandfather, and like the grandfather, Grabot exists almost entirely in the form of a tale told within the novel. As a character whose story is narrated more than enacted, Grabot is surrounded from the start by an aura of myth. In fact, on many levels, he represents a highly literary mythology. A figure who blinds himself in order to manipulate his destiny, Grabot is a kind of Oedipus in reverse. Oedipus, of course, blinds himself of his own volition, after losing his struggle with destiny. Grabot partially blinds himself as an act of will, but the Mois tribesmen turn this act of will against him, blinding him in his remaining eye. His punishment also recalls still another mythological figure, for both Grabot and Ixion are condemned to revolve eternally, bound to a wheel.

We can also see in Grabot a symptomatic trace of one of Malraux's own immediate and influential predecessors: Joseph Conrad. Indeed Grabot could almost be Kurtz himself, wandered by mistake into this novel from *Heart of Darkness*. Of course, Malraux revises one important aspect of the Kurtz story. Whereas Kurtz's madness leads him to delirious and criminal abuse of the jungle and its inhabitants, Grabot has *been abused* by the jungle. By so vividly conjuring up the character of Kurtz, Grabot becomes even more of a literary *mise-en-abîme*, a story within a story.

Once discovered, Grabot dispels all of the legends that preceded him. Tied to a millstone that turns perpetual circles, he loses his status as mythical hero and becomes instead a figure of the inexorability of time and human helplessness. Grabot's ceaseless circling continues even after he has been released, since he has internalized the movement forced upon him by his captors, becoming his own tormentor. "The man was free, but he did not move. 'You can move now, old chap.' Grabot started moving along his old track, parallel with the wall."

Circling a dark room at the command of a bell, Grabot turns into a kind of subjugated human timepiece, similar to the worker in Fritz Lang's film *Metropolis* whose nightmarish task it is to substitute his human hands for the mechanical hands of a clock. Grabot's clocklike circling suggests also the motion of searching backward in time—turning back the hands of a clock—for a myth to grab hold of, as Claude does with his family history, as Perken does with Grabot. Both are spinning tales out of the past with which to counter the present.

One could say that Grabot embodies time more than he moves through it. In fact, in this novel, time eventually detaches itself from everything, becoming a purely reified entity whose existence mocks all attempts by the characters to master it. As Claude and Perken wait for the Mois to attack, time takes on a life of its own; it becomes a character in the drama of waiting: "In the emptiness, . . . time alone lived . . . the passing minutes seemed immured within the ring of those bestial faces, in which eternity was incarnate." This detachment of time is reminiscent of Malraux's detached "chariot of history."

Perken and Claude never manage to extract any artifacts from the jungle. They carry Grabot out instead in another reversal of the inanimate and the animate. Grabot, more like a jungle temple than a man, is a human version of what they had been looking for: "His skin was an unhealthy gray. . . . A wreck, but a mighty wreck. . . . But as on the temples, Asia had set her mark on him." Conversely, the stones of the temple wall are as obdurate as a willful human being, "immensely solid, sure of itself, instinct with ponderous malevolence . . . the stone remained impassive, self-willed as a living creature, able to say 'No.' " The self-will sought in Grabot appears instead in the stone that is expected to be yielding. These artifacts of another civilization do not yield to exploitation as easily as Grabot does—Grabot, who had come to subjugate that civilization. Human will has been ironically displaced onto the object world.

It is interesting to look at the precise stone that is described in the passage quoted above. The bas-relief in question depicts women dancing and its presentation in the text is significant:

> The last block had been removed, another block tipped over, and,
> one by one, the surfaces which . . . had been moldering face-
> downward in the soil were once again exposed to daylight. . . .
> Carved on two faces, the corner-stones represented two dancing
> girls. The figures extended over three stones, placed one on top
> of the other. It looked as if a vigorous push might bring the top
> one down.

The sculpture very insistently recalls one of the earliest tableaux of the novel:
the line of dancing prostitutes in a Somalian brothel. This event takes place
prior to the time of the novel and is narrated as a memory of Claude's,

> He visualized the scene again, . . . the women, straight-nosed
> wenches. . . . In time to a blind man's flute they paraded round
> and round in Indian file, each drumming furiously on the buttocks
> of the girl in front. . . . The brothel-keeper had pushed a smiling
> little girl towards Perken.

The similarities between the lapidary and the human dancers are unmistakable. Under the blows of Claude's hammer, the stones one by one
reveal their faces, "une à une montraient leurs faces." In French, the construction "une à une" imparts a curious feminine individuality to the stones
and "montraient leurs faces" implies a comparable anthropomorphism since
the verb "montrer" suggests an action of will on the part of the stone, and
the word "face" carries the sense of *human* face, just as it does in English.
The stone at the top is precariously balanced, a vigorous push, Malraux
writes, would cause it to fall. Similarly, the young girl in the brothel is
"pushed" toward Perken (the verb "pousser" is used in both cases in the
French text) and consequently toward a fall of another sort.

What is happening here is that the story of the brothel, already somewhat
objectified by virtue of being a *memory* within the novel, reappears in the
new, petrified form of the carved figures. It is as if Claude and Perken, who
search for the aesthetic alterity of a distant and ancient civilization, succeed
only in refinding their own personal past myths. But they do not recognize
any elements of their past adventure in this sculpture, like two dreamers
who refuse to interpret the manifest content of a communal dream. Their
experience crystallizes into an inanimate object, much as Grabot becomes a
jungle ruin. Erotism is for sale in a brothel, the women are the goods. At
the temple site, this is literalized as the women are made of stone, seemingly
removable and marketable. But ironically, although the will of the live prostitute is overcome (let us remember that she is reluctant, and must be

"pushed" toward Perken), the women depicted in the bas-relief never reach the market-place, they must be left behind in the jungle. The sculpture allegorizes the loss of the explorers' will to the jungle's unyieldingness, a loss also embodied by Grabot.

In seeing the living memory behind the sculpture, the reader, like the artists of which Claude Vannec speaks, succeeds in reawakening a sleeping art object, affording it a version of that Malrauvian "double time." And there is still another element of temporal play operating in this episode. As the relic of a long-dead civilization, the bas-relief should naturally predate Claude and Perken by several thousand years, yet it seems to represent the *advancement* of their experiences into an aestheticized state. Claude and Perken confront the artifacts of their past in ancient artwork, a fact which calls into question the notion that they are travelling backward in time, with their archaeological expedition. Instead, it is as though the motif of the dancing women races ahead of the protagonists, moving from their past in advance of them, cloaked in antiquity. This motif moves temporally in a direction counter to the time of the characters within the fictional frame of the novel. Malraux insists upon the temporally mobile quality of the stone, for as Claude chips away at it, the particles stream out as if in a timepiece: "The stone-dust softly trickling bright and white as salt from the triangular notch cut in the stone was falling like the sand in an hour-glass." Just as Grabot's endless turning suggests clockwork, this sculpture seems to mark the passage of time as it is removed. Grabot was a legend discovered and dismantled, the bas-relief lays bare an unconscious legend in the text (the memory of the brothel); both when "re-activated," appear as literalizations of the calibration of time.

The self-conscious enframement, represented by the sculpture of the dancers, is a thematic version of the novel's main narrative structure. *The Royal Way* is itself a constant series of static enframements. Episodes are enframed and so are characters, who regularly gaze at each other through binoculars, via their reflections in mirrors, etc. Individual descriptions are also enframed, encased like frames of film. Nearly every chapter opens with a detailed analysis of the conditions of the light, such as one might find in a filmscript. Malraux is, of course, known for his cinematographic technique. Geoffrey Hartman writes, "Malraux [uses] short, narrative units which he juxtaposes neatly and elliptically by cinema methods of 'fade-out' and 'montage.'" Hartman goes on to call Malraux, "the first important practitioner of the journalistic novel."

Hartman is referring here to the "anti-mimetic" art of Malraux, who incorporated so much of his personal life and the actuality of his time into his novels. His works reflect the Nietzschean denial of any external, "real" world, that could be opposed to fiction: "[There is] not the slightest escape hatch . . . that leads to the real world," writes Nietzsche in *Dawn*, "we are in our web like spiders." There is accordingly, little distinction in Malraux's thought between a journalist's objectivity and aesthetic selectivity. He makes this especially clear by choosing to divide the novel's point of view between Claude and Perken, the latter's consciousness taking narrative precedence just after he is wounded by the Mois. The absence of a single, consistent point of view breaks the bond that normally might form between the reader and one protagonist.

This instability of narrative point of view has been criticized by such critics as W. M. Frohock who writes that "the shifting point of view in *The Royal Way* blurs the picture of [Perken]." This criticism is based upon the assumption that Malraux was trying to create *clear* pictures of particular characters, to write a realist novel in effect. But we must keep in mind that *The Royal Way* was written very soon after Malraux's two attempts to follow the style of the surrealists: *Les Royaumes farfelus*, and *Lunes en papier*. The lack of clear character development and a shifting narrative consciousness are both features commonly found in surrealist works. Rather than interpret these features as weaknesses, we might use them to locate *The Royal Way* somewhere between the genres of the surreal and the real.

The breaking of the narrative continuity is also a version of Malraux's self-conscious, cinematographic enframement. Both techniques rupture narrative linearity, and draw attention to the aesthetic decision-making that is constantly in play; a novel proceeds in a series of author-created frames. One might argue that Malraux's cinematic technique is a kind of twentieth-century, mechanized version of the device of the eighteenth-century novel, in which the author claims to have "found" and merely edited the documents, diaries or letters which comprise the text. Like a single letter in an epistolary novel, a single "frame" of filmic text suggests the exposed seams of a narrative and the possibility of its being broken down into individual units. In both cases, the genealogy of the novel becomes one of its own themes and the problem of authorship is rendered explicit. One recalls that early in his career, Malraux published an essay on Choderlos Laclos.

In the *Archaeology of Knowledge*, Foucault describes tradition; it is, he says,

> a notion intended to give special temporal status to a group of phenomena that are both successful and identical . . . tradition enables us to isolate the new against a background of permanence.

The Royal Way is a Foucauldian counter-genealogy in the sense that it valorizes a dismantling of societally sanctioned genealogical progression and divisions. Perken declares at one point, "In the great game I'm playing against death I'd rather have twenty tribes to back me than a child." Adventure is the opposite of family.

Being shared between two points of view, the narrative of *The Royal Way* creates a structural version of this counter-linearity. The reader's relationship with the teller of the tale is broken, by the dual viewpoints, and dependence upon a single narrative authority is broken as well, just as Claude's dependence upon his institutional and familial backgrounds is eventually broken. Perken aptly summarizes the Malrauvian dismantling of genealogical and academic conventions when he says that he wants to leave "a scar on the map." As a metaphor that transfers human qualities onto the textual, this much-quoted phrase creates a confusion of the animate and the documentary. But this metaphor also implies a destruction and violent redrawing of the lines that already divide the land masses on the map—the scarring of war.

Early in the novel, we learn that, as a result of torture, Perken's fingers are severely scarred in spiral patterns. His wish to leave a scar on the map therefore conflates Perken's body with the map, merging him once again with his physical surroundings. This is yet another instance of Malraux's constant theme of self-aestheticization. But here, Perken's biography is also involved. As a Schleswig German, he comes from a place that is a kind of literalized scar on the map. His history entails then, from the start, not a linear narrative but a cutting off. He is from a region that represents a wound on the body of Europe, he is from a home to which he can never return.

This brings me to the essential question of just how Malraux uses his insistence upon self-documentation and enframement to deal with the problem of history and lineage. I will use as my starting point here the final scene of *The Royal Way*:

> With a rush of hatred Claude recalled a prayer of his childhood. "O Lord, be with us in our last agony. . . ." Ah, could he but express by look or gesture if not by words, the desperate fraternity that was wrenching him out of himself! He passed his arm round Perken's shoulders.
>
> Perken gazed at him as if he were a stranger, an intruder from another world.

The fraternity proffered by Claude is unilateral, and ineffective, met with Perken's alienated stare. This is the same state of nonrecognition, the same denial of connectedness that fills the novel. Claude and Perken search for their own legends where they will not find them—in Grabot for example—and cannot see them even when staring directly at them, as in the form of the sculpted dancers. Their searching backward for lost civilizations leads them only in a circle, back to themselves. In not recognizing their own experience in the bas-relief, and in not being able to maintain their distinction from the inanimate world, Claude and Perken are like the blind circling Grabot. The aestheticized self in Malraux is a blind self. Claude's foray beyond the academic leads him only to death and failure. He and Perken are essentially alone, their fraternity artificial. The Foucauldian dismantling of the temporal axis only frees time to be a crushing, destructive force which attacks, "when one's cut off from others [one experiences] a death-in-life . . . time, that loathsome thing, spread[s] . . . like a cancer, inevitably."

Critics have called *The Royal Way* Malraux's only nonpolitical novel. And while it is true that it borrows from specific historical events less blatantly than do Malraux's other works, this novel is clearly about issues of post-War Europe and colonialism. Claude and Perken are blind to their own manufacturing of legends. They fail in bringing their own stories to the jungle, for the myths surrounding Grabot prove untrue, and the Lord's prayer can only be uttered in vain. They look for the stories *of* the jungle, the artistic otherness of a temple sculpture for example, but confront, however blindly, only themselves once again. In not breaking out of their own structure of myth, Claude and Perken enact a problem inherent in any European attempt to make use of, or in some way "read" the East. Edward Said's remarks are highly relevant here:

> Orientalism is a school of interpretations whose material happens to be the Orient. . . . Its objective discoveries . . . are and always have been conditioned by the fact that its truth, like any truths delivered by language, are embodied in language, and what is the truth of language Nietzsche once said but "a mobile army of metaphors, metonyms and anthropomorphisms . . . truths are illusions about which one has forgotten that this is what they are."

Malraux's *The Royal Way* could be his novelization of the scars left on the map and on humanity by a war that carved into the boundaries of nations and by colonialist expeditions that violently tried to yoke Eastern cultures into European intellectual and commercial spheres. *The Royal Way* is about that generation that began with the dead—"nous, nous commençons par des tués." That metaphor of *le char de l'histoire* is also referring to the *tank* of history, *les chars de combat*, first used during World War I. It is also, finally, the chariot of death, *un char funèbre*, that carts away the fallen after a battle. It is the chariot that left behind it a sense of the impossibility of genealogical tracing, either backward or forward in time. Less devoted to accounting particular historical events, *The Royal Way* is more Malraux's chronicle of this chariot.

Chronology

1901   Georges-André Malraux is born in Paris, November 3. His parents, Fernand Malraux and Berthe Lamy, are separated in 1905. His maternal grandmother and aunt raise André in Bondy, a small suburb of Paris.

1909   Malraux's grandfather dies at Dunkirk.

1914–18   Malraux's father is conscripted.

1919   Malraux attends lectures at the Musée Guimet and the Ecole du Louvre. He is employed by the bookseller-publisher René-Louis Doyon. Begins study of Sanskrit. Meets François Mauriac.

1920   Malraux's first article "Des origines de la poésie cubiste" is published in *La Connaissance*, a review edited by Doyon. Articles on Lautréamont and André Salmon are also published in the review *Action*. Becomes the artistic director of the publisher Simon Kra; publishes works by Remy de Gourmont, Max Jacob, Ensor, Derain, Léger, and Baudelaire.

1921   Malraux begins his friendship with Kahnweiler who publishes his *Lunes en papier*, a surrealist work illustrated by Léger, in a limited edition of 100 copies. Other articles by Malraux are published in journals. He travels to Italy. On October 21, he marries Clara Goldschmidt.

1922   Begins acquaintance with Picasso. Articles on Gide and Jacob are published in *Action*. First article appears in *Nouvelle Revue Française*, on *L'Abbaye de Typhaines* by Gobineau.

1923   Travels to Indochina with Clara and Louis Chevasson. After visiting the Cambodian temple of Banteai-Srey, from which they remove statues and bas-reliefs, the group is accused of theft and arrested in Pnom-Penh.

1924   Trial in Pnom-Penh. Doyon, contacted by Clara, begins an appeal for Malraux's release in *L'Eclair*. Twenty-three celebrated authors sign a similar appeal, including Mauriac, Gide, and Breton. Malraux is reprieved and returns to France where he publishes "Ecrit pour une idole à trompe" in *Accords*.

1925   Returns to Indochina and organizes the "Young Annam" movement with Nguyen Pho. Also launches, with Paul Monin, the newspaper he entitles *L'Indochine*, whose publication will cease in August due to printers' refusals to print it. In November, the paper reappears as *L'Indochine enchaînée*.

1926   In Paris Malraux directs *A la sphère*, which publishes works by Samain, Morand, Giraudoux, Gide, Mauriac, etc. *La Tentation de L'Occident* is published by Grasset in August.

1927   *Commerce* publishes "Le Voyage aux Iles Fortunées." The *Review 600* publishes "Ecrit pour un ours en peluche." His essay "D'une jeunesse européenne" is published in *Ecrits*.

1928   *Les Conquérants* and *Les Royaumes farfelus* are published by Grasset and Gallimard respectively. Visits Persia. Becomes member of the Comité de Lecture as well as artistic director at Gallimard until the Spanish Civil War.

1930   Publication of *La Voie royale*. Malraux travels to Afghanistan, India, Japan, and the United States.

1931   Debate between Trotsky and Malraux at *NRF* about *Les Conquérants*. Travels To China, writes a preface to Charles Clement's *Mediterranée*.

1932   Exhibition of Gothic-Buddhist art at *NRF*. Malraux writes preface to D. H. Lawrence's *Lady Chatterley's Lover*. Meets Heidegger.

1933   Writes preface to Faulkner's *Sanctuary*. Publishes *La Condition humaine* which is a great success, and wins the Prix Goncourt in December. Daughter Florence is born.

1934   Flies over the Desert of Dhana with Edouard Corniglion-Molinier, searching for the "Kingdom of the Queen of Sheba."

This adventure is described in *L'Intransigeant*. Meets with Trotsky in March. Becomes president of the World Committee for the Liberation of Dimitrov and Thaemann. Travels to Berlin with Gide to present a letter to Goebbels. Member of the Presidium of the International League against Antisemitism. President of the World Committee against War and Fascism. In August he addresses the first Congress of Soviet Writers in Moscow. Meets Meyerhof and Eisenstein (whose plans to make a film of *La Condition humaine* are halted by Stalin). Meets Gorky and Pasternak. Meets T. E. Lawrence.

1935   *Le Temps du mépris.*

1936   Speech in June at the International Congress of Writers for the Defense of Culture in London. Travels to Spain at the start of the Spanish Civil War and heads an international air squadron, fighting with the Republicans. Flies on sixty-five air missions and is twice wounded.

1937   *L'Espoir.* Travels to the United States and Canada to raise money for the Spanish Republican cause. Meets Hemingway, Einstein, and Robert Oppenheimer. Camus adapts *Le Temps du mépris* for the Théâtre du Travail in Algiers.

1938   Makes film of *L'Espoir (Sierra de Teruel)* in Barcelona, music by Darius Milhaud. "La Psychologie des Renaissances" and "De la Représentation en Occident et en Extrême-Occident" are published in *Verve*.

1939   Gallimard publishes "Etude sur Laclos." Film is finished in April and shown privately in July.

1940   Captured in Sens with his tank unit. Five months later he escapes to the free zone.

1943   *Les Noyers de l'Altenburg* published in Switzerland.

1944   Active as a Resistance leader, using the name Colonel Berger (after the hero in *Les Noyers de l'Altenburg*). Taken prisoner in Toulouse, he was later freed by the French. Josete Clotis, with whom Malraux had two sons, is killed in an accident. Half-brother Claude, also a member of the Resistance, is executed. Malraux is involved in the liberation of the Vosges and Alsace, especially Strasbourg.

1945   Death of another half-brother, Roland, also a member of the Resistance. Malraux becomes Minister of Information for the first De Gaulle government.

1947–50   Malraux is director of propaganda for the R.P.F. (Rassemblement du peuple français), the Gaullist party. He publishes essays on art, *La Psychologie de l'art*. Marries Madeleine Malraux, widow of his half-brother Roland.

1951   *Les Voix du silence.*

1952–54   *Le Musée imaginaire de la sculpture mondiale* published in three volumes.

1957   *La Metamorphose des dieux*, volume 1.

1958   Malraux is Minister of Information in the second De Gaulle government.

1959–69   Malraux is Minister for Cultural Affairs.

1961   An automobile accident kills both of Malraux's sons, Pierre-Gauthier and Vincent.

1962–63   Malraux travels to the United States twice. He is a guest of the Kennedys at the White House.

1965   Malraux suffers acute depression. Travels to China and other Asian countries. Resumes writing.

1966   Reunion with poet and novelist Louise de Vilmorin, author of *Madame de.*

1967   *Antimémoires* is published and is an immediate best-seller.

1969   Louise de Vilmorin dies. Malraux continues to live at her family estate at Verrières.

1970   *Le Triangle noir* is published. De Gaulle dies.

1971   *Les Chênes qu'on abat.*

1973   Exhibition at the Fondation Maeght in Saint-Paul de Vence displays the works of Malraux's imaginary museum.

1974   *Lazare, La Tête d'obsidienne*, and *L'Irréel.*

1975   *Hôtes de passage.*

1976   *La Corde et les souris* and *L'Intemporel* published. Malraux dies
       of a pulmonary embolism on November 23. He is buried in a
       private ceremony at Verrières-le-Buisson. National homage at
       the Louvre. Memorial mass at Saint-Louis des Invalides, hom-
       ily preached by R. P. Bockel.

1977   *Le Surnaturel* and *L'Homme précaire et la littérature* published
       posthumously.

Contributors

HAROLD BLOOM, Sterling Professor of the Humanities at Yale University, is the author of *The Anxiety of Influence*, *Poetry and Repression*, and many other volumes of literary criticism. His forthcoming study, *Freud: Transference and Authority*, attempts a full-scale reading of all of Freud's major writings. A MacArthur Prize Fellow, he is general editor of five series of literary criticism published by Chelsea House. During 1987–88, he was appointed Charles Eliot Norton Professor of Poetry at Harvard University.

W. M. FROHOCK is Professor Emeritus of French at Harvard University and is a fellow of the Comargo Foundation in Cassis, France. He is the author of *André Malraux and the Tragic Imagination* and several shorter works on Malraux, as well as studies on French and American literature.

GEOFFREY H. HARTMAN is Karl Young Professor of English and Comparative Literature at Yale University. His books include *Wordsworth's Poetry* and *Saving the Text*, a study of Jacques Derrida.

R. W. B. LEWIS is Neil Gray Professor of Rhetoric at Yale University. He is the author of *The American Adam*, *The Picaresque Saint*, *The Poetry of Hart Crane*, *Trials of the Word*, and *Edith Wharton: A Biography*.

DAVID WILKINSON is the author of *Malraux: An Essay in Political Criticism*.

ROGER SHATTUCK has written extensively on Proust and other modern French authors.

MICHAEL RIFFATERRE is University Professor at Columbia University. His books which have appeared in English are *Semiotics of Poetry* and *Text Production*.

THOMAS JEFFERSON KLINE is Professor of Romance Languages at Boston University.

LUCIEN GOLDMANN is the author of many works of philosophy, political theory, and literary criticism. Among them are *Le Dieu Caché*, *Immanuel Kant*, and *The Philosophy of Enlightenment*.

C. J. GRESHOFF teaches at the University of Capetown in South Africa.

E. H. GOMBRICH is Professor of History of Classical Tradition at the University of London, and the Director of the Warburg Institute. His many works on art and aesthetic theory include *Art and Illusion*, *Art History and Social Sciences*, *The Heritage of Apelles*, and *The Sense of Order*.

VICTOR BROMBERT is Henry Putnam Professor of Comparative Literature and Romance Languages at Princeton University. He is the author of *The Intellectual Hero*, *Stendhal: A Collection of Critical Essays*, *Victor Hugo and the Visionary World*, and *The Novels of Flaubert*.

NINA S. TUCCI teaches at the University of Houston, Texas.

SUSAN RUBIN SULEIMAN is Assistant Professor of Romance Languages and Literature at Harvard University. She is the author of *Authoritarian Fictions* and co-editor of *The Reader in the Text*.

RHONDA K. GARELICK is a doctoral candidate in the French Department at Yale University.

Bibliography

Alberes, R. M. *La Révolte des écrivains d'aujourd'hui*. Paris: Correa, 1949.

Allan, Derek W. "The Psychology of a Terrorist: Tchen in *La Condition humaine*." *Nottingham French Studies* 21 (May 1982): 48–66.

Astier, Emmanuel d'. *Portraits*. Paris: Gallimard, 1963.

Baumgartner, P. "Solitude and Involvement: Two Aspects of Tragedy in Malraux's Novels." *The French Review* (1965): 766–76.

Bevan, David. "André Malraux: Féministe." *Atlantis*, no. 7 (1982): 117–20.

Blend, C. D. *André Malraux: Tragic Humanist*. Columbus: Ohio State University Press, 1963.

———. "Early Expression of Malraux's Art Theory." *The Romanic Review* 53, no. 3 (1962): 199–213.

Blumenthal, Gerda. *André Malraux: The Conquest of Dread*. Baltimore: The Johns Hopkins University Press, 1960.

Boak, C. D. "Jean Hougron and *La nuit indochinoise*." *France-Asie*, no. 174 (July-August 1962): 489–501.

———. "Malraux—A Note on Editions." *AUMLA*, no. 21 (May 1964): 79–83.

———. "Malraux and T. E. Lawrence." *The Modern Language Review* 61 (1966): 218–24.

Boak, Denis. *André Malraux*. Oxford: Clarendon Press, 1968.

Bree, Germaine, and Margaret Guiton. *An Age of Fiction*. New Brunswick, N.J.: Rutgers University Press, 1957.

Brombert, Victor. *The Intellectual Hero: Studies in the French Novel 1880–1955*. Philadelphia: Lippincott, 1961.

Burgum, Edwin Berry, *The Novel and the World's Dilemma*. Oxford: Oxford University Press, 1947.

Buroca, C. "Reflexions sur l'art chez Camus et chez Malraux." *Simoun*, no. 1 (January 1952): 116–20.

Casey, B. "André Malraux's *Heart of Darkness*." *Twentieth Century Literature* 5, no. 1 (1959): 21–26.

Caute, David. *Communism and the French Intellectuals*. New York: Macmillan, 1964.

Cazenave, Michel. *André Malraux*. Paris: L'Herne, 1982.

Chase, Richard V. *The Quest for Myth*. New Orleans: Louisiana State University Press, 1949.

Chevalier, H. M. "André Malraux: The Legend and the Man." *Modern Language Quarterly* 14 (1953): 199–208.

Chiaromonte, Nicola. "Malraux and the Demons of Action." *Partisan Review* 15 (1948): 776–89.

Clouard, H. "Itinéraire d'André Malraux." *Revue de Paris* 59 (December 1958): 82–95.

Cordle, T. H. "Malraux and Nietzsche's *Birth of Tragedy.*" *Bucknell Review* 8, no. 2 (1959): 89–104.

Cornick, Martyn. "Malraux and Conrad: Imagery of Confrontation in *La Voie royale* and *Heart of Darkness.*" *Mélanges Malraux Miscellany*, no. 15 (1983): 7-15.

Daniels, G. "The Sense of the Past in the Novels of André Malraux." In L. J. Austin et al., *Studies in Modern French Literature Presented to P. Mansel Jones*, 71–86. Manchester: Manchester University Press, 1961.

Dial, Roger. "André Malraux on Revolution: Elements in *The Conquerors* and *Man's Fate.*" *Mélanges Malraux Miscellany*, no. 14 (1982): 14–32.

Drieu la Rochelle, Pierre. "Malraux, the New Man." In *From the N.R.F.—An Image of the Twentieth Century from the Pages of the Nouvelle Revue Française*. Edited by Justin O'Brien. New York: Farrar, Straus & Cudahy, 1958.

Ehrenberg, Ilya. *Memoirs 1921–1941*. Translated by Tatania Shebunina and Yvonne Kapp. New York: World Publishing, 1964.

Ellis, L. B. "Some Existentialist Concepts in Gide, Malraux and Saint-Exupéry." *Bucknell Review* 10, no. 2 (1961): 164–73.

Erikson, E. H. "Identity and the Life Cycle." *Psychological Issues* 1, no. 1 (1959): Monograph I.

Fischer, Louis. *Men and Politics—An Autobiography*. New York: Duelle, Sloan & Pearce, 1941.

Flanner, Janet. *Men and Monuments*. New York: Harper & Row, 1957.

———. *Paris Journal 1944–1965*. New York: Atheneum, 1965.

Frank, Joseph. *The Widening Gyre*. New Brunswick, N. J.: Rutgers University Press, 1963.

Frohock, W. M. *André Malraux*. New York: Columbia University Press, 1974.

———. *André Malraux and the Tragic Imagination*. Stanford, Calif.: Stanford University Press, 1951.

———. "Note for a Malraux Bibliography." *MLN* 65 (1950): 392–95.

———. "Notes on Malraux's Symbols." *The Romanic Review* 42 (1951): 274–81.

———. *Style and Temper; Studies in French Fiction 1925–1960*. Cambridge: Harvard University Press, 1967.

Gannon, Edward. *The Honor of Being a Man*. Chicago: Loyola University Press, 1957.

Garaudy, Roger. *Literatuare from the Graveyard: J. P. Sartre, F. Mauriac, A. Malraux, A. Koestler*. Translated by Joseph Bernstein. New York: International Publishers, 1948.

Gide, André. *Journal 1889–1939*. Paris: Bibliotheque de la Pléiade, 1959.

———. *Journal 1939–1949*. Paris: Bibliotheque de la Pléiade, 1959.

Gidley, Mick. "Malraux and the Attractions of Rhetoric in Faulkner's Later Public Comments." *William Faulkner*, no. 6 (May 1984): 20–35.

Goldberger, Avriel. *Visions of a New Hero; The Heroic Life According to André Malraux and Earlier Advocates of Human Grandeur*. Paris: Minard, 1965.

Greenlee, James W. *Malraux's Heroes and History.* De Kalb: Northern Illinois University Press, 1975.

Halda, Bernard. *Berenson et Malraux.* Paris: Minard, 1964.

Hewitt, James. *André Malraux.* New York: Ungar, 1978.

Horvath, Violet. *André Malraux: The Human Adventure.* New York: New York University Press, 1969.

Jarrell, Randall. *A Sad Heart at the Supermarket: Essays and Fables.* New York: Atheneum, 1962.

Jenkins, Cecill. *André Malraux.* New York: Twayne, 1972.

Knapp, Bettina. "Archetypal Saturn / Chronos and the Goya / Malraux Dynamics." *Kentucky Romance Quarterly* 4 (1983): 373–87.

Knight, Everett W. *Literature Considered as Philosophy: The French Example.* New York: Macmillan, 1958.

Langlois, Walter G. *André Malraux: The Indochina Adventure.* New York: Praeger, 1966.

———. "Young Malraux and Eroticism: An Unpublished Chapter from *La Voie royale.*" *Mélanges Malraux Miscellany,* no. 15 (1983): 32–42.

Lewis, R. W. B., ed. *André Malraux—A Collection of Critical Essays.* Englewood Cliffs, N.J.: Prentice-Hall, 1964.

Merleau-Ponty, Maurice. *Signs.* Translated by Richard C. McCleary. Evanston, Ill.: Northwestern University Press, 1964.

Montalbetti, Jean. "La Vision dostoïevskienne d'André Malraux." *Nouvelle Revue Française* 59, no. 350 (March 1982): 79–87.

Morrisey, Will. *Reflections on Malraux: Cultural Founding in Modernity.* Lanham, Md.: University Press of America, 1984.

Peyre, Henri. *French Novelists of Today.* New York: Oxford University Press, 1967.

Reck, Rima Drell. *Literature and Responsibility: The French Novelist in the Twentieth Century.* Baton Rouge: Louisiana State University Press, 1969.

Regler, Gustav. *The Owl of Minerva.* Translated by Norman Denny. New York: Farrar, Straus & Cudahy, 1960.

Riffaterre, Michael. *Essais de stylistique structurale.* Paris: Flammarion, 1971.

Righter, William. *The Rhetorical Hero—An Essay on the Aesthetics of André Malraux.* London: Routledge & Kegan Paul, 1964. New York: Chilmark Press, 1964.

Savage, Catherine. *Malraux, Sartre and Aragon as Political Novelists.* University of Florida Monographs, no. 17. Gainesville: University of Florida, 1964.

Scheinman, Marc. "Trotsky and Malraux: The Political Imagination." In *The Artist and Political Vision,* edited by Benjamin Barber and Michael J. McGrath. New Brunswick, N.J.: Transaction, 1982.

Smith, Roch C. "Tchen's Sacred Isolation: Prelude to Malraux's Fraternal Humanism." *Studies in Twentieth Century Literature* 7 (1982): 45–57.

Soulsby, Sarah E. "Political Commitment as a Means of Revolt against Destiny as Seen in Some of André Malraux's Earlier Novels." *Journal of English,* no. 2 (1976): 95–109.

Sulzberger, Cyrus L. *A Long Row of Candles: Memoirs and Diaries 1934–1954.* New York: Macmillan, 1969.

Tarica, Ralph. "Ironic Figures in Malraux's Novels." In *Image and Theme—Studies in*

Modern French Fiction, edited by W. M. Frohock. Cambridge: Harvard University Press, 1969.

Vivas, E. *The Artistic Transaction*. Columbus: Ohio State University Press, 1963.

Wilbur, C. M., and Julie L. Y. How. *Documents on Communism, Nationalism, and Soviet Advisors in China 1918–1927*. New York: Columbia University Press, 1956.

Williams, W. D. *Nietzsche and the French*. Oxford: Oxford University Press, 1952.

Wilson, Edmund. *The Bit between My Teeth*. New York: Farrar, Straus, 1966.

———. *The Shores of Light*. New York: Farrar, Straus, 1952.

Acknowledgments

"The Metallic Realm: *The Conquerors*" (originally entitled "The Metallic Realm") by
W. M. Frohock from *André Malraux and the Tragic Imagination* by W. M. Frohock,
© 1952 by the Board of Trustees of the Leland Stanford Junior University.
Reprinted by permission of the publishers, Stanford University Press.

"The Silence of the Infinite Spaces" (originally entitled "Chapter V") by Geoffrey
H. Hartman from *André Malraux* by Geoffrey H. Hartman, © 1960 by Geoffrey
H. Hartman. Reprinted by permission.

"Malraux and His Critics" by R. W. B. Lewis from *The Trials of the Word* by R. W. B.
Lewis, © 1965 by R. W. B. Lewis. Reprinted by permission of the author and
Yale University Press.

"The Bolshevik Hero" by David Wilkinson from *Malraux: An Essay in Political Criticism* by David Wilkinson, © 1967 by the President and Fellows of Harvard
College. Reprinted by permission of Harvard University Press.

"Malraux, The Conqueror" by Roger Shattuck from *The Innocent Eye: On Modern
Literature and the Arts* by Roger Shattuck, © 1968, 1984 by Roger Shattuck.
Reprinted by permission of Joan Daves and Farrar, Straus & Giroux, Inc. This
essay first appeared in the *New York Review of Books*.

"Malraux's *Anti-Memoirs*" (originally entitled "Malraux's *Antimemoirs*") by Michael
Riffaterre from *Columbia Forum* 11, no. 4 (Winter 1968), © 1968 by the Trustees
of Columbia University in the City of New York. Reprinted by permission of
Columbia University Press.

"*Le Temps du mépris* Recaptured" by Thomas Jefferson Kline from *André Malraux and
the Metamorphosis of Death* by Thomas Jefferson Kline, © 1973 by Columbia
University Press. Reprinted by permission of Columbia University Press.

"The Structure of *La Condition humaine*" (originally entitled "Structural Study of
Malraux's Novels") by Lucien Goldmann from *Toward a Sociology of the Novel*,
translated by Alan Sheridan, © 1975 by Tavistock Publications Ltd. Reprinted
by permission.

"*Les Noyers de l'Altenburg*" (originally entitled "The Epilogue: *Les Noyers de l'Altenburg*")
by C. J. Greshoff from *An Introduction to the Novels of Malraux* by C. J. Greshoff,

© 1975 by C. J. Greshoff. Reprinted by permission of A. A. Balkema, Rotterdam, Netherlands.

"Malraux's Philosophy of Art in Historical Perspective" by E. H. Gombrich from *Malraux: Life and Work*, edited by Martine de Courcel, © 1976 by George Weidenfeld & Nicolson Ltd. Reprinted by permission of Harcourt Brace Jovanovich, Inc., and George Weidenfeld & Nicolson.

"Remembering Malraux: On Violence and the Image of Man" by Victor Brombert from *Dialogues with the Unseen and the Unknown: Essays in Memory of Andre Malraux* edited by Lynne L. Gelber, © 1978 by Skidmore College. Reprinted by permission of Skidmore College, Saratoga Springs, New York.

"The Orient as Western Man's 'Shadow' in Malraux's *La Tentation de l'Occident*" by Nina S. Tucci from *L'Esprit Createur* 22, no. 2 (Summer 1982), © 1982 by *L'Esprit Createur*. Reprinted by permission.

"The Model Relativized: Malraux's *L'Espoir*" by Susan Rubin Suleiman from *Authorian Fictions* by Susan Rubin Suleiman, © 1983 by Columbia University Press. Reprinted by permission of Columbia University Press.

"*La Voie royal* and the Double Time of Art" by Rhonda K. Garelick, © 1987 by Rhonda K. Garelick. Published for the first time in this volume. Printed by permission.

Index

Modern Critical Views